Name Server Operations and
DNS Configuration using BIND

BIND DNS Administration Reference

Second Edition

Edited by Jeremy C. Reed
Published by Reed Media Services

BIND DNS Administration Reference
Name Server Operations and DNS Configuration using BIND
Second Edition
January 2016

ISBN: 978-1-937516-03-1

Publisher: Reed Media Services
Editor: Jeremy C. Reed

Cover design by Getty Creations

This is an open source book based on Internet Systems Consortium's BIND 9 documentation. See page xi for complete copyright and license details.

Contents

Preface

The Berkeley Internet Name Domain (BIND) implements a domain name server for a number of operating systems. This book provides basic information about the installation and care of the Internet Systems Consortium (ISC) BIND version 9 software package for system administrators.

This book corresponds to the latest supported BIND release versions, at the time of this book's printing: versions 9.9.8 and 9.10.3.

Note

The book also documents some features to be introduced in BIND 9.11.0 as documented in the open source code, but not officially released at the time of this book's printing. These features, command-line options, and configuration keywords may be changed before that release becomes final.

This book is based on documentation that is included with the BIND source code, including ISC's BIND 9 Administrator Reference Manual (originally by the BIND 9 Development Team) and manpages. The editor for this printed book provided hundreds of improvements to ISC which were integrated into the official documentation. The main differences between this book and the original reference manual are: reorganization of content, extra examples, new content, man pages, other documentation merged in, cross-referencing, indexing, and formatting for book use. For complete details about this book, please see the website at http://www.reedmedia.net/books/bind-dns/.

Copyrights and Licenses

The original materials and this book are open source. The following are the copyrights and licenses found in the original materials:

Copyright (C) 2004-2015 Internet Systems Consortium, Inc. ("ISC")

THE SOFTWARE IS PROVIDED "AS IS" AND ISC DISCLAIMS ALL WARRANTIES WITH RE-GARD TO THIS SOFTWARE INCLUDING ALL IMPLIED WARRANTIES OF MERCHANTABIL-ITY AND FITNESS. IN NO EVENT SHALL ISC BE LIABLE FOR ANY SPECIAL, DIRECT, INDIRECT, OR CONSEQUENTIAL DAMAGES OR ANY DAMAGES WHATSOEVER RESULT-ING FROM LOSS OF USE, DATA OR PROFITS, WHETHER IN AN ACTION OF CONTRACT, NEGLIGENCE OR OTHER TORTIOUS ACTION, ARISING OUT OF OR IN CONNECTION WITH THE USE OR PERFORMANCE OF THIS SOFTWARE.

Copyright (C) 1999-2003 Internet Software Consortium

Permission to use, copy, modify, and distribute this software for any purpose with or without fee is hereby granted, provided that the above copyright notice and this permission notice appear in all copies.

THE SOFTWARE IS PROVIDED "AS IS" AND INTERNET SOFTWARE CONSORTIUM DIS-CLAIMS ALL WARRANTIES WITH REGARD TO THIS SOFTWARE INCLUDING ALL IM-PLIED WARRANTIES OF MERCHANTABILITY AND FITNESS. IN NO EVENT SHALL IN-TERNET SOFTWARE CONSORTIUM BE LIABLE FOR ANY SPECIAL, DIRECT, INDIRECT, OR CONSEQUENTIAL DAMAGES OR ANY DAMAGES WHATSOEVER RESULTING FROM LOSS OF USE, DATA OR PROFITS, WHETHER IN AN ACTION OF CONTRACT, NEGLI-GENCE OR OTHER TORTIOUS ACTION, ARISING OUT OF OR IN CONNECTION WITH THE USE OR PERFORMANCE OF THIS SOFTWARE.

Portions Copyright (c) 1985, 1986, 1988, 1989, 1996 The Regents of the University of California

Redistribution and use in source and binary forms, with or without modification, are permitted pro-vided that the following conditions are met:

1. Redistributions of source code must retain the above copyright notice, this list of conditions and the following disclaimer.

2. Redistributions in binary form must reproduce the above copyright notice, this list of conditions and the following disclaimer in the documentation and/or other materials provided with the distribution.

3. Neither the name of the University nor the names of its contributors may be used to endorse or promote products derived from this software without specific prior written permission.

THIS SOFTWARE IS PROVIDED BY THE REGENTS AND CONTRIBUTORS ``AS IS'' AND ANY EXPRESS OR IMPLIED WARRANTIES, INCLUDING, BUT NOT LIMITED TO, THE IM-PLIED WARRANTIES OF MERCHANTABILITY AND FITNESS FOR A PARTICULAR PUR-POSE ARE DISCLAIMED. IN NO EVENT SHALL THE REGENTS OR CONTRIBUTORS BE LIABLE FOR ANY DIRECT, INDIRECT, INCIDENTAL, SPECIAL, EXEMPLARY, OR CON-SEQUENTIAL DAMAGES (INCLUDING, BUT NOT LIMITED TO, PROCUREMENT OF SUB-STITUTE GOODS OR SERVICES; LOSS OF USE, DATA, OR PROFITS; OR BUSINESS IN-TERRUPTION) HOWEVER CAUSED AND ON ANY THEORY OF LIABILITY, WHETHER IN CONTRACT, STRICT LIABILITY, OR TORT (INCLUDING NEGLIGENCE OR OTHERWISE) ARISING IN ANY WAY OUT OF THE USE OF THIS SOFTWARE, EVEN IF ADVISED OF THE POSSIBILITY OF SUCH DAMAGE.

Portions Copyright (c) 1993 by Digital Equipment Corporation

Permission to use, copy, modify, and distribute this software for any purpose with or without fee is hereby granted, provided that the above copyright notice and this permission notice appear in all copies, and that the name of Digital Equipment Corporation not be used in advertising or publicity pertaining to distribution of the document or software without specific, written prior permission.

THE SOFTWARE IS PROVIDED "AS IS" AND DIGITAL EQUIPMENT CORP. DISCLAIMS ALL WARRANTIES WITH REGARD TO THIS SOFTWARE, INCLUDING ALL IMPLIED WARRANTIES OF MERCHANTABILITY AND FITNESS. IN NO EVENT SHALL DIGITAL EQUIPMENT CORPORATION BE LIABLE FOR ANY SPECIAL, DIRECT, INDIRECT, OR CONSEQUENTIAL DAMAGES OR ANY DAMAGES WHATSOEVER RESULTING FROM LOSS OF USE, DATA OR PROFITS, WHETHER IN AN ACTION OF CONTRACT, NEGLIGENCE OR OTHER TORTIOUS ACTION, ARISING OUT OF OR IN CONNECTION WITH THE USE OR PERFORMANCE OF THIS SOFTWARE.

Acknowledgments

This book includes open source licensed documentation written by numerous authors and contributors. Acknowledgment and enormous thanks are due to: Mark Andrews, Rob Austein, Curtis Blackburn, James Brister, Andrew Cherenson, David Conrad, Francis Dupont, Paul Ebersman, Tony Finch, Michael Graff, Andreas Gustafsson, Bob Halley, David Hankins, Tomas Hozza, Evan Hunt, Stephen Jacob, Jinmei Tatuya, Ashley Kitto, Witold Krecicki, David Lawrence, Eric Luce, Scott Mann, Michael Sawyer, Vernon Schryver, Mukund Sivaraman, Mary Stahl, Sun Guonian, Andrew Tridgell, Glen Turner, Brian Wellington, Chris Yarnell, and the BIND 9 development team. The complete list of contributors is unknown. (Please let us know of any other documentation contributors.) Thank you for your contributions to the ISC BIND documentation.

Thank you to ISC for providing the original manuals that this book is mostly based on. Thank you to Paul Vixie for inspiring BIND 9 and giving the editor the opportunity to continue to work on the documentation. Thank you to Mark Andrews and Rob Austein for providing valuable feedback and information for the first edition of this book and also for helping with committing improvements back into the original source.

Organization of this Book

In this book, Chapter 1 introduces the history of DNS and BIND, and the basic DNS and BIND concepts. The second chapter introduces zone files and resource records and related BIND tools. Chapter 3 describes resource requirements for running BIND in various environments and steps for installing BIND. Information in Chapter 4 is about starting, stopping, and remotely controlling the DNS server. Chapter 5 introduces the configuration files and syntax and Chapter 6 describes all the nameserver configuration options. Chapter 7 discusses implementing split DNS setups without having to run multiple servers. Chapter 8 covers the diagnostic tools and clients useful for debugging and researching DNS. Chapter 9 covers dynamic updates and server communication authentication. Chapter 10 introduces DNSSEC, and the tools for creating and managing signed resource records. Chapter 11 describes the BIND 9 lightweight resolver.

Where Can I Get Help?

The Internet Systems Consortium (ISC) offers a wide range of support and service agreements for BIND and DHCP servers. Multiple levels of premium support are available and each level includes support for all ISC programs, significant discounts on products and training, and a recognized priority on bug fixes and non-funded feature requests. In addition, ISC offers a standard support agreement package which includes services ranging from bug fix announcements to remote support. It also includes training in BIND and DHCP.

To discuss arrangements for professional support, contact ISC at info@isc.org or visit the ISC web page at http://www.isc.org/services/ to read more.

An open community for BIND discussion and free support is available via the BIND Users mailing list. Subscription details and archives can be found via https://lists.isc.org/.

Note that the BIND 9 bug database is kept closed for a number of reasons. These include, but are not limited to, that the database contains proprietory information from people reporting bugs. The database has in the past and may in future contain unfixed bugs which are capable of bringing down most of the Internet's DNS infrastructure. The release pages for each version contain up-to-date lists of bugs that have been fixed. That is as close as ISC can get to providing a bug database.

1   The Domain Name System (DNS)

The Internet Domain Name System (DNS) consists of the syntax to specify the names of entities in the Internet in a hierarchical manner, the rules used for delegating authority over names, and the system implementation that actually maps names to Internet addresses. DNS data is maintained in a group of distributed hierarchical databases.

The purpose of this book is to explain the installation and upkeep of the BIND (Berkeley Internet Name Domain) software package, and we begin by reviewing the background and the fundamentals of the Domain Name System (DNS) as they relate to BIND.

1.1   A Brief History of DNS and BIND

Although the *official* beginning of the Domain Name System occurred in 1984 with the publication of RFC 920, "Domain Requirements", the core of the new system was described in 1983 in RFCs 882, "Domain Names - Concepts and Facilities", and 883, "Domain Names - Implementation and Specification". From 1984 to 1987, the ARPAnet (the precursor to today's Internet) became a testbed of experimentation for developing the new naming/addressing scheme in a rapidly expanding, operational network environment. New RFCs were written and published in 1987 that modified the original documents to incorporate improvements based on the working model. RFC 1034 and RFC 1035 were published and became the standards upon which all DNS implementations are built.

The first working domain name server, called Jeeves, was written in 1983-84 by Paul Mockapetris for operation on DEC Tops-20 machines located at the University of Southern California's Information Sciences Institute (USC-ISI) and SRI International's Network Information Center (SRI-NIC). A DNS server for Unix machines, the Berkeley Internet Name Domain (BIND) package, was written soon after by a group of graduate students at the University of California at Berkeley under a grant from the US Defense Advanced Research Projects Administration (DARPA). Douglas Terry, Mark Painter, David Riggle, and Songnian Zhou made up the initial BIND project team.

Versions of BIND through 4.8.3 were maintained by the Computer Systems Research Group (CSRG) at UC Berkeley, starting with additional work by Ralph Campbell. Kevin Dunlap, a Digital Equipment Corporation employee on loan to the CSRG, worked on BIND for two years, from 1985 to 1987. Many other people also contributed to BIND development during that time: Doug Kingston, Craig Partridge, Smoot Carl-Mitchell, Mike Muuss, Jim Bloom and Mike Schwartz. BIND maintenance was subsequently handled by Mike Karels and Øivind Kure. BIND was widely distributed as part of the BSD (Berkeley Software Distribution) releases.

BIND versions 4.9 and 4.9.1 were released by Digital Equipment Corporation. Paul Vixie, then a DEC employee, became BIND's primary caretaker. He was assisted by Phil Almquist, Robert Elz, Alan Barrett, Paul Albitz, Bryan Beecher, Andrew Partan, Andy Cherenson, Tom Limoncelli, Berthold Paffrath, Fuat Baran, Anant Kumar, Art Harkin, Win Treese, Don Lewis, Christophe Wolfhugel, and others.

In 1994, BIND version 4.9.2 was sponsored by Vixie Enterprises. Vixie became BIND's principal architect and programmer.

BIND versions from 4.9.3 onward have been developed and maintained by the Internet Systems Consortium and its predecessor, the Internet Software Consortium, with support being provided by ISC's sponsors.

As co-architects/programmers, Bob Halley and Vixie released the first production-ready version of BIND version 8 in May 1997. It had a completely new configuration file format, dynamic updates, online change notification, categorized logging, more efficient zone transfers, and a better build mechanism than BIND 4.

BIND version 9 was released in September 2000 and was a major rewrite of nearly all aspects of the underlying BIND architecture. Notably it provided DNSSEC for signed zones, IPv6 support, views support, and multiprocessor support.

BIND versions 4 and 8 are officially deprecated. No additional development is done on BIND version 4 or BIND version 8.

1.2   DNS Fundamentals

The Domain Name System (DNS) is a hierarchical, distributed database. It stores information for mapping Internet host names to IP addresses and vice versa, mail routing information, and other data used by Internet applications.

Clients look up information in the DNS by calling a *resolver* library, which sends queries to one or more *name servers* and interprets the responses. The BIND 9 software distribution contains a name server, **named**, and a resolver library, **liblwres**.

1.3   Domains and Domain Names

The data stored in the DNS is identified by *domain names* that are organized as a tree according to organizational or administrative boundaries. Each node of the tree, called a *domain*, is given a label. The domain name of the node is the concatenation of all the labels on the path from the node to the *root* node. This is represented in written form as a string of labels listed from right to left and separated by dots. A label need only be unique within its parent domain.

For example, a domain name for a host at the company *Example, Inc.* could be `ourhost.exam ple.com`, where `com` is the top level domain to which `ourhost.example.com` belongs, `exam ple` is a subdomain of `com`, and `ourhost` is the name of the host.

For administrative purposes, the name space is partitioned into areas called *zones*, each starting at a node and extending down to the leaf nodes or to nodes where other zones start. The data for each zone is stored in a *name server*, which answers queries about the zone using the *DNS protocol*.

The data associated with each domain name is stored in the form of *resource records* (RRs). The supported resource record types are described in Section 2.1.

1.4 Zones

To properly operate a name server, it is important to understand the difference between a *zone* and a *domain*.

As stated previously, a zone is a point of delegation in the DNS tree. A zone consists of those contiguous parts of the domain tree for which a name server has complete information and over which it has authority. It contains all domain names from a certain point downward in the domain tree except those which are delegated to other zones. A delegation point is marked by one or more *NS records* in the parent zone, which should be matched by equivalent NS records at the root of the delegated zone.

For instance, consider the `example.com` domain which includes names such as `host.aaa.exa mple.com` and `host.bbb.example.com` even though the `example.com` zone includes only delegations for the `aaa.example.com` and `bbb.example.com` zones. A zone can map exactly to a single domain, but could also include only part of a domain, the rest of which could be delegated to other name servers. Every name in the DNS tree is a *domain*, even if it is *terminal*, that is, has no *subdomains*. Every subdomain is a domain and every domain except the root is also a subdomain. The terminology is not intuitive and it is suggested that you read RFCs 1033 ("Domain Administrators Operations Guide"), 1034, and 1035 to gain a complete understanding of this difficult and subtle topic.

Though BIND is called a "domain name server", it deals primarily in terms of zones. The master and slave declarations in the `named.conf` file specify zones, not domains.[1] When you ask some other site if it is willing to be a slave server for your *domain*, you are actually asking for slave service for some collection of zones.

1.5 Authoritative Name Servers

Each zone is served by at least one *authoritative name server*, which contains the complete data for the zone. To make the DNS tolerant of server and network failures, most zones have two or more authoritative servers, on different networks.

Responses from authoritative servers have the "authoritative answer" (AA) bit set in the response packets. This makes them easy to identify when debugging DNS configurations using tools like **dig** (introduced in Chapter 8).

---

[1] The master and slave terminology is covered in the upcoming sections.

The Primary Master

The authoritative server where the master copy of the zone data is maintained is called the *primary master* server, or simply the *primary*. Typically it loads the zone contents from some local file edited by humans or perhaps generated mechanically from some other local file which is edited by humans. This file is called the *zone file* or *master file*.

In some cases, however, the master file may not be edited by humans at all, but may instead be the result of *dynamic update* operations (as covered in Chapter 9).

Slave Servers

The other authoritative servers, the *slave* servers (also known as *secondary* servers) load the zone contents from another server using a replication process known as a *zone transfer*. Typically the data are transferred directly from the primary master, but it is also possible to transfer it from another slave. In other words, a slave server may itself act as a master to a subordinate slave server.

Stealth Servers

Usually all of the zone's authoritative servers are listed in NS records in the parent zone. These NS records constitute a *delegation* of the zone from the parent. The authoritative servers are also listed in the zone file itself, at the *top level* or *apex* of the zone. You can list servers in the zone's top-level NS records that are not in the parent's NS delegation, but you cannot list servers in the parent's delegation that are not present at the zone's top level.

A *stealth server* is a server that is authoritative for a zone but is not listed in that zone's NS records. Stealth servers can be used for keeping a local copy of a zone to speed up access to the zone's records or to make sure that the zone is available even if all the "official" servers for the zone are inaccessible.

A configuration where the primary master server itself is a stealth server is often referred to as a "hidden primary" configuration. One use for this configuration is when the primary master is behind a firewall and therefore unable to communicate directly with the outside world.

1.6   Caching Name Servers

The resolver libraries provided by most operating systems are *stub resolvers*, meaning that they are not capable of performing the full DNS resolution process by themselves by talking directly to the authoritative servers. Instead, they rely on a local name server to perform the resolution on their behalf. Such a server is called a *recursive* name server; it performs *recursive lookups* for local clients.

To improve performance, recursive servers cache the results of the lookups they perform. Since the processes of recursion and caching are intimately connected, the terms *recursive server* and *caching server* are often used synonymously.

The length of time for which a record may be retained in the cache of a caching name server is controlled by the Time To Live (TTL) field associated with each resource record.

Forwarding

Even a caching name server does not necessarily perform the complete recursive lookup itself. Instead, it can *forward* some or all of the queries that it cannot satisfy from its cache to another caching name server, commonly referred to as a *forwarder*.

There may be one or more forwarders, and they are queried in turn until the list is exhausted or an answer is found. Forwarders are typically used when you do not wish all the servers at a given site to interact directly with the rest of the Internet servers. A typical scenario would involve a number of internal DNS servers and an Internet firewall. Servers unable to pass packets through the firewall would forward to the server that can do it, and that server would query the Internet DNS servers on the internal server's behalf.

1.7 Name Servers in Multiple Roles

The BIND name server can simultaneously act as a master for some zones, a slave for other zones, and as a caching (recursive) server for a set of local clients.

However, since the functions of authoritative name service and caching/recursive name service are logically separate, it is often advantageous to run them on separate server machines. A server that only provides authoritative name service (an *authoritative-only* server) can run with recursion disabled, improving reliability and security. A server that is not authoritative for any zones and only provides recursive service to local clients (a *caching-only* server) does not need to be reachable from the Internet at large and can be placed inside a firewall.

2 Zone Files

This chapter describes the concept of a Resource Record (RR) and explains when each is used. Since the publication of RFC 1034, several new RRs have been identified and implemented in the DNS. These are also included.

BIND provides the **named-rrchecker** command for checking if an individual DNS resource record is syntactically correct. The **arpaname** tool may be used to display a corresponding ARPA name for an IP address. The **named-checkzone** and **named-compilezone** tools are provided for checking a master file for syntax and consistency, and for dumping the zone content to a specified file (typically in a different format). The **named** server may automatically generate *journal* files that record the changes made to a dynamic zone; the journal can be displayed using the **named-journalprint** command. These tools are explained in detail in this chapter.

2.1 Resource Records

A domain name identifies a node. Each node has a set of resource information, which may be empty. The set of resource information associated with a particular name is composed of separate RRs. The order of RRs in a set is not significant and need not be preserved by name servers, resolvers, or other parts of the DNS. However, sorting of multiple RRs is permitted for optimization purposes, for example, to specify that a particular nearby server be tried first.

The components of a Resource Record are:

owner name
> The domain name where the RR is found.

TTL
> The time-to-live of the RR. This field is a 32-bit integer in units of seconds, and is primarily used by resolvers when they cache RRs. The TTL describes how long a RR can be cached before it should be discarded. (Also see about the maximum cache size on page 124.)

class
> An encoded 16-bit value that identifies a protocol family or instance of a protocol.

type
> An encoded 16-bit value that specifies the type of the resource record. (The common resource record types are listed in the following section.)

RDATA

The resource data. The format of the data is type (and sometimes class) specific.

The following are *types* of valid RRs:

A

A host address. In the IN class, this is a 32-bit IP address. Described in RFC 1035.

AAAA

IPv6 address. Described in RFC 1886. (For more details, see Section 2.13.)

A6

IPv6 address. This can be a partial address (a suffix) and an indirection to the name where the rest of the address (the prefix) can be found. Experimental. Described in RFC 2874. (For more details, see Section 2.13.)

AFSDB

Location of AFS database servers. Experimental. Described in RFC 1183.

APL

Address prefix list. Experimental. Described in RFC 3123.

ATMA

ATM Address.

CAA

Identifies which Certificate Authorities can issue certificates for this domain and what rules they need to follow when doing so. Defined in RFC 6844.

CDNSKEY

Identifies which DNSKEY records should be published as DS records in the parent zone.

CDS

Contains the set of DS records that should be published by the parent zone.

CERT

Holds a digital certificate. Described in RFC 2538.

CNAME

Identifies the canonical name of an alias. Described in RFC 1035.

CSYNC

Child-to-Parent Synchronization in DNS as described in RFC 7477.

DHCID

Identifies which DHCP client is associated with this name. Described in RFC 4701.

DLV

A DNS Look-aside Validation record which contains the records that are used as trust anchors for zones in a DLV namespace. Described in RFC 4431.

DNAME

Replaces the domain name specified with another name to be looked up, effectively aliasing an entire subtree of the domain name space rather than a single record as in the case of the CNAME RR. Described in RFC 2672.

DNSKEY

Stores a public key associated with a signed DNS zone. Described in RFC 4034.

DS

Stores the hash of a public key associated with a signed DNS zone. Described in RFC 4034.

EID

End Point Identifier.

EUI48

A 48-bit EUI address. Described in RFC 7043.

EUI64

A 64-bit EUI address. Described in RFC 7043.

GID

Reserved.

GPOS

Specifies the global position. Superseded by LOC.

HINFO

Identifies the CPU and OS used by a host. Described in RFC 1035.

HIP

Host Identity Protocol Address. Described in RFC 5205.

IPSECKEY

Provides a method for storing IPsec keying material in DNS. Described in RFC 4025.

ISDN

Representation of ISDN addresses. Experimental. Described in RFC 1183.

KEY

Stores a public key associated with a DNS name. Used in original DNSSEC; replaced by DNSKEY in the latest DNSSEC, but still used with SIG(0). Described in RFCs 2535 and 2931.

KX

Identifies a key exchanger for this DNS name. Described in RFC 2230.

L32

Holds 32-bit Locator values for Identifier-Locator Network Protocol. Described in RFC 6742.

L64

Holds 64-bit Locator values for Identifier-Locator Network Protocol. Described in RFC 6742.

LOC
> For storing GPS info. Described in RFC 1876. Experimental.

LP
> Identifier-Locator Network Protocol. Described in RFC 6742.

MB
> Mail Box. Historical.

MD
> Mail Destination. Historical.

MF
> Mail Forwarder. Historical.

MG
> Mail Group. Historical.

MINFO
> Mail Information.

MR
> Mail Rename. Historical.

MX
> Identifies a mail exchange for the domain with a 16-bit preference value (lower is better) followed by the host name of the mail exchange. Described in RFC 974 and RFC 1035. (For more details, see Section 2.6.)

NAPTR
> Name authority pointer. Described in RFC 2915.

NID
> Holds values for Node Identifiers in Identifier-Locator Network Protocol. Described in RFC 6742.

NINFO
> Contains zone status information.

NIMLOC
> Nimrod Locator.

NSAP
> A network service access point. Described in RFC 1706.

NSAP-PTR
> Historical.

NS
> The authoritative name server for the domain. Described in RFC 1035. (For more details, see Section 1.4.)

NSEC

Used in DNSSEC to securely indicate that RRs with an owner name in a certain name interval do not exist in a zone and indicate what RR types are present for an existing name. Described in RFC 4034.

NSEC3

Used in DNSSEC to securely indicate that RRs with an owner name in a certain name interval do not exist in a zone and indicate what RR types are present for an existing name. NSEC3 differs from NSEC in that it prevents zone enumeration but is more computationally expensive on both the server and the client than NSEC. Described in RFC 5155.

Note

Queries for NSEC3 records fail to return the NSEC3 record, because NSEC3 records are strictly meta data and can only be returned in the authority section. This is done so that signing the zone using NSEC3 records does not bring names into existence that do not exist in the unsigned version of the zone.

NSEC3PARAM

Used in DNSSEC to tell the authoritative server which NSEC3 chains are available to use. Described in RFC 5155.

NULL

This is an opaque container.

NXT

Used in DNSSEC to securely indicate that RRs with an owner name in a certain name interval do not exist in a zone and indicate what RR types are present for an existing name. Used in original DNSSEC; replaced by NSEC in the latest DNSSEC. Described in RFC 2535.

OPENPGPKEY

Used to hold an OPENPGPKEY.

PTR

A pointer to another part of the domain name space. Described in RFC 1035. (For more details, see Section 2.7.)

PX

Provides mappings between RFC 822 and X.400 addresses. Described in RFC 2163.

RKEY

Resource key.

RP

Information on persons responsible for the domain. Experimental. Described in RFC 1183.

RRSIG

Contains DNSSEC signature data. Described in RFC 4034.

RT

Route-through binding for hosts that do not have their own direct wide area network addresses. Experimental. Described in RFC 1183.

SIG

Contains DNSSEC signature data. Used in original DNSSEC; replaced by RRSIG in the latest DNSSEC, but still used for SIG(0). Described in RFCs 2535 and 2931.

SINK

The kitchen sink record.

SOA

Identifies the start of a zone of authority. Described in RFC 1035.

SPF

Contains the Sender Policy Framework information for a given email domain. Described in RFC 4408.

SRV

Information about well known network services (replaces WKS). Described in RFC 2782.

SSHFP

Provides a way to securely publish a secure shell key's fingerprint. Described in RFC 4255.

TA

Trust Anchor. Experimental.

TALINK

Trust Anchor Link. Experimental.

TLSA

Transport Layer Security Certificate Association. Described in RFC 6698.

TXT

Text records. Described in RFC 1035.

UID

Reserved.

UINFO

Reserved.

UNSPEC

Reserved. Historical.

URI

Holds a URI. Described in RFC 7553.

WKS

Information about which well known network services, such as SMTP, that a domain supports. Historical.

X25

Representation of X.25 network addresses. Experimental. Described in RFC 1183.

The following *classes* of resource records are currently valid in the DNS:

IN

> The Internet.

CH

> Chaosnet, a LAN protocol created at MIT in the mid-1970s. Rarely used for its historical purpose, but reused for BIND's built-in server information zones, e.g., `version.bind` (see page 131).

HS

> Hesiod, an information service developed by MIT's Project Athena. It was used to share information about various systems databases, such as users, groups, printers, and so on.

The owner name is often implicit, rather than forming an integral part of the RR. For example, many name servers internally form tree or hash structures for the name space, and chain RRs off nodes. The remaining RR parts are the fixed header (type, class, TTL) which is consistent for all RRs, and a variable part (RDATA) that fits the needs of the resource being described.

The meaning of the TTL field is a time limit on how long an RR can be kept in a cache. This limit does not apply to authoritative data in zones; it is also timed out, but by the refreshing policies for the zone. The TTL is assigned by the administrator for the zone where the data originates. While short TTLs can be used to minimize caching, and a zero TTL prohibits caching, the realities of Internet performance suggest that these times should be on the order of days for the typical host. If a change can be anticipated, the TTL can be reduced prior to the change to minimize inconsistency during the change, and then increased back to its former value following the change.

The data in the RDATA section of RRs is carried as a combination of binary strings and domain names. The domain names are frequently used as "pointers" to other data in the DNS.

2.2 Textual expression of RRs

Resource Records are represented in binary form in the packets of the DNS protocol, and are usually represented in an highly encoded form when stored in a name server or resolver. In the examples provided in RFC 1034, a style similar to that used in master files was employed in order to show the contents of RRs. In this format, most RRs are shown on a single line, although continuation lines are possible using parentheses.

The start of the line gives the owner of the RR. If a line begins with a blank, then the owner is assumed to be the same as that of the previous RR. Blank lines are often included for readability.

Following the owner, the TTL, class, and type of the RR are listed. Class and type use the mnemonics defined above, and TTL is an integer before the type field. In order to avoid ambiguity in parsing, type and class mnemonics are disjoint, TTLs are integers, and the type mnemonic is always last. The IN class and TTL values are often omitted from examples in the interests of clarity.

The resource data or RDATA section of the RR are given using knowledge of the typical representation for the data.

For example, we might show the RRs carried in a message as:

```
ISI.EDU.          MX     10 VENERA.ISI.EDU.
                  MX     10 VAXA.ISI.EDU
VENERA.ISI.EDU    A      128.9.0.32
                  A      10.1.0.52
VAXA.ISI.EDU      A      10.2.0.27
                  A      128.9.0.33
```

The MX RRs have an RDATA section which consists of a 16-bit number followed by a domain name. The address RRs use a standard IP address format to contain a 32-bit internet address.

The above example shows six RRs, with two RRs at each of three domain names.

Similarly we might see:

```
XX.LCS.MIT.EDU.       IN A          10.0.0.44
                      CH A          MIT.EDU. 2420
```

This example shows two addresses for XX.LCS.MIT.EDU, each of a different class.

A semicolon (;) starts a comment; the remainder of the line is ignored.

2.3 SOA Record

```
;name <ttl> class  SOA  Origin                 Person in charge
@            IN     SOA  ucbvax.Berkeley.Edu. kjd.ucbvax.Berkeley.Edu. (
                        1995122103 ; Serial
                        10800      ; Refresh
                        1800       ; Retry
                        3600000    ; Expire
                        259200 )   ; Minimum
```

The Start of Authority, SOA, record designates the start of a zone. There must be exactly one SOA record per zone. The *name* is the name of the zone and is often given as "@" since this is always the current $ORIGIN and the SOA RR is usually the first record of the primary zone file. *Origin* is the name of the host on which this data file resides (in other words, the primary master server for this zone.) *Person in charge* is the email address for the person responsible for the name server, with the first "@" changed to a period (.). (The example is the email address "kjd@ucbvax.Berkeley.Edu".)

The serial number is the version number of this data file and must be a positive integer. This number should be incremented whenever a change is made to the data.

The *refresh* indicates how often, in seconds, the secondary name servers are to check with the primary name server to see if an update is needed. The *retry* indicates how long, in seconds, a secondary server should wait before retrying a failed zone transfer. *Expire* is the upper limit, in seconds, that a secondary name server is to use the data before it expires for lack of getting a refresh.

The final field in the SOA is the negative caching TTL. This controls how long other servers will cache no-such-domain (NXDOMAIN) responses from you.

(Historically, the final field was the default number of seconds to be used for the Time To Live field on resource records which do not specify one in the zone file. It also enforced the *Minimum* Time To Live when specified on some resource record in the zone.)

Incrementing and Changing the Serial Number

Zone serial numbers are just numbers — they aren't date related. A lot of people set them to a number that represents a date, usually of the form YYYYMMDDRR (year, month, day, and number of revisions per that day). Occasionally they will make a mistake and set them to a "date in the future" then try to correct them by setting them to the "current date". This causes problems because serial numbers are used to indicate that a zone has been updated. If the serial number on the slave server is lower than the serial number on the master, the slave server will attempt to update its copy of the zone.

Setting the serial number to a lower number on the master server than the slave server means that the slave will not perform updates to its copy of the zone.

The solution to this is to add 2147483647 (2^31-1) to the number, reload the zone and make sure all slaves have updated to the new zone serial number, then reset the number to what you want it to be, and reload the zone again.

2.4   Setting TTLs

The time-to-live of the RR field is a 32-bit integer represented in units of seconds, and is primarily used by resolvers when they cache RRs. The TTL describes how long a RR can be cached before it should be discarded. The following three types of TTL are currently used in a zone file.

SOA

As mentioned previously, the last field in the SOA is the negative caching TTL and it controls how long other servers will cache NXDOMAIN responses.

The maximum time for negative caching is 3 hours (3h). (See the **max-ncache-ttl** option on page 128 for more information.)

$TTL

The $TTL directive at the top of the zone file (before the SOA) gives a default TTL for every RR without a specific TTL set.

RR TTLs

Each RR can have a TTL as the second field in the RR, which will control how long other servers can cache it. (See the **max-cache-ttl** option on page 128 for more information.)

All of these TTLs default to units of seconds, though units can be explicitly specified, for example, `1h30m`.

2.5   Timing Mnemonics

Timing values for TTLs and SOA Refresh, Retry, Expire and Minimum may optionally be presented with timing mnemonics instead of just seconds as an alternative presentation format. They may be defined in the master file using weeks, days, hours, minutes, and seconds using single character identifiers.

Upper and lower case letters are allowed. No spaces or tabs are allowed (as they separate the RR fields). The timing letter is used as suffix to a integer number. The timing is:

S or s
>   seconds

M or m
>   minutes (* 60)

H or h
>   hours (* 60 * 60)

D or d
>   days (* 60 * 60 * 24)

W or w
>   weeks (* 60 * 60 * 24 * 7)

Note that "M" and "m" do not represent a month.

The value "1s1s1s" is 3. This would be better represented as "3s" or just "3".

The value of "1s2w1s3w4h5h1w" is 3661202; for example: 1 + (2*60*60*24*7) + 1 + (3*60*60*24*7) + (4*60*60) + (5*60*60) + (1*60*60*24*7). If using mnemonics, this would be better represented as "6w9h2s".

It is suggested that: the presentation output be reduced to the least amount of mnemonics, ordered from longest duration to shortest, mnemonics characters are not repeated, and a consistent case is used. For example: use "1W" instead of "7D"; or use "1w3d" instead of "72h5D86400s1d".

Warning
These timing mnemonics are not used for the SOA SERIAL. The serial number is not timing information (even though some operators use a time for it). Also note that the timing mnemonics can not be used for the Original TTL field for an RRSIG RR; an unsigned decimal integer is used per RFC 4034.

2.6   MX Records

As described above, domain servers store information as a series of resource records, each of which contains a particular piece of information about a given domain name (which is usually, but not always, a host). The simplest way to think of a RR is as a typed pair of data, a domain name matched with a relevant datum, and stored with some additional type information to help systems determine when the RR is relevant.

MX records are used to control delivery of email. The data specified in the record is a priority and a domain name. The priority controls the order in which email delivery is attempted, with the lowest number first. If two priorities are the same, a server is chosen randomly. If no servers at a given priority are responding, the mail transport agent will fall back to the next largest priority. Priority numbers do not have any absolute meaning — they are relevant only respective to other MX records for that domain name. The domain name given is the machine to which the mail will be delivered. It *must* have an associated address record (A or AAAA) — CNAME is not sufficient.

For a given domain, if there is both a CNAME record and an MX record, the MX record is in error, and will be ignored. Instead, the mail will be delivered to the server specified in the MX record pointed to by the CNAME. For example:

```
example.com.          IN    MX    10          mail.example.com.
                      IN    MX    10          mail2.example.com.
                      IN    MX    20          mail.backup.org.
mail.example.com.     IN    A     10.0.0.1
mail2.example.com.    IN    A     10.0.0.2
```

Mail delivery will be attempted to `mail.example.com` and `mail2.example.com` (in any order), and if neither of those succeed, delivery to `mail.backup.org` will be attempted.

2.7   Inverse Mapping in IPv4

Reverse name resolution (that is, translation from IP address to name) is achieved by means of the *in-addr.arpa* domain and PTR records. Entries in the in-addr.arpa domain are made in least-to-most significant order, read left to right. This is the opposite order to the way IP addresses are usually written. Thus, a machine with an IP address of 10.1.2.3 would have a corresponding in-addr.arpa name of 3.2.1.10.in-addr.arpa. This name should have a PTR resource record whose data field is the name of the machine or, optionally, multiple PTR records if the machine has more than one name. For example, in the *example.com* domain:

```
$ORIGIN           2.1.10.in-addr.arpa
3                 IN PTR foo.example.com.
```

Note

The **$ORIGIN** lines in the examples are for providing context to the examples only — they do not necessarily appear in the actual usage. They are only used here to indicate that the example is relative to the listed origin.

2.8   arpaname — translate IP addresses to corresponding ARPA names

Synopsis

```
arpaname ipaddress ...
```

arpaname Description

arpaname translates IP addresses (IPv4 and IPv6) to the corresponding IN-ADDR.ARPA or IP6.ARPA names.

2.9   Load Balancing

A primitive form of load balancing can be achieved in the DNS by using multiple records (such as multiple A records) for one name.[1]

For example, if you have three WWW servers with network addresses of 10.0.0.1, 10.0.0.2, and 10.0.0.3, a set of records such as the following means that clients will connect to each machine one third of the time:

```
www           600        IN        A          10.0.0.1
              600        IN        A          10.0.0.2
              600        IN        A          10.0.0.3
```

When a resolver queries for these records, BIND will rotate them and respond to the query with the records in a different order. In the example above, clients will randomly receive records in the order 1, 2, 3; 2, 3, 1; and 3, 1, 2. Most clients will use the first record returned and discard the rest.

For more detail on ordering responses, check the **rrset-order** sub-statement in the **options** statement in Section 6.7.

2.10   Other Zone File Directives

The Master File Format was initially defined in RFC 1035 and has subsequently been extended. While the Master File Format itself is class independent all records in a Master File must be of the same class.

Master File Directives include **$ORIGIN**, **$INCLUDE**, and **$TTL.**

@ (at-sign)

When used in the label (or name) field, the asperand or at-sign (@) symbol represents the current origin. At the start of the zone file, it is the <zone_name> (followed by trailing dot).

The $ORIGIN Directive

Syntax: **$ORIGIN** *domain-name* [*comment*]

$ORIGIN sets the domain name that will be appended to any unqualified records. When a zone is first read in, there is an implicit **$ORIGIN** <zone_name>. (followed by trailing dot). The current **$ORIGIN** is appended to the domain specified in the **$ORIGIN** argument if it is not absolute.

---

[1] Some consider this load balancing as fragile at best and completely pointless in the general case.

```
$ORIGIN example.com.
WWW      CNAME   MAIN-SERVER
```

is equivalent to

```
WWW.EXAMPLE.COM. CNAME MAIN-SERVER.EXAMPLE.COM.
```

The $INCLUDE Directive

Syntax: **$INCLUDE** *filename* [*origin*] [*comment*]

Read and process the file `filename` as if it were included into the file at this point. If **origin** is specified the file is processed with **$ORIGIN** set to that value, otherwise the current **$ORIGIN** is used.

The origin and the current domain name revert to the values they had prior to the **$INCLUDE** once the file has been read.

Note
RFC 1035 specifies that the current origin should be restored after an **$INCLUDE**, but it is silent on whether the current domain name should also be restored. BIND 9 restores both of them. This could be construed as a deviation from RFC 1035, a feature, or both.

The $TTL Directive

Syntax: **$TTL** *default-ttl* [*comment*]

Set the default Time To Live (TTL) for subsequent records with undefined TTLs. Valid TTLs are of the range 0-2147483647 seconds.

$TTL is defined in RFC 2308. (For more details, see Section 2.4.)

Q: *Why does named log the warning message "no TTL specified - using SOA MINTTL instead"?*

A: Your zone file is illegal according to RFC1035. It must either have a line like:

```
$TTL 86400
```

at the beginning, or the first record in it must have a TTL field, like the "84600" in this example:

```
example.com. 86400 IN SOA ns hostmaster ( 1 3600 1800 1814400 3600 )
```

2.11   BIND Master File Extension: the $GENERATE Directive

Syntax: **$GENERATE** *range lhs* [*ttl*] [*class*] *type rhs* [*comment*]

$GENERATE is used to create a series of resource records that only differ from each other by an
iterator. **$GENERATE** can be used to easily generate the sets of records required to support sub /24
reverse delegations described in RFC 2317: Classless IN-ADDR.ARPA delegation.

```
$ORIGIN 0.0.192.IN-ADDR.ARPA.
$GENERATE 1-2 @ NS SERVER$.EXAMPLE.
$GENERATE 1-127 $ CNAME $.0
```

is equivalent to

```
0.0.0.192.IN-ADDR.ARPA. NS SERVER1.EXAMPLE.
0.0.0.192.IN-ADDR.ARPA. NS SERVER2.EXAMPLE.
1.0.0.192.IN-ADDR.ARPA. CNAME 1.0.0.0.192.IN-ADDR.ARPA.
2.0.0.192.IN-ADDR.ARPA. CNAME 2.0.0.0.192.IN-ADDR.ARPA.
...
127.0.0.192.IN-ADDR.ARPA. CNAME 127.0.0.0.192.IN-ADDR.ARPA.
```

The following example generates a set of A and MX records. Note the MX's right hand side is a
quoted string. The quotes will be stripped when the right hand side is processed.

```
$ORIGIN EXAMPLE.
$GENERATE 1-127 HOST-$ A 1.2.3.$
$GENERATE 1-127 HOST-$ MX "0 ."
```

is equivalent to

```
HOST-1.EXAMPLE.     A   1.2.3.1
HOST-1.EXAMPLE.     MX 0 .
HOST-2.EXAMPLE.     A   1.2.3.2
HOST-2.EXAMPLE.     MX 0 .
HOST-3.EXAMPLE.     A   1.2.3.3
HOST-3.EXAMPLE.     MX 0 .
...
HOST-127.EXAMPLE.   A   1.2.3.127
HOST-127.EXAMPLE.   MX 0 .
```

range

> This can be one of two forms: start-stop or start-stop/step. If the first form is used, then step is
> set to 1. start, stop and step must be positive integers between 0 and (2^{31})-1. start must not be
> larger than stop.

lhs

> This describes the owner name of the resource records to be created. Any single $ (dollar sign)
> symbols within the **lhs** string are replaced by the iterator value. To get a $ in the output, you
> need to escape the $ using a backslash \, e.g. \$. The $ may optionally be followed by modifiers
> which change the offset from the iterator, field width and base. Modifiers are introduced by a {

(left brace) immediately following the **$** as **${offset[,width[,base]]}**. For example, **${-20,3,d}** subtracts 20 from the current value, prints the result as a decimal in a zero-padded field of width 3. Available output forms are decimal (**d**), octal (**o**), hexadecimal (**x** or **X** for uppercase) and nibble (**n** or **N** for uppercase). The default modifier is **${0,0,d}**. If the **lhs** is not absolute, the current **$ORIGIN** is appended to the name.

In nibble mode the value will be treated as if it was a reversed hexadecimal string with each hexadecimal digit as a separate label. The width field includes the label separator.

For compatibility with earlier versions, **$$** is still recognized as indicating a literal $ in the output.

ttl

> Specifies the time-to-live of the generated records. If not specified this will be inherited using the normal TTL inheritance rules.
>
> **class** and **ttl** can be entered in either order.

class

> Specifies the class of the generated records. This must match the zone class if it is specified.
>
> **class** and **ttl** can be entered in either order.

type

> Any valid type.

rhs

> **rhs** is the right-hand side like a domain name, or, optionally, a quoted string. It is processed similarly to **lhs**.

The **$GENERATE** directive is a BIND extension and not part of the standard zone file format. Some server implementations, like BIND 8, may not support the optional TTL and CLASS fields.

2.12 Additional File Formats

In addition to the standard textual format, BIND 9 supports the ability to read or dump to zone files in other formats.

The `raw` format is a binary representation of zone data in a manner similar to that used in zone transfers. Since it does not require parsing text, load time is significantly reduced.

An even faster alternative is the `map` format, which is an image of a BIND 9 in-memory zone database; it is capable of being loaded directly into memory via the **mmap()** function; the zone can begin serving queries almost immediately. (Support for the `map` format was introduced in BIND 9.10.)

For a primary server, a zone file in `raw` or `map` format is expected to be generated from a textual zone file by the **named-compilezone** command. (See page 24 for details.) For a secondary server or for a dynamic zone, it is automatically generated (if this format is specified by the **masterfile-format** option) when **named** dumps the zone contents after zone transfer or when applying prior updates.

If a zone file in a binary format needs manual modification, it first must be converted to a textual form by the **named-compilezone** command. All necessary modification should go to the text file, which should then be converted to the binary form by the **named-compilezone** command again.

Note

The **map** format is extremely architecture-specific. A map file *cannot* be used on a system with different pointer size, endianness or data alignment than the system on which it was generated, and should in general be used only inside a single system. While raw format uses network byte order and avoids architecture-dependent data alignment so that it is as portable as possible, it is also primarily expected to be used inside the same single system.

To export a zone file in either raw or map format, or make a portable backup of such a file, conversion to text format is recommended.

2.13   IPv6 Support in BIND 9

BIND 9 fully supports all currently defined forms of IPv6 name to address and address to name lookups. It will also use IPv6 addresses to make queries when running on an IPv6 capable system.

For forward lookups, BIND 9 supports only AAAA records. RFC 3363 deprecated the use of A6 records, and client-side support for A6 records was accordingly removed from BIND 9. However, authoritative BIND 9 name servers still load zone files containing A6 records correctly, answer queries for A6 records, and accept zone transfer for a zone containing A6 records.

For IPv6 reverse lookups, BIND 9 supports the traditional "nibble" format used in the *ip6.arpa* domain, as well as the older, deprecated *ip6.int* domain. Older versions of BIND 9 supported the "binary label" (also known as "bitstring") format, but support of binary labels has been completely removed per RFC 3363. Many applications in BIND 9 do not understand the binary label format at all any more, and will return an error if given. In particular, an authoritative BIND 9 name server will not load a zone file containing binary labels.

IPv6 Addresses (AAAA)

IPv6 addresses are 128-bit identifiers for interfaces and sets of interfaces which were introduced in the DNS to facilitate scalable Internet routing. There are three types of addresses: *Unicast*, an identifier for a single interface; *Anycast*, an identifier for a set of interfaces; and *Multicast*, an identifier for a set of interfaces. This section describes the global Unicast address scheme. For more information, see RFC 3587, "Global Unicast Address Format."

IPv6 unicast addresses consist of a *global routing prefix*, a *subnet identifier*, and an *interface identifier*.

The global routing prefix is provided by the upstream provider or ISP, and (roughly) corresponds to the IPv4 *network* section of the address range. The subnet identifier is for local subnetting, much the same as subnetting an IPv4 /16 network into /24 subnets. The interface identifier is the address of an individual interface on a given network; in IPv6, addresses belong to interfaces rather than to machines.

The subnetting capability of IPv6 is much more flexible than that of IPv4: subnetting can be carried out on bit boundaries, in much the same way as Classless InterDomain Routing (CIDR), and the DNS PTR representation ("nibble" format) makes setting up reverse zones easier.

The Interface Identifier must be unique on the local link, and is usually generated automatically by the IPv6 implementation, although it is usually possible to override the default setting if necessary. A typical IPv6 address might look like: **2001:db8:201:9:a00:20ff:fe81:2b32**

IPv6 address specifications often contain long strings of zeros, so the architects have included a shorthand for specifying them. The double colon (`::`) indicates the longest possible string of zeros that can fit, and can be used only once in an address.

Address Lookups Using AAAA Records

The IPv6 AAAA record is a parallel to the IPv4 A record, and, unlike the deprecated A6 record, specifies the entire IPv6 address in a single record. For example,

```
$ORIGIN example.com.
host            3600    IN      AAAA    2001:db8::1
```

Use of IPv4-in-IPv6 mapped addresses is not recommended. If a host has an IPv4 address, use an A record, not a AAAA, with `::ffff:192.168.42.1` as the address.

Address to Name Lookups Using Nibble Format

When looking up an address in nibble format, the address components are simply reversed, just as in IPv4, and `ip6.arpa.` is appended to the resulting name. For example, the following would provide reverse name lookup for a host with address `2001:db8::1`.

```
$ORIGIN 0.0.0.0.0.0.0.0.8.b.d.0.1.0.0.2.ip6.arpa.
1.0.0.0.0.0.0.0.0.0.0.0.0.0.0.0  14400   IN      PTR     (
          host.example.com. )
```

2.14   named-checkzone — zone file validity checker and converter

Synopsis

named-checkzone [-d] [-h] [-j] [-q] [-v] [-c *class*] [-f *format*] [-F *format*] [-J *filename*] [-i *mode*] [-k *mode*] [-m *mode*] [-M *mode*] [-n *mode*] [-l *ttl*] [-L *serial*] [-o *filename*] [-r *mode*] [-s *style*] [-S *mode*] [-t *directory*] [-T *mode*] [-w *directory*] [-D] [-W *mode*] zonename filename

named-compilezone [-d] [-j] [-q] [-v] [-c *class*] [-C *mode*] [-f *format*] [-F *format*] [-J *filename*] [-i *mode*] [-k *mode*] [-m *mode*] [-n *mode*] [-l *ttl*] [-L *serial*] [-r *mode*] [-s *style*] [-t *directory*] [-T *mode*] [-w *directory*] [-D] [-W *mode*] -o *filename* zonename filename

named-checkzone Description

named-checkzone checks the syntax and integrity of a zone file. It performs the same checks as **named** does when loading a zone. This makes **named-checkzone** useful for checking zone files before configuring them into a name server.

named-compilezone is similar to **named-checkzone**, but it always dumps the zone contents to a specified file in a specified format. Additionally, it applies stricter check levels by default, since the dump output will be used as an actual zone file loaded by **named**. When manually specified otherwise, the check levels must at least be as strict as those specified in the **named** configuration file.

named-checkzone Options

-d
> Enable debugging.

-h
> Print the usage summary and exit.

-q
> Quiet mode - exit code only.

-v
> Print the version of the **named-checkzone** program and exit.

-j
> When loading a zone file, read the journal if it exists. The journal file name is assumed to be the zone file name appended with the string `.jnl`.

-J *filename*
> When loading the zone file read the journal from the given file, if it exists. (Implies -j.) (This −J option was introduced in BIND 9.10.)

-c *class*
> Specify the class of the zone. If not specified, "IN" is assumed.

-i *mode*
> Perform post-load zone integrity checks. Possible modes are **"full"** (default), **"full-sibling"**, **"local"**, **"local-sibling"** and **"none"**.

Note
Working hostname lookups and network access may be needed to verify these checks. The external checks use getaddrinfo(3) and may give false positives due to inconsistencies between the various sources of address information (such as the hosts file vs. NIS vs. DNS).

Mode **"full"** checks that MX records refer to A or AAAA record (both in-zone and out-of-zone hostnames). Mode **"local"** only checks MX records which refer to in-zone hostnames.

Mode **"full"** checks that SRV records refer to A or AAAA record (both in-zone and out-of-zone hostnames). Mode **"local"** only checks SRV records which refer to in-zone hostnames.

Mode **"full"** checks that delegation NS records refer to A or AAAA record (both in-zone and out-of-zone hostnames). It also checks that glue address records in the zone match those advertised by the child. Mode **"local"** only checks NS records which refer to in-zone hostnames or that some required glue exists, that is when the nameserver is in a child zone.

Mode **"full-sibling"** and **"local-sibling"** disable sibling glue checks but are otherwise the same as **"full"** and **"local"** respectively.

Mode **"none"** disables the checks.

-f *format*

Specify the format of the zone file. Possible formats are **"text"** (default), **"raw"**, and **"map"**. (The **"map"** format was introduced in BIND 9.10.)

-F *format*

Specify the format of the output file specified. For **named-checkzone**, this does not cause any effects unless it dumps the zone contents.

Possible formats are **"text"** (default), which is the standard textual representation of the zone, and **"map"**, **"raw"**, and **"raw=N"**, which store the zone in a binary format for rapid loading by **named**. **"raw=N"** (introduced in BIND 9.9) specifies the format version of the raw zone file: if N is 0, the raw file can be read by any version of **named**; if N is 1, the file can be read by release 9.9.0 or higher; the default is 1. (The **"map"** format was introduced in BIND 9.10.)

-k *mode*

Perform **"check-names"** checks with the specified failure mode. Possible modes are **"fail"** (default for **named-compilezone**), **"warn"** (default for **named-checkzone**) and **"ignore"**.

-l *ttl*

Sets a maximum permissible TTL for the input file. Any record with a TTL higher than this value will cause the zone to be rejected. This is similar to using the **max-zone-ttl** option in `named.conf`. (This `-l` option was introduced in BIND 9.10.)

-L *serial*

When compiling a zone to "raw" or "map" format, set the "source serial" value in the header to the specified serial number. (The `-L` option was introduced in BIND 9.9. It is expected to be used primarily for testing purposes.)

-m *mode*

Specify whether MX records should be checked to see if they are addresses. Possible modes are **"fail"**, **"warn"** (default) and **"ignore"**.

-M *mode*

Check if a MX record refers to a CNAME. Possible modes are **"fail"**, **"warn"** (default) and **"ignore"**.

-n *mode*

> Specify whether NS records should be checked to see if they are addresses. Possible modes are **"fail"** (default for **named-compilezone**), **"warn"** (default for **named-checkzone**) and **"ignore"**.

-o *filename*

> Write zone output to `filename`. If `filename` is – (dash) then write to standard out. This is mandatory for **named-compilezone**.

-r *mode*

> Check for records that are treated as different by DNSSEC but are semantically equal in plain DNS. Possible modes are **"fail"**, **"warn"** (default) and **"ignore"**.

-s *style*

> Specify the style of the dumped zone file. Possible styles are **"full"** (default) and **"relative"**. The full format is most suitable for processing automatically by a separate script. On the other hand, the relative format is more human-readable and is thus suitable for editing by hand. For **named-checkzone** this does not cause any effects unless it dumps the zone contents. It also does not have any meaning if the output format is not text.

-S *mode*

> Check if a SRV record refers to a CNAME. Possible modes are **"fail"**, **"warn"** (default) and **"ignore"**.

-t *directory*

> Chroot to `directory` so that include directives in the configuration file are processed as if run by a similarly chrooted **named**.

-T *mode*

> Check if Sender Policy Framework (SPF) records exist and issues a warning if an SPF-formatted TXT record is not also present. Possible modes are **"warn"** (default), **"ignore"**.

-w *directory*

> chdir to `directory` so that relative filenames in master file $INCLUDE directives work. This is similar to the directory clause in `named.conf`.

-D

> Dump zone file in canonical format. This is always enabled for **named-compilezone**.

-W *mode*

> Specify whether to check for non-terminal wildcards. Non-terminal wildcards are almost always the result of a failure to understand the wildcard matching algorithm (RFC 1034). Possible modes are **"warn"** (default) and **"ignore"**.

zonename

> The domain name of the zone being checked.

filename

> The name of the zone file.

named-checkzone Return Values

named-checkzone returns an exit status of 1 if errors were detected and 0 otherwise.

2.15 named-journalprint — print human-readable zone journal

Synopsis

```
named-journalprint journal
```

named-journalprint Description

named-journalprint prints the contents of a zone journal file in a human-readable form.

Journal files are automatically created by **named** when changes are made to dynamic zones (e.g., by **nsupdate**). They record each addition or deletion of a resource record, in binary format, allowing the changes to be re-applied to the zone when the server is restarted after a shutdown or crash. By default, the name of the journal file is formed by appending the extension .jnl to the name of the corresponding zone file.

named-journalprint converts the contents of a given journal file into a human-readable text format. Each line begins with "add" or "del", to indicate whether the record was added or deleted, and continues with the resource record in master-file format.

2.16 named-rrchecker — DNS resource record syntax checker

Synopsis

```
named-rrchecker [-h] [-o origin] [-p] [-u] [-C] [-T] [-P]
```

named-rrchecker Description

named-rrchecker read a individual DNS resource record from standard input and checks if it is syntactically correct. It may be called by provisioning systems so that their front-end does not need to be upgraded to support new DNS record types. This tool was introduced in BIND 9.10.

The -h prints out the help menu.

The -o *origin* option specifies a origin to be used when interpreting the record.

The -p prints out the resulting record in canonical form. If there is no canonical form defined then the record will be printed in unknown record format.

The -u prints out the resulting record in unknown record form.

The -C, -T and -P print out the known class, standard type and private type mnemonics respectively.

3 BIND Installation

The BIND software is provided from Internet Systems Consortium as a source distribution in a compressed .tar file. The downloads are available from the file server at http://ftp.isc.org/isc/bind9/ or via FTP at ftp://ftp.isc.org/isc/bind9/. ISC also provides pre-compiled binaries for 64-bit and 32-bit Windows platforms.

ISC supports a couple different versions of the software — see the "cur/" directory link at the downloads site which links to the latest release versions. Use the latest version for the newest maintained features (9.10 at the time of this book's printing) or use the previous version for the previous stable release (9.9 at the time of this book's printing).

BIND is available for free under the MIT-style open source ISC License (as shown on page xi).

This chapter covers the system requirements and steps for building and installing BIND, including DNS library support. It also shares examples of using ready-to-use software packages provided by some operating systems.

3.1 BIND Resource Requirements

Hardware Requirements

DNS hardware requirements have traditionally been quite modest. For many installations, servers that have been pensioned off from active duty have performed admirably as DNS servers.

The DNSSEC features of BIND 9 may prove to be quite CPU intensive however, so organizations that make heavy use of these features may wish to consider faster systems for these applications. BIND 9 is fully multithreaded, allowing full utilization of multiprocessor systems for installations that need it.

CPU Requirements

CPU requirements for BIND 9 range from i486-class machines for serving of static zones without caching, to enterprise-class machines if you intend to process many dynamic updates and DNSSEC signed zones, serving many thousands of queries per second. BIND is used on SPARC, ARM, MIPS, VAX, PowerPC, and many other platforms.

Memory Requirements

The memory of the server has to be large enough to fit the cache and zones loaded off disk. The **max-cache-size** option can be used to limit the amount of memory used by the cache, at the expense of reducing cache hit rates and causing more DNS traffic. (The cache memory limit option is described on page 124.) Additionally, if additional section caching is enabled, the **max-acache-size** option can be used to limit the amount of memory used by the mechanism. (Details about additional section caching can be found in Section 6.7.) It is still good practice to have enough memory to load all zone and cache data into memory — unfortunately, the best way to determine this for a given installation is to watch the name server in operation. After a few weeks the server process should reach a relatively stable size where entries are expiring from the cache as fast as they are being inserted.

Name Server Intensive Environment Issues

For name server intensive environments, there are two alternative configurations that may be used. The first is where clients and any second-level internal name servers query a main name server, which has enough memory to build a large cache. This approach minimizes the bandwidth used by external name lookups. The second alternative is to set up second-level internal name servers to make queries independently. In this configuration, none of the individual machines needs to have as much memory or CPU power as in the first alternative, but this has the disadvantage of making many more external queries, as none of the name servers share their cached data.

3.2   Supported Operating Systems

ISC BIND 9 compiles and runs on a large number of Unix-like operating systems and on Microsoft Windows Server 2003 and 2008, and Windows XP and Vista.

Building BIND 9 on Unix requires an ANSI C compiler, basic POSIX support, and a 64 bit integer type. ISC has had successful builds and tests on the following systems: CentOS 5; COMPAQ Tru64 UNIX 5.1B; Fedora Core 6; Fedora Linux 18, 19; FreeBSD 4.11, 5.2.1, 6.2, 6.3, 8.4, 10; HP-UX 11.11; MacOSX 10.5, 10.6; NetBSD 3.x, 4.x, 5.x, 6.x; OpenBSD 3.3 and up; Solaris 8, 9, 9 (x86), 10, 11; Ubuntu 7.04, 7.10, 13.10; Windows XP, 2003, 2008[1] and many others. ISC has also had reports from the user community that a supported version of BIND will build and run on the following systems: AIX 4.3, 5L; CentOS 4, 4.5, 5; Darwin 9.0.0d1/ARM; Debian 4, 5, 6; Fedora Core 5, 7, 8; FreeBSD 6, 7, 8; HP-UX 11.23 PA; MacOS X 10.5, 10.6, 10.7; Red Hat Enterprise Linux 4, 5, 6; SCO OpenServer 5.0.6; Slackware 9, 10; Solaris 8, 9; and SuSE 9, 10.

 Warning
Linux requires kernel build 2.6.39 or later to get the performance benefits from using multiple sockets.

---

[1] As of BIND 9.5.1, 9.4.3, and 9.3.6, older versions of Windows, including Windows NT and Windows 2000, are no longer supported.

3.3 Building

To build, just run at the shell command-line (after extracting the tar file):

```
./configure
make
```

Note
Do not use a parallel "make".

"make install" will install **named** and the various BIND 9 libraries and tools. By default, installation is into /usr/local, but this can be changed with the "--prefix" option when running "configure".

You may specify the option "--sysconfdir" to set the directory where configuration files like "named.conf" are used by default, and "--localstatedir" to set the default parent directory of "run/named.pid". For backwards compatibility with BIND 8, --sysconfdir defaults to "/etc" and --localstatedir defaults to "/var" if no --prefix option is given. If there is a --prefix option, sysconfdir defaults to "$prefix/etc" and localstatedir defaults to "$prefix/var".

On most platforms, BIND 9 is built with multithreading support, allowing it to take advantage of multiple CPUs. You can configure this by specifying "--enable-threads" or "--disable-threads" on the configure command line. The default is to enable threads, except on some older operating systems on which threads are known to have had problems in the past.

Note
Prior to BIND 9.10, the default was to disable threads on Linux systems; this has been reversed. On Linux systems, the threaded build is known to change BIND's behavior with respect to file permissions; it may be necessary to specify a user with the -u option when running **named**.

To build shared libraries, specify "--with-libtool" on the configure command line.

Certain compiled-in constants and default settings can be increased to values better suited to large servers with abundant memory resources (e.g, 64-bit servers with 12GB or more of memory) by specifying "--with-tuning=large" on the configure command line. This can improve performance on big servers, but will consume more memory and may degrade performance on smaller systems.

For the server to support DNSSEC, you need to build it with crypto support. You must have OpenSSL 0.9.5a or newer installed and specify "--with-openssl" on the configure command line. This is the default behavior. If OpenSSL is installed under a nonstandard prefix, you can tell configure where to look for it using "--with-openssl=/prefix".

The "--enable-openssl-version-check" (which defaults to yes) will have the configure check for safe OpenSSL library versions. It is recommended to use OpenSSL version 0.9.7l or 0.9.8d or greater. Further details about building with OpenSSL or SoftHSM for PKCS#11 or HSM support, see Section 10.17.

To support the HTTP statistics channel, configure with "--with-libxml2" and/or "--with-libjson". The server must be linked with at least one of the following: libxml2 (http://xmlsoft.org) or json-c (https://github.com/json-c). If these are installed at a nonstandard prefix, use "--with-libxml2=/prefix" or "--with-libjson=/prefix". The JSON-based statistics supported was introduced in BIND 9.10.

A new XML schema is used (version 3) which adds additional zone statistics and uses a flatter tree for more efficient parsing. The stylesheet included uses the Google Charts API to render data into into charts and graphs when using a Javascript-capable web browser. On BIND 9.9 to use the *new* stats, used the "--enable-newstats" switch. (It is enabled by default for later versions.)

Geolocation support using MaxMind GeoIP can be enabled since BIND 9.10 by configuring with the "--with-geoip" switch. It requires the GeoIP C development headers and library to be installed. The switch can optionally point to the base path that contains the `include/GeoIP.h` header and libraries. (For more details, see Section 6.1.)

On some platforms it is necessary to explicitly request large file support to handle files bigger than 2GB. This can be done by "--enable-largefile" on the configure command line.

Support for the "fixed" **rrset-order** option can be enabled or disabled by specifying "--enable-fixed-rrset" or "--disable-fixed-rrset" on the configure command line. The default is "disabled", to reduce memory footprint.

If your operating system has integrated support for IPv6, it will be used automatically. If you have installed KAME IPv6 separately, use "--with-kame[=PATH]" to specify its location.

To enable internationalized domain name (IDN) support for the **dig** and **host** tools, use "--with-idn[=PATH]" and optionally point to directory containing the include and lib directories for libidnkit. The "--with-idnlib=ARG" switch may be used to specify compiler switches for libidnkit.

To disable support for the NSIP and NSDNAME response policy zone records, use "--disable-rpz-nsip" or "--disable-rpz-nsdname".

To allow the **filter-aaaa-on-v4** and **filter-aaaa-on-v6** options to enable filtering of AAAA records, use the "--enable-filter-aaaa" switch.

Very verbose query trace logging can be enabled by using "--enable-querytrace".

The **dnssec-checkds** and **dnssec-coverage** tools use the Python scripting language. If configure cannot find the python interpreter, use the "--with-python=PATH" to specify its path.

On Linux platforms, libseccomp-based system-call filtering can be enabled with "--enable-seccomp".

The configure script will report some of the features that are enabled or disabled. To see all the configure option values use "--enable-full-report".

To see additional configure options, run "configure --help". Note that the help message does not reflect the BIND 8 compatibility defaults for sysconfdir and localstatedir.

The build of BIND may be further customized by setting the STD_CDEFINES environment variable to define some preprocessor symbols before running configure. Some possible settings include:

-DCHECK_LOCAL=0
    named-checkzone checks out-of-zone addresses by default. To disable this default, set this.

-DCHECK_SIBLING=0

Sibling glue checking in **named-checkzone** is enabled by default. To disable the default check, set this.

-DDIG_SIGCHASE=1

Enable DNSSEC signature chasing support in **dig**. (This sets -DDIG_SIGCHASE_TD=1 and -DDIG_SIGCHASE_BU=1.) ISC recommends using the **delv** tool instead.

-DISC_FACILITY=LOG_LOCAL0

Change the default syslog facility of **named** (and **lwresd**).

-DISC_SOCKET_POLLWATCH_TIMEOUT=20

The watch timeout is also configurable.

-DISC_SOCKET_USE_POLLWATCH=1

Enable workaround for Solaris kernel bug about `/dev/poll`.

-DNO_VERSION_DATE

Exclude the date stamp in the **named** binary (for version output). This is for repeatable identical builds.

-DNS_CLIENT_DROPPORT=0

Disable dropping queries from particular well known ports.

-DNS_RUN_PID_DIR=0

To create the default PID files in `${localstatedir}/run` rather than `${localstatedir}/run/{named,lwresd}/` set this.

If you need to re-run configure please run "make distclean" first. This will ensure that all the option changes take.

A limited test suite can be run with "make test". Many of the tests require you to configure a set of virtual IP addresses on your system, and some require Perl; see bin/tests/system/README for details.

Note

"make install" does not generate a default `named.conf` file. There really isn't a default configuration which fits any site perfectly. There are lots of decisions that need to be made and there is no consensus on what the defaults should be. For example, some systems use `/etc/namedb` as the location where the configuration files for the server are stored. Others use `/var/named`.

What addresses to listen on? For a laptop on the move a lot you may only want to listen on the loop back interfaces.

To whom do you offer recursive service? Is there a firewall to consider? If so, is it stateless or stateful? Are you directly on the Internet? Are you on a private network? Are you on a NAT'd network? The answers to all these questions change how you configure even a caching name server.

The configurations are introduced in Chapter 5.

3.4   BIND 9 DNS Library Support

BIND 9 exports its internal libraries so that they can be used by third-party applications more easily (we call them "export" libraries in this document). In addition to all major DNS-related APIs BIND 9 is currently using, the export libraries provide the following features:

- The "DNS client" module. This is a higher level API that provides an interface to name resolution, single DNS transaction with a particular server, and dynamic update. Regarding name resolution, it supports advanced features such as DNSSEC validation and caching. This module supports both synchronous and asynchronous mode.

- The "IRS" (Information Retrieval System) library. It provides an interface to parse the traditional resolv.conf file and more advanced, DNS-specific configuration file for the rest of this package (see the description for the dns.conf file below).

- As part of the IRS library, standard address-name mapping functions, getaddrinfo() and getnameinfo(), are provided. They use the DNSSEC-aware validating resolver backend, and could use other advanced features of the BIND 9 libraries such as caching. The getaddrinfo() function resolves both A and AAAA RRs concurrently (when the address family is unspecified).

- An experimental framework to support other event libraries than BIND 9's internal event task system.

Prerequisite

GNU make is required to build the export libraries (other parts of BIND 9 can still be built with other types of make). In the reminder of this document, "make" means GNU make. Note that in some platforms you may need to invoke a different command name than "make" (e.g. "gmake") to indicate it's GNU make.

Compilation

```
$ ./configure --enable-exportlib [other flags]
$ make
```

This will create (in addition to usual BIND 9 programs) and a separate set of libraries under the lib/export directory. For example, `lib/export/dns/libdns.a` is the archive file of the export version of the BIND 9 DNS library. Sample application programs using the libraries will also be built under the `lib/export/samples` directory (see below). Also some of the header files provide pretty detailed explanations.

Installation

```
$ cd lib/export
$ make install
```

This will install library object files under the directory specified by the --with-export-libdir configure option (default: EPREFIX/lib/bind9), and header files under the directory specified by the --with-export-includedir configure option (default: PREFIX/include/bind9). Root privilege is normally required. "**make install**" at the top directory will do the same.

To see how to build your own application after the installation, see `lib/export/samples/Makefile-postinstall.in`.

Known Defects/Restrictions

- Currently, win32 is not supported for the export library. (Normal BIND 9 application can be built as before).

- The "fixed" RRset order is not (currently) supported in the export library. If you want to use "fixed" RRset order for, e.g. **named** while still building the export library even without the fixed order support, build them separately:

```
$ ./configure --enable-fixed-rrset [other flags, but not --enable- ↵
    exportlib]
$ make
$ ./configure --enable-exportlib [other flags, but not --enable- ↵
    fixed-rrset]
$ cd lib/export
$ make
```

- The client module and the IRS library currently do not support DNSSEC validation using DLV (the underlying modules can handle it, but there is no tunable interface to enable the feature).

- RFC 5011 trust anchor management is not supported in the validating stub resolver of the export library. In fact, it is not clear whether it should: trust anchors would be a system-wide configuration which would be managed by an administrator, while the stub resolver will be used by ordinary applications run by a normal user.

- Not all common `/etc/resolv.conf` options are supported in the IRS library. The only available options in this version are "debug" and "ndots".

The dns.conf File

The IRS library supports an "advanced" configuration file related to the DNS library for configuration parameters that would be beyond the capability of the `resolv.conf` file. Specifically, it is intended to provide DNSSEC related configuration parameters. By default the path to this configuration file is `/etc/dns.conf`. This module is very experimental and the configuration syntax or library interfaces may change in future versions. Currently, only the **trusted-keys** statement is supported, whose syntax is the same as the same name of statement for `named.conf`. (See Section 6.10 for details.)

Sample Applications

Some sample application programs using this API are provided for reference. The following is a brief description of these applications.

sample: a simple stub resolver utility

It sends a query of a given name (of a given optional RR type) to a specified recursive server, and prints the result as a list of RRs. It can also act as a validating stub resolver if a trust anchor is given via a set of command line options.

Usage: sample [options] server_address hostname

Options and Arguments:

-t RRtype
> specify the RR type of the query. The default is the A RR.

[-a algorithm] [-e] -k keyname -K keystring
> specify a command-line DNS key to validate the answer. For example, to specify the following DNSKEY of example.com:

```
example.com. 3600 IN DNSKEY 257 3 5 xxx
```

> specify the options as follows:

```
-e -k example.com -K "xxx"
```

> -e means that this key is a zone's "key signing key" (as known as "secure Entry point"). When -a is omitted rsasha1 will be used by default.

-s domain:alt_server_address
> specify a separate recursive server address for the specific "domain". Example: -s example.com:2001:db8::1234

server_address
> an IP(v4/v6) address of the recursive server to which queries are sent.

hostname
> the domain name for the query

sample-async: a simple stub resolver, working asynchronously

Similar to "sample", but accepts a list of (query) domain names as a separate file and resolves the names asynchronously.

Usage: sample-async [-s server_address] [-t RR_type] input_file

Options and Arguments:

-s server_address
> an IPv4 address of the recursive server to which queries are sent. (IPv6 addresses are not supported in this implementation)

-t RR_type
> specify the RR type of the queries. The default is the A RR.

input_file
> a list of domain names to be resolved. each line consists of a single domain name. Example:

```
www.example.com
mx.example.net
ns.xxx.example
```

sample-request: a simple DNS transaction client

It sends a query to a specified server, and prints the response with minimal processing. It doesn't act as a "stub resolver": it stops the processing once it gets any response from the server, whether it's a referral or an alias (CNAME or DNAME) that would require further queries to get the ultimate answer. In other words, this utility acts as a very simplified **dig**.

Usage: sample-request [-t RRtype] server_address hostname

Options and Arguments:

-t RRtype
> specify the RR type of the queries. The default is the A RR.

server_address
> an IP(v4/v6) address of the recursive server to which the query is sent.

hostname
> the domain name for the query

sample-gai: getaddrinfo() and getnameinfo() test code

This is a test program to check getaddrinfo() and getnameinfo() behavior. It takes a host name as an argument, calls getaddrinfo() with the given host name, and calls getnameinfo() with the resulting IP addresses returned by getaddrinfo(). If the dns.conf file exists and defines a trust anchor, the underlying resolver will act as a validating resolver, and getaddrinfo()/getnameinfo() will fail with an EAI_INSECUREDATA error when DNSSEC validation fails.

Usage: sample-gai hostname

sample-update: a simple dynamic update client program

It accepts a single update command as a command-line argument, sends an update request message to the authoritative server, and shows the response from the server. In other words, this is a simplified **nsupdate**.

Usage: sample-update [options] (add|delete) "update data"

Options and Arguments:

-a auth_server
> An IP address of the authoritative server that has authority for the zone containing the update name. This should normally be the primary authoritative server that accepts dynamic updates. It can also be a secondary server that is configured to forward update requests to the primary server.

-k keyfile
> A TSIG key file to secure the update transaction. The keyfile format is the same as that for the nsupdate utility.

-p prerequisite
> A prerequisite for the update (only one prerequisite can be specified). The prerequisite format is the same as that is accepted by the nsupdate utility.

-r recursive_server
> An IP address of a recursive server that this utility will use. A recursive server may be necessary to identify the authoritative server address to which the update request is sent.

-z zonename
> The domain name of the zone that contains

(add|delete)
> Specify the type of update operation. Either "add" or "delete" must be specified.

"update data"
> Specify the data to be updated. A typical example of the data would look like "name TTL RRtype RDATA".

Note
In practice, either -a or -r must be specified. Others can be optional; the underlying library routine tries to identify the appropriate server and the zone name for the update.

Examples: assuming the primary authoritative server of the dynamic.example.com zone has an IPv6 address 2001:db8::1234,

```
$ sample-update -a sample-update -k Kxxx.+nnn+mmmm.key add "foo.dynamic ←
    .example.com 30 IN A 192.168.2.1"
```

adds an A RR for foo.dynamic.example.com using the given key.

```
$ sample-update -a sample-update -k Kxxx.+nnn+mmmm.key delete "foo. ←
  dynamic.example.com 30 IN A"
```

removes all A RRs for foo.dynamic.example.com using the given key.

```
$ sample-update -a sample-update -k Kxxx.+nnn+mmmm.key delete "foo. ←
  dynamic.example.com"
```

removes all RRs for foo.dynamic.example.com using the given key.

nsprobe: domain/name server checker in terms of RFC 4074

It checks a set of domains to see the name servers of the domains behave correctly in terms of RFC 4074. This is included in the set of sample programs to show how the export library can be used in a DNS-related application.

Usage: nsprobe [-d] [-v [-v...]] [-c cache_address] [input_file]

Options

-d
> run in the "debug" mode. with this option nsprobe will dump every RRs it receives.

-v
> increase verbosity of other normal log messages. This can be specified multiple times

-c cache_address
> specify an IP address of a recursive (caching) name server. nsprobe uses this server to get the NS RRset of each domain and the A and/or AAAA RRsets for the name servers. The default value is 127.0.0.1.

input_file
> a file name containing a list of domain (zone) names to be probed. when omitted the standard input will be used. Each line of the input file specifies a single domain name such as "example.com". In general this domain name must be the apex name of some DNS zone (unlike normal "host names" such as "www.example.com"). nsprobe first identifies the NS RRsets for the given domain name, and sends A and AAAA queries to these servers for some "widely used" names under the zone; specifically, adding "www" and "ftp" to the zone name.

3.5   Software Packages for BIND

Various operating systems provide BIND installed by default or readily available as packaged software. This may provide an easier and faster way to get and use the BIND suite on a platform. Check your operating system's or package system's documentation about its BIND setup.

Note

Third-party installations of BIND may include custom patches, configurations, and start/stop mechanisms. The versions and features may not match the official upstream (ISC) versions.

This section introduces a few packaged versions of BIND.

FreeBSD packages

FreeBSD provides the following "dns" packages: bind-tools, bind98 (for 9.8 branch), bind99 (for 9.9 branch), and bind910 (for 9.10 branch). The bind-tools package has various BIND commands without providing the entire server suite, including dig, host, nslookup, and several "dnssec" command-line tools. (The "bind9*" packages also provide the tools.)

The bind910 package may be installed on FreeBSD as root using: `pkg install bind910` at the command-line. (This will need around 53 MB of disk space and it will install dependencies as required.) The server is installed to `/usr/local/sbin/named`. Several configurations are included by default under the `/usr/local/etc/namedb/` directory. The default *named.conf* configuration will allow local system queries and may be used as a local caching resolver.

The service script at `/usr/local/etc/rc.d/named` may be used to start, stop, and reload the **named** server. This script also will also create a `rndc.key` file (if it doesn't exist). To enable the "named" service to start at boot time, set `named_enable=YES` in your `/etc/rc.conf` file. It is configured by default to run as the "bind" user. The default logging will go to the `/var/log/messages` log file.

Debian / Ubuntu packages

Debian and Ubuntu provide several BIND-related packages, including bind9 which provides the startup scripts, popular configurations, miscellaneous tools included with BIND, and the **named** server itself. The bind9utils package provides standard administration tools (**dnssec-keygen, dnssec-signzone, named-checkconf, named-checkzone, named-compilezone, rndc,** and **rndc-confgen**). The bind9-host package provides the **host** tool and the dnsutils package provides the **dig, nslookup,** and **nsupdate** tools. (Packages are also available for static and shared libraries and corresponding include headers provided with BIND.)

The server can be installed on Debian or Ubuntu by running the following as root: `apt-get install bind9`. This will also enable and start the **named** service (running as the "bind" user) which can be queried with `rndc status` with its provided configuration. The **named** server can be restarted with `service bind9 restart`.

The default configurations are under the `/etc/bind/` directory which splits up the configurations into multiple files. The zone files and cached data is located in the `/var/cache/bind/` directory. DNSSEC validation is enabled by default and the server listens on IPv6 too. It is recommended that your custom configurations be done in `/etc/bind/named.conf.local`.

Red Hat / CentOS packages

The Red Hat and CentOS "bind" package provides the **named** server, common configurations, and 20 BIND administration tools. The bind-chroot package provides configurations to run the server in a chroot environment. The bind-utils package provides the **dig, host, nslookup**, and **nsupdate** utilities. (Other packages are also available for libraries and development headers.)

The server can be installed as root by running **yum install bind**. This will install the /etc/ named.conf and other configurations, and system-specific startup scripts. To use a chroot environment install the package with **yum install bind-chroot**.

On Red Hat 6 (and CentOS 6) enable the server to start at boot with **chkconfig named on** and then start it with **service named start**.

On Red Hat 7 (or CentOS 7) enable the desired service with **systemctl enable named** or **systemctl enable named-chroot**. Then start one with **systemctl start named** or **systemctl start named-chroot**.

Then you should be able to run **rndc status** to see its status. It will run as the "named" user. The chroot directory is at /var/named/chroot/.

The provided /etc/named.conf configuration on Red Hat or CentOS only listens on the local host and has DNSSEC validation enabled.

4　Name Server Operations

This chapter introduces **named**, the server daemon that (usually) runs in the background to find and share answers to DNS queries.

The common and simple way to start it is to run `named` (or its full path name, for example `/usr/local/sbin/named`), as the root superuser at the Unix shell prompt. It will silently startup and go to the background (and your shell prompt will return). By default, its startup output — whether successful or not — will be sent to the system log. (Details about logging are covered in Section 6.5.)

BIND doesn't ship with startup scripts, but your operating system or BIND package may include a startup (or service) script, such as `/etc/rc.d/named`, `/etc/rc.d/rc.bind`, `/etc/init.d/named`, or another script. Consult your system or package manifest or documentation to see how to use it or enable it. (Some operating system examples are introduced in Section 3.5.)

4.1　named — Internet domain name server

Synopsis

```
named [-4] [-6] [-c config-file] [-d debug-level] [-D string] [-E engine-name]
[-f] [-g] [-L logfile] [-M option] [-m flag] [-n #cpus] [-p port] [-s] [-S #max-
socks] [-t directory] [-U #listeners] [-u user] [-v] [-V] [-X lock-file] [-x cache-
file]
```

named Description

named is a Domain Name System (DNS) server, part of the BIND 9 distribution from ISC. For more information on the DNS, see RFCs 1033, 1034, and 1035.

When invoked without arguments, **named** will read the default configuration file `/etc/named.conf`, read any initial data, and listen for queries.

named Options

-4

Use IPv4 only even if the host machine is capable of IPv6. −4 and −6 are mutually exclusive.

-6

Use IPv6 only even if the host machine is capable of IPv4. −4 and −6 are mutually exclusive.

-c *config-file*

Use *config-file* as the configuration file instead of the default, /etc/named.conf. To ensure that reloading the configuration file continues to work after the server has changed its working directory due to to a possible directory option in the configuration file, *config-file* should be an absolute pathname.

-d *debug-level*

Set the daemon's debug level to *debug-level*. Debugging traces from **named** become more verbose as the debug level increases.

-D *string*

Specifies a string that is used to identify a instance of **named** in a process listing. The contents of *string* are not examined. (The −D option was introduced in BIND 9.10.)

-E *engine-name*

When applicable, specifies the hardware to use for cryptographic operations, such as a secure key store used for signing.

When BIND is built with OpenSSL PKCS#11 support, this defaults to the string "pkcs11", which identifies an OpenSSL engine that can drive a cryptographic accelerator or hardware service module. When BIND 9.10 or later is built with native PKCS#11 cryptography (--enable-native-pkcs11), it defaults to the path of the PKCS#11 provider library specified via "--with-pkcs11". (The native PKCS#11 support was introduced in BIND 9.10. See Section 10.17 for further details.)

-f

Run the server in the foreground (i.e. do not daemonize).

-g

Run the server in the foreground and force all logging to stderr.

-L *logfile*

Log to the file logfile by default instead of the system log. The −L option was introduced in BIND 9.11.

-M *option*

Sets the default memory context options. Currently the only supported option is *external*, which causes the internal memory manager to be bypassed in favor of system-provided memory allocation functions.

-m *flag*

Turn on memory usage debugging flags. Possible flags are *usage*, *trace*, *record*, *size*, and *mctx*. These correspond to the ISC_MEM_DEBUGXXXX flags described in <isc/mem.h>.

-n *#cpus*

Create *#cpus* worker threads to take advantage of multiple CPUs. If not specified, **named** will try to determine the number of CPUs present and create one thread per CPU. If it is unable to determine the number of CPUs, a single worker thread will be created.

-p *port*

Listen for queries on port *port*. If not specified, the default is port 53.

-s

Write memory usage statistics to stdout on exit.

Note

This option is mainly of interest to BIND 9 developers and may be removed or changed in a future release.

-S *#max-socks*

Allow **named** to use up to *#max-socks* sockets. The default value is 4096 on systems built with default configuration options, and 21000 on systems built with "configure --with-tuning=large". (This build-time tuning was introduced in BIND 9.10; for more details, see Section 3.3.)

Warning

This option should be unnecessary for the vast majority of users. The use of this option could even be harmful because the specified value may exceed the limitation of the underlying system API. It is therefore set only when the default configuration causes exhaustion of file descriptors and the operational environment is known to support the specified number of sockets. Note also that the actual maximum number is normally a little fewer than the specified value because **named** reserves some file descriptors for its internal use.

-t *directory*

Chroot to *directory* after processing the command line arguments, but before reading the configuration file.

Warning

This option should be used in conjunction with the −u option, as chrooting a process running as root doesn't enhance security on most systems; the way chroot(2) is defined allows a process with root privileges to escape a chroot jail.

-U *#listeners*

Use *#listeners* worker threads to listen for incoming UDP packets on each address. If not specified, **named** will calculate a default value based on the number of detected CPUs: 1 for 1 CPU, and the number of detected CPUs minus one for machines with more than 1 CPU. This cannot be increased to a value higher than the number of CPUs. If −n has been set to a higher value than the number of detected CPUs, then −U may be increased as high as that value, but no higher. On Windows, the number of UDP listeners is hardwired to 1 and this option has no effect. (The −U option was introduced in BIND 9.9.)

-u *user*

Setuid to *user* after completing privileged operations, such as creating sockets that listen on privileged ports.

Note

On Linux, **named** uses the kernel's capability mechanism to drop all root privileges except the ability to bind(2) to a privileged port and set process resource limits. Unfortunately, this means that the −u option only works when **named** is run on kernel 2.2.18 or later, or kernel 2.3.99-pre3 or later, since previous kernels did not allow privileges to be retained after setuid(2).

-v

Report the version number and exit.

-V

Report the version number and build options, and exit.

-X *lock-file*

Acquire a lock on the specified file at runtime; this helps to prevent duplicate **named** instances from running simultaneously. Use of this option overrides the **lock-file** option in named. conf. If set to none, the lock file check is disabled. The −X option was introduced in BIND 9.11.

-x *cache-file*

Load data from *cache-file* into the cache of the default view.

 Warning

This option must not be used. It is only of interest to BIND 9 developers and may be removed or changed in a future release.

---

named Signals

Certain UNIX signals cause the name server to take specific actions, as described in the following list. These signals can be sent using the **kill** command.

In routine operation, signals should not be used to control the nameserver; **rndc** should be used instead.

SIGHUP

Force a reload of the server. Causes the server to read named.conf and reload the database.

SIGINT, SIGTERM
> Shut down the server. Causes the server to clean up and exit.

The result of sending any other signals to the server is undefined.

named Configuration

named inherits the `umask` (file creation mode mask) from the parent process. If files created by **named**, such as journal files, need to have custom permissions, the `umask` should be set explicitly in the script used to start the **named** process.

named Files

`/etc/named.conf`
> The default configuration file.

`/var/run/named/named.pid`
> The default process-id file.

Note

The best solution to troubleshooting and solving installation and configuration issues is to take preventative measures by setting up logging files beforehand. The log files provide a source of hints and information that can be used to figure out what went wrong and how to fix the problem.

4.2 Chroot and Setuid

On UNIX servers, it is possible to run BIND in a *chrooted* environment (using the **chroot()** function) by specifying the `-t` option for **named**. This can help improve system security by placing BIND in a "sandbox", which will limit the damage done if a server is compromised.

Another useful feature in the UNIX version of BIND is the ability to run the daemon as an unprivileged user (`-u user`). It is suggested to run as an unprivileged user when using the **chroot** feature.

Here is an example command line to load BIND in a **chroot** sandbox, **/var/named**, and to run **named setuid** to user 202:

```
/usr/local/sbin/named -u 202 -t /var/named
```

The chroot Environment

In order for a **chroot** environment to work properly in a particular directory (for example, `/var/named`), you will need to set up an environment that includes everything BIND needs to run. From

BIND's point of view, /var/named is the root of the filesystem. You will need to adjust the values of options like like **directory** and **pid-file** to account for this.

Unlike with earlier versions of BIND, you typically will *not* need to compile **named** statically nor install shared libraries under the new root. However, depending on your operating system, you may need to set up things like /dev/zero, /dev/random, /dev/log, and /etc/localtime.

Using the setuid Function

Prior to running the **named** daemon, use the **touch** utility (to change file access and modification times) or the **chown** utility (to set the user id and/or group id) on files to which you want BIND to write.

Note

If the **named** daemon is running as an unprivileged user, it will not be able to bind to new restricted ports if the server is reloaded.

4.3   Remote name daemon control (rndc)

The remote name daemon control (**rndc**) program allows the system administrator to control the operation of a name server. Since BIND 9.2, **rndc** supports all the commands of the BIND 8 **ndc** utility except **ndc start** and **ndc restart**, which were also not supported in **ndc**'s channel mode. If you run **rndc** without any options it will display a usage message.

rndc requires a configuration file, since all communication with the server is authenticated with digital signatures that rely on a shared secret, and there is no way to provide that secret other than with a configuration file. The default location for the **rndc** configuration file is /etc/rndc.conf, but an alternate location can be specified with the -c option. If the configuration file is not found, **rndc** will also look in /etc/rndc.key (or whatever sysconfdir was defined when the BIND build was configured). The rndc.key file is generated by running **rndc-confgen -a** as described in Section 6.2.

The format of the configuration file is similar to that of named.conf, but limited to only four statements, the **options**, **key**, **server** and **include** statements. These statements are what associate the secret keys to the servers with which they are meant to be shared. The order of statements is not significant.

The **options** has three clauses: **default-server**, **default-key**, and **default-port**. **default-server** takes a host name or address argument and represents the server that will be contacted if no -s option is provided on the command line. **default-key** takes the name of a key as its argument, as defined by a **key** statement. **default-port** specifies the port to which **rndc** should connect if no port is given on the command line or in a **server** statement.

The **key** defines a key to be used by **rndc** when authenticating with **named**. Its syntax is identical to the **key** statement in named.conf. The keyword **key** is followed by a key name, which must be a valid domain name, though it need not actually be hierarchical; thus, a string like "**rndc_key**" is a valid name. The **key** has two clauses: **algorithm** and **secret**. While the configuration parser will accept any string as the argument to algorithm, currently only the strings "**hmac—md5**", "**hmac—sha1**", "**hmac—sha224**", "**hmac—sha256**", "**hmac—sha384**" and "**hmac—sha512**" have any meaning. (Prior to BIND 9.10, only **hmac—md5** was supported.) The secret is a base-64 encoded string as specified in RFC 3548.

The **server** associates a key defined using the **key** statement with a server. The keyword **server** is followed by a host name or address. The **server** has two clauses: **key** and **port**. The **key** clause specifies the name of the key to be used when communicating with this server, and the **port** clause can be used to specify the port **rndc** should connect to on the server.

A sample minimal configuration file is as follows:

```
key rndc_key {
     algorithm "hmac-sha256";
     secret
       "c3Ryb25nIGVub3VnaCBmb3IgYSBtYW4gYnV0IG1hZGUgZm9yIGEgd29tYW4K";
};
options {
     default-server 127.0.0.1;
     default-key    rndc_key;
};
```

This file, if installed as `/etc/rndc.conf`, would allow the command:

$ **rndc reload**

to connect to 127.0.0.1 port 953 and cause the name server to reload, if a name server on the local machine were running with following controls statements:

```
controls {
  inet 127.0.0.1
      allow { localhost; } keys { rndc_key; };
};
```

and it had an identical key statement for `rndc_key`.

Running the **rndc-confgen** program will conveniently create a `rndc.conf` file for you, and also display the corresponding **controls** statement that you need to add to `named.conf`. Alternatively, you can run **rndc-confgen -a** to set up a `rndc.key` file and not modify `named.conf` at all.

4.4 rndc — name server control utility

Synopsis

rndc [-b *source-address*] [-c *config-file*] [-k *key-file*] [-s *server*] [-p *port*] [-q] [-r] [-V] [-y *key_id*] command

rndc Description

rndc controls the operation of a name server. It supersedes the **ndc** utility that was provided in old BIND releases. If **rndc** is invoked with no command line options or arguments, it prints a short summary of the supported commands and the available options and their arguments.

rndc communicates with the name server over a TCP connection, sending commands authenticated with digital signatures. In the current versions of **rndc** and **named**, the only supported authentication algorithms are HMAC-MD5 (for compatibility), HMAC-SHA1, HMAC-SHA224, HMAC-SHA256 (default), HMAC-SHA384 and HMAC-SHA512. (The default algorithm changed from HMAC-MD5 in BIND 9.10.) They use a shared secret on each end of the connection. This provides TSIG-style authentication for the command request and the name server's response. All commands sent over the channel must be signed by a key_id known to the server.

rndc reads a configuration file to determine how to contact the name server and decide what algorithm and key it should use.

rndc Options

-b *source-address*
> Use *source-address* as the source address for the connection to the server. Multiple instances are permitted to allow setting of both the IPv4 and IPv6 source addresses.

-c *config-file*
> Use *config-file* as the configuration file instead of the default, `/etc/rndc.conf`.

-k *key-file*
> Use *key-file* as the key file instead of the default, `/etc/rndc.key`. The key in `/etc/rndc.key` will be used to authenticate commands sent to the server if the *config-file* does not exist.

-s *server*
> *server* is the name or address of the server which matches a server statement in the configuration file for **rndc**. If no server is supplied on the command line, the host named by the default-server clause in the options statement of the **rndc** configuration file will be used.

-p *port*
> Send commands to TCP port *port* instead of BIND 9's default control channel port, 953.

-q

> Quiet mode: Message text returned by the server will not be printed except when there is an error. (The `-q` option was introduced in BIND 9.10.)

-r

> Instructs **rndc** to print the result code returned by **named** after executing the requested command (e.g., ISC_R_SUCCESS, ISC_R_FAILURE, etc). (The `-r` option was introduced in BIND 9.11.)

-r

> Instructs **rndc** to print the result code returned by **named** after executing the requested command (e.g., ISC_R_SUCCESS, ISC_R_FAILURE, etc).

-V

> Enable verbose logging.

-y *key_id*

> Use the key *key_id* from the configuration file. *key_id* must be known by **named** with the same algorithm and secret string in order for control message validation to succeed. If no *key_id* is specified, **rndc** will first look for a key clause in the server statement of the server being used, or if no server statement is present for that host, then the default-key clause of the options statement. Note that the configuration file contains shared secrets which are used to send authenticated control commands to name servers. It should therefore not have general read or write access.

rndc Commands

A list of commands supported by **rndc** can be seen by running **rndc** without arguments.

Currently supported commands are:

`addzone` *zone* [*class* [*view*]] *configuration*

> Add a zone while the server is running. This command requires the **allow-new-zones** option to be set to **yes**. The *configuration* string specified on the command line is the zone configuration text that would ordinarily be placed in `named.conf`.
>
> The configuration is saved in a file called *name*.`nzf`, where *name* is the name of the view, or if it contains characters that are incompatible with use as a file name, a cryptographic hash generated from the name of the view. When **named** is restarted, the file will be loaded into the view configuration, so that zones that were added can persist after a restart.
>
> This sample **addzone** command would add the zone `example.com` to the default view:
>
> ```
> $ rndc addzone example.com '{ type master; file "example.com.db";
> };'
> ```
>
> (Note the brackets and semi-colon around the zone configuration text.)
>
> See also **rndc delzone** and **rndc modzone**.

`delzone` [`-clean`] *zone* [*class* [*view*]]

> Delete a zone while the server is running.
>
> If the `-clean` argument is specified, the zone's master file (and journal file, if any) will be deleted along with the zone. Without the `-clean` option, zone files must be cleaned up by hand. (If the zone is of type "slave" or "stub", the files needing to be cleaned up will be reported in the output of the **rndc delzone** command.)
>
> If the zone was originally added via **rndc addzone**, then it will be removed permanently. However, if it was originally configured in `named.conf`, then that original configuration is still in place; when the server is restarted or reconfigured, the zone will come back. To remove it permanently, it must also be removed from `named.conf`
>
> See also **rndc addzone** and **rndc modzone**.

`dumpdb [-all|-cache|-zone|-adb|-bad|-fail] [view ...]`

Dump the server's caches (default) and/or zones to the dump file for the specified views. If no view is specified, all views are dumped. (See the **dump-file** option in Section 6.7 for details.)

`flush`
Flushes the server's cache.

`flushname name [view]`
Flushes the given name from the view's DNS cache and, if applicable, from the view's name-server address database, bad server cache and SERVFAIL cache. (The SERVFAIL cache was introduced in BIND 9.11.)

`flushtree name [view]`
Flushes the given name, and all of its subdomains, from the view's DNS cache, address database, bad server cache, and SERVFAIL cache. (The **flushtree** feature was introduced in BIND 9.9. Note that the `-all` option was removed in BIND 9.10. The SERVFAIL cache was introduced in BIND 9.11.)

`freeze [zone [class [view]]]`
Suspend updates to a dynamic zone. If no zone is specified, then all zones are suspended. This allows manual edits to be made to a zone normally updated by dynamic update. It also causes changes in the journal file to be synced into the master file. All dynamic update attempts will be refused while the zone is frozen. (Prior to BIND 9.9, the **freeze** feature removed the journal file.)

See also **rndc thaw**.

`halt [-p]`
Stop the server immediately. Recent changes made through dynamic update or IXFR are not saved to the master files, but will be rolled forward from the journal files when the server is restarted. If `-p` is specified **named**'s process id is returned. This allows an external process to determine when **named** had completed halting.

See also **rndc stop**.

`loadkeys zone [class [view]]`
Fetch all DNSSEC keys for the given zone from the key directory. If they are within their publication period, merge them into the zone's DNSKEY RRset. Unlike **rndc sign**, however, the zone is not immediately re-signed by the new keys, but is allowed to incrementally re-sign over time.

This command requires that the **auto-dnssec** zone option be set to `maintain`, and also requires the zone to be configured to allow dynamic DNS. (See Section 9.2 about Dynamic Update Policies for more details.)

`managed-keys (status | refresh | sync) [class [view]]`
When run with the "status" keyword, print the current status of the managed-keys database for the specified view, or for all views if none is specified. When run with the "refresh" keyword, force an immediate refresh of all the managed-keys in the specified view, or all views. When run with the "sync" keyword, force an immediate dump of the managed-keys database to disk

(in the file `managed-keys.bind` or (`viewname.mkeys`). (The **managed-keys** feature was introduced in BIND 9.11.)

modzone *zone* **[***class* **[***view***]]** *configuration*

Modify the configuration of a zone while the server is running. This command requires the **allow-new-zones** option to be set to **yes**. As with **addzone**, the *configuration* string specified on the command line is the zone configuration text that would ordinarily be placed in `named.conf`.

If the zone was originally added via **rndc addzone**, the configuration changes will be recorded permanently and will still be in effect after the server is restarted or reconfigured. However, if it was originally configured in `named.conf`, then that original configuration is still in place; when the server is restarted or reconfigured, the zone will revert to its original configuration. To make the changes permanent, it must also be modified in `named.conf`

See also **rndc addzone** and **rndc delzone**. (The **modzone** feature was introduced in BIND 9.11.)

notify *zone* **[***class* **[***view***]]**

Resend NOTIFY messages for the zone.

notrace

Sets the server's debugging level to 0.

See also **rndc trace**.

nta **[(-d | -f | -r | -l** *duration***)]** *domain* **[***view***]**

Sets a DNSSEC negative trust anchor (NTA) for `domain`, with a lifetime of `duration`. The default lifetime is configured in `named.conf` via the `nta-lifetime` option, and defaults to one hour. The lifetime cannot exceed one week.

A negative trust anchor selectively disables DNSSEC validation for zones that are known to be failing because of misconfiguration rather than an attack. When data to be validated is at or below an active NTA (and above any other configured trust anchors), **named** will abort the DNSSEC validation process and treat the data as insecure rather than bogus. This continues until the NTA's lifetime is elapsed.

NTAs persist across restarts of the **named** server. The NTAs for a view are saved in a file called `name.nta`, where `name` is the name of the view, or if it contains characters that are incompatible with use as a file name, a cryptographic hash generated from the name of the view.

An existing NTA can be removed by using the `-remove` option.

An NTA's lifetime can be specified with the `-lifetime` option. TTL-style suffixes can be used to specify the lifetime in seconds, minutes, or hours. If the specified NTA already exists, its lifetime will be updated to the new value. Setting `lifetime` to zero is equivalent to `-remove`.

If `-dump` is used, any other arguments are ignored, and a list of existing NTAs is printed (note that this may include NTAs that are expired but have not yet been cleaned up).

Normally, **named** will periodically test to see whether data below an NTA can now be validated (see the `nta-recheck` option in Section 6.7 for details). If data can be validated, then the NTA is regarded as no longer necessary, and will be allowed to expire early. The `-force` overrides this behavior and forces an NTA to persist for its entire lifetime, regardless of whether data could be validated if the NTA were not present.

All of these options can be shortened, i.e., to -l, -r, -d, and -f.

The negative trust anchors support was introduced in BIND 9.11.

querylog [on|off]

Enable or disable query logging. (For backward compatibility, this command can also be used without an argument to toggle query logging on and off.)

Query logging can also be enabled by explicitly directing the **queries category** to a **channel** in the **logging** section of named.conf or by specifying **querylog yes;** in the **options** section of named.conf.

reconfig

Reload the configuration file and load new zones, but do not reload existing zone files even if they have changed. This is faster than a full **reload** when there is a large number of zones because it avoids the need to examine the modification times of the zones files.

recursing

Dump the list of queries **named** is currently recursing on, and the list of domains to which iterative queries are currently being sent. (The second list includes the number of fetches currently active for the given domain, and how many have been passed or dropped because of the fetches-per-zone option.)

refresh *zone* [*class* [*view*]]

Schedule zone maintenance for the given zone.

reload

Reload configuration file and zones.

reload *zone* [*class* [*view*]]

Reload the given zone.

Q: *Why don't my zones reload when I do an "rndc reload" or SIGHUP?*

A: A zone can be updated either by editing zone files and reloading the server or by dynamic update, but not both. If you have enabled dynamic update for a zone using the **allow-update** option, you are not supposed to edit the zone file by hand, and the server will not attempt to reload it.

retransfer *zone* [*class* [*view*]]

Retransfer the given slave zone from the master server.

If the zone is configured to use **inline-signing** (introduced in BIND 9.9), the signed version of the zone is discarded; after the retransfer of the unsigned version is complete, the signed version will be regenerated with all new signatures.

scan

Scan the list of available network interfaces for changes, without performing a full **reconfig** or waiting for the **interface-interval** timer (see page 125). On operating systems that support routing sockets, see the **automatic-interface-scan** option on page 102 for automatically updating the interface information. (The **rndc scan** feature and **automatic-interface-scan** options were introduced in BIND 9.10.)

secroots [-] [*view* ...]

Dump the server's security roots and negative trust anchors for the specified views. If no view is specified, all views are dumped. (The negative trust anchors support was introduced in BIND 9.11.)

If the first argument is "-", then the output is returned via the **rndc** response channel and printed to the standard output. Otherwise, it is written to the secroots dump file, which defaults to named.secroots, but can be overridden via the secroots-file option in named.conf.

See also **rndc managed-keys**.

showzone *zone* [*class* [*view*]]

Print the configuration of a running zone. (This feature was introduced in BIND 9.11.)

See also **rndc zonestatus**.

sign *zone* [*class* [*view*]]

Fetch all DNSSEC keys for the given zone from the key directory. (See the **key-directory** option in Section 6.7 for details.) If they are within their publication period, merge them into the zone's DNSKEY RRset. If the DNSKEY RRset is changed, then the zone is automatically re-signed with the new key set.

This command requires that the **auto-dnssec** zone option be set to allow or maintain, and also requires the zone to be configured to allow dynamic DNS. (See Section 9.2 about Dynamic Update Policies for more details.)

See also **rndc loadkeys**.

signing [(-list | -clear *keyid/algorithm* | -clear all | -nsec3param (*parameters* | none) | -serial *value*)] *zone* [*class* [*view*]]

List, edit, or remove the DNSSEC signing state records for the specified zone. (The **signing** feature was introduced in BIND 9.9.)

The status of ongoing DNSSEC operations (such as signing or generating NSEC3 chains) is stored in the zone in the form of DNS resource records of type **sig-signing-type**. **rndc signing -list** converts these records into a human-readable form, indicating which keys are currently signing or have finished signing the zone, and which NSEC3 chains are being created or removed.

rndc signing -clear can remove a single key (specified in the same format that **rndc signing -list** uses to display it), or all keys. In either case, only completed keys are removed; any record indicating that a key has not yet finished signing the zone will be retained.

rndc signing -nsec3param sets the NSEC3 parameters for a zone. This is the only supported mechanism for using NSEC3 with **inline-signing** zones. Parameters are specified in the same format as an NSEC3PARAM resource record: hash algorithm, flags, iterations, and salt, in that order.

Currently, the only defined value for hash algorithm is 1, representing SHA-1. The flags may be set to 0 or 1, depending on whether you wish to set the opt-out bit in the NSEC3 chain.

`iterations` defines the number of additional times to apply the algorithm when generating an NSEC3 hash. The `salt` is a string of data expressed in hexadecimal, a hyphen (`-`) if no salt is to be used, or the keyword `auto`, which causes **named** to generate a random 64-bit salt.

So, for example, to create an NSEC3 chain using the SHA-1 hash algorithm, no opt-out flag, 10 iterations, and a salt value of "FFFF", use: **rndc signing -nsec3param 1 0 10 FFFF *zone***. To set the opt-out flag, 15 iterations, and no salt, use: **rndc signing -nsec3param 1 1 15 - *zone***.

rndc signing -nsec3param none removes an existing NSEC3 chain and replaces it with NSEC.

rndc signing -serial value sets the serial number of the zone to value. If the value would cause the serial number to go backwards it will be rejected. The primary use is to set the serial on inline signed zones.

stats

Write server statistics to the statistics file. (See the **statistics-file** option on page 96.)

BIND 9 maintains lots of statistics information and provides multiple interfaces for users to get access to the statistics, such as incoming requests, cache memory usage, UDP traffic size, socket I/O, and various other counters. For access to the stats via an HTTP interface in JSON or XML formats, see Section 6.9

status

Display status of the server. Note that the number of zones includes the internal **bind/CH** zone and the default **./IN** hint zone if there is not an explicit root zone configured.

stop [-p]

Stop the server, making sure any recent changes made through dynamic update or IXFR are first saved to the master files of the updated zones. If `-p` is specified **named**'s process id is returned. This allows an external process to determine when **named** had completed stopping.

See also **rndc halt**.

sync [-clean] [*zone* [*class* [*view*]]]

Sync changes in the journal file for a dynamic zone to the master file. If the "-clean" option is specified, the journal file is also removed. If no zone is specified, then all zones are synced. (The **sync** feature was introduced in BIND 9.9.)

thaw [*zone* [*class* [*view*]]]

Enable updates to a frozen dynamic zone. If no zone is specified, then all frozen zones are enabled. This causes the server to reload the zone from disk, and re-enables dynamic updates after the load has completed. After a zone is thawed, dynamic updates will no longer be refused. If the zone has changed and the **ixfr-from-differences** option is in use, then the journal file will be updated to reflect changes in the zone. Otherwise, if the zone has changed, any existing journal file will be removed.

See also **rndc freeze**.

trace

Increment the servers debugging level by one.

trace *level*
> Sets the server's debugging level to an explicit value.

> See also **rndc notrace**.

tsig-delete *keyname* [*view*]
> Delete a given TKEY-negotiated key from the server. (This does not apply to statically configured TSIG keys.)

tsig-list
> List the names of all TSIG keys currently configured for use by **named** in each view. The list both statically configured keys and dynamic TKEY-negotiated keys.

validation (on | off | check) [*view* ...]

> Enable, disable, or check the current status of DNSSEC validation. Note **dnssec-enable** also needs to be set to **yes** or **auto** to be effective. It defaults to enabled.

zonestatus *zone* [*class* [*view*]]

> Displays the current status of the given zone, including the master file name and any include files from which it was loaded, when it was most recently loaded, the current serial number, the number of nodes, whether the zone supports dynamic updates, whether the zone is DNSSEC signed, whether it uses automatic DNSSEC key management or inline signing, and the scheduled refresh or expiry times for the zone. (The **zonestatus** feature was introduced in BIND 9.10.)

> See also **rndc showzone**.

rndc Limitations

There is currently no way to provide the shared secret for a key_id without using the configuration file.

Several error messages could be clearer.

4.5 `rndc.conf` — rndc configuration file

rndc.conf Description

`rndc.conf` is the configuration file for **rndc**, the BIND 9 name server control utility. This file has a similar structure and syntax to `named.conf`. Statements are enclosed in braces and terminated with a semi-colon. Clauses in the statements are also semi-colon terminated. The usual comment styles are supported:

C style: /* */

C++ style: // to end of line

Unix style: # to end of line

`rndc.conf` is much simpler than `named.conf`. The file uses three statements: an options statement, a server statement and a key statement.

The `options` statement contains five clauses. The `default-server` clause is followed by the name or address of a name server. This host will be used when no name server is given as an argument to **rndc**. The `default-key` clause is followed by the name of a key which is identified by a `key` statement. If no `keyid` is provided on the rndc command line, and no `key` clause is found in a matching `server` statement, this default key will be used to authenticate the server's commands and responses. The `default-port` clause is followed by the port to connect to on the remote name server. If no `port` option is provided on the rndc command line, and no `port` clause is found in a matching `server` statement, this default port will be used to connect. The `default-source-address` and `default-source-address-v6` clauses which can be used to set the IPv4 and IPv6 source addresses respectively.

After the `server` keyword, the server statement includes a string which is the hostname or address for a name server. The statement has three possible clauses: `key`, `port` and `addresses`. The key name must match the name of a key statement in the file. The port number specifies the port to connect to. If an `addresses` clause is supplied these addresses will be used instead of the server name. Each address can take an optional port. If an `source-address` or `source-address-v6` of supplied then these will be used to specify the IPv4 and IPv6 source addresses respectively.

The `key` statement begins with an identifying string, the name of the key. The statement has two clauses. `algorithm` identifies the authentication algorithm for **rndc** to use; currently only HMAC-MD5 (for compatibility), HMAC-SHA1, HMAC-SHA224, HMAC-SHA256 (default), HMAC-SHA384 and HMAC-SHA512 are supported. This is followed by a secret clause which contains the base-64 encoding of the algorithm's authentication key. The base-64 string is enclosed in double quotes.

There are two common ways to generate the base-64 string for the secret. The BIND 9 program **rndc-confgen** can be used to generate a random key, or the **mmencode** program, also known as **mimencode**, can be used to generate a base-64 string from known input. **mmencode** does not ship with BIND 9 but is available on many systems. See the EXAMPLE section for sample command lines for each.

rndc.conf Example

```
options {
  default-server  localhost;
  default-key     samplekey;
};

server localhost {
  key             samplekey;
};

server testserver {
  key    testkey;
  addresses { localhost port 5353; };
};
```

```
key samplekey {
  algorithm        hmac-sha256;
  secret           "6FMfj43Osz4lyb24OIe2iGEz9lf1llJO+lz";
};

key testkey {
  algorithm hmac-sha256;
  secret    "R3HI8P6BKw9ZwXwN3VZKuQ==";
};
```

In the above example, **rndc** will by default use the server at localhost (127.0.0.1) and the key called samplekey. Commands to the localhost server will use the samplekey key, which must also be defined in the server's configuration file with the same name and secret. The key statement indicates that samplekey uses the HMAC-SHA256 algorithm and its secret clause contains the base-64 encoding of the HMAC-SHA256 secret enclosed in double quotes.

If **rndc -s testserver** is used then **rndc** will connect to server on localhost port 5353 using the key testkey.

To generate a random secret with **rndc-confgen**:

rndc-confgen

A complete `rndc.conf` file, including the randomly generated key, will be written to the standard output. Commented-out `key` and `controls` statements for `named.conf` are also printed.

To generate a base-64 secret with **mmencode**:

echo "known plaintext for a secret" | mmencode

rndc.conf Name Server Configuration

The name server must be configured to accept rndc connections and to recognize the key specified in the `rndc.conf` file, using the controls statement in `named.conf`. See the sections on the `controls` statement in the Section 6.7 for details.

4.6   rndc-confgen — rndc key generation tool

Synopsis

rndc-confgen [-a] [-A *algorithm*] [-b *keysize*] [-c *keyfile*] [-h] [-k *keyname*] [-p *port*] [-r *randomfile*] [-s *address*] [-t *chrootdir*] [-u *user*]

rndc-confgen Description

rndc-confgen generates configuration files for **rndc**. It can be used as a convenient alternative to writing the `rndc.conf` file and the corresponding **controls** and **key** statements in `named.conf` by hand. Alternatively, it can be run with the **-a** option to set up a `rndc.key` file and avoid the need for a `rndc.conf` file and a **controls** statement altogether.

rndc-confgen Options

-a

Do automatic **rndc** configuration. This creates a file `rndc.key` in `/etc` (or whatever `sysco nfdir` was specified as when BIND was built) that is read by both **rndc** and **named** on startup. The `rndc.key` file defines a default command channel and authentication key allowing **rndc** to communicate with **named** on the local host with no further configuration.

Running **rndc-confgen -a** allows BIND 9 and **rndc** to be used as drop-in replacements for BIND 8 and **ndc**, with no changes to the existing BIND 8 `named.conf` file.

If a more elaborate configuration than that generated by **rndc-confgen -a** is required, for example if rndc is to be used remotely, you should run **rndc-confgen** without the **-a** option and set up a `rndc.conf` and `named.conf` as directed.

-A *algorithm*

Specifies the algorithm to use for the TSIG key. Available choices are: hmac-md5, hmac-sha1, hmac-sha224, hmac-sha256, hmac-sha384 and hmac-sha512. The default is hmac-md5.

-b *keysize*

Specifies the size of the authentication key in bits. Must be between 1 and 512 bits; the default is the hash size.

-c *keyfile*

Used with the **-a** option to specify an alternate location for `rndc.key`.

-h

Prints a short summary of the options and arguments to **rndc-confgen**.

-k *keyname*

Specifies the key name of the rndc authentication key. This must be a valid domain name. The default is `rndc-key`.

-p *port*

Specifies the command channel port where **named** listens for connections from **rndc**. The default is 953.

-r *randomfile*

Specifies a source of random data for generating the authorization. If the operating system does not provide a `/dev/random` or equivalent device, the default source of randomness is keyboard input. `randomdev` specifies the name of a character device or file containing random data to be used instead of the default. The special value `keyboard` indicates that keyboard input should be used.

-s *address*

Specifies the IP address where **named** listens for command channel connections from **rndc**. The default is the loopback address 127.0.0.1.

-t *chrootdir*

Used with the **-a** option to specify a directory where **named** will run chrooted. An additional copy of the `rndc.key` will be written relative to this directory so that it will be found by the chrooted **named**.

-u *user*

> Used with the **-a** option to set the owner of the `rndc.key` file generated. If **-t** is also specified only the file in the chroot area has its owner changed.

rndc-confgen Examples

To allow **rndc** to be used with no manual configuration, run

`rndc-confgen -a`

To print a sample `rndc.conf` file and corresponding **controls** and **key** statements to be manually inserted into `named.conf`, run

`rndc-confgen`

Note

If you get "rndc: connect failed: connection refused" when trying to run **rndc**, it is usually a configuration error.

First ensure that **named** is running and no errors are being reported at startup (/var/log/messages or equivalent). Running "**named -g <usual arguments>**" from a title can help at this point.

Secondly ensure that named is configured to use **rndc** either by "**rndc-confgen -a**", **rndc-confgen** or manually.

Old versions of **rndc-confgen** used localhost rather than 127.0.0.1 in `/etc/rndc.conf` for the default server. Update `/etc/rndc.conf` if necessary so that the default server listed in `/etc/rndc.conf` matches the addresses used in `named.conf`. "localhost" has two address (127.0.0.1 and ::1).

If you use "**rndc-confgen -a**" and **named** is running with **-t** or **-u** ensure that `/etc/rndc.conf` has the correct ownership and that a copy is in the chroot area. You can do this by re-running "**rndc-confgen -a**" with appropriate **-t** and **-u** arguments.

4.7 genrandom — generate a file containing random data

Synopsis

`genrandom [-n number] size filename`

genrandom Description

genrandom generates a file or a set of files containing a specified quantity of pseudo-random data, which can be used as a source of entropy for other commands on systems with no random device.

genrandom Arguments

-n *number*

In place of generating one file, generates `number` (from 2 to 9) files, appending `number` to the name.

size

The size of the file, in kilobytes, to generate.

filename

The file name into which random data should be written.

5 Name Server Configuration

This chapter introduces the name server configuration and provides some suggested configurations along with guidelines for their use. The standard configuration file elements and address match lists are used with various options and configurations as covered in the following chapter.

BIND includes a tool, the **named-checkconf** program, for checking the syntax of a `named.conf` configuration file. This is covered in detail at the end of this chapter.

5.1 Configuration File Elements

Following is a list of elements used throughout the BIND configuration file documentation:

`acl_name`

> The name of an `address_match_list` as defined by the **acl** statement.

`address_match_list`

> A list of one or more `ip_addr`, `ip_prefix`, `key_id`, or `acl_name` elements. See Section 5.2 for details.

`masters_list`

> A named list of one or more `ip_addr` with optional `key_id` and/or `ip_port`. A `masters_list` may include other `masters_lists`.

`domain_name`

> A quoted string which will be used as a DNS name, for example `"my.test.domain"`.

`namelist`

> A list of one or more `domain_name` elements.

`dotted_decimal`

> One to four integers valued 0 through 255 separated by dots (`.'), such as **123**, **45.67** or **89.123.45.67**.

`ip4_addr`

> An IPv4 address with exactly four elements in `dotted_decimal` notation.

ip6_addr

> An IPv6 address, such as **2001:db8::1234**. IPv6 scoped addresses that have ambiguity on their scope zones must be disambiguated by an appropriate zone ID with the percent character (`%') as delimiter. It is strongly recommended to use string zone names rather than numeric identifiers, in order to be robust against system configuration changes. However, since there is no standard mapping for such names and identifier values, currently only interface names as link identifiers are supported, assuming one-to-one mapping between interfaces and links. For example, a link-local address **fe80::1** on the link attached to the interface **ne0** can be specified as **fe80::1%ne0**. Note that on most systems link-local addresses always have the ambiguity, and need to be disambiguated.

ip_addr

> An ip4_addr or ip6_addr.

ip_dscp

> A number between 0 and 63, used to select a differentiated services code point (DSCP) value for use with outgoing traffic on operating systems that support DSCP. (DSCP support was introduced in BIND 9.10. See the **dscp** in Section 6.7 for more information.)

ip_port

> An IP port number. The number is limited to 0 through 65535, with values below 1024 typically restricted to use by processes running as root. In some cases, an asterisk (`*') character can be used as a placeholder to select a random high-numbered port.

ip_prefix

> An IP network specified as an ip_addr, followed by a slash (`/') and then the number of bits in the netmask. Trailing zeros in a ip_addr may omitted. For example, **127/8** is the network **127.0.0.0** with netmask **255.0.0.0** and **1.2.3.0/28** is network **1.2.3.0** with netmask **255.255.255.240**.
>
> When specifying a prefix involving a IPv6 scoped address the scope may be omitted. In that case the prefix will match packets from any scope.

key_id

> A domain_name representing the name of a shared key, to be used for transaction security.

key_list

> A list of one or more key_ids, separated by semicolons and ending with a semicolon.

number

> A non-negative 32-bit integer (i.e., a number between 0 and 4294967295, inclusive). Its acceptable value might further be limited by the context in which it is used.

path_name

> A quoted string which will be used as a pathname, such as zones/master/my.test.domain.

port_list

> A list of an ip_port or a port range. A port range is specified in the form of **range** followed by two ip_ports, port_low and port_high, which represents port numbers from port_low through port_high, inclusive. port_low must not be larger than port_high. For

example, `range 1024 65535` represents ports from 1024 through 65535. In either case an asterisk (`*`) character is not allowed as a valid `ip_port`.

`size_spec`

A 64-bit unsigned integer, or the keywords **unlimited** or **default**.

Integers may take values 0 <= value <= 18446744073709551615, though certain parameters (such as **max-journal-size**) may use a more limited range within these extremes. In most cases, setting a value to 0 does not literally mean zero; it means "undefined" or "as big as possible", depending on the context. See the explanations of particular parameters that use `size_spec` for details on how they interpret its use.

Numeric values can optionally be followed by a scaling factor: **K** or **k** for kilobytes, **M** or **m** for megabytes, and **G** or **g** for gigabytes, which scale by 1024, 1024*1024, and 1024*1024*1024 respectively.

`unlimited` generally means "as big as possible", and is usually the best way to safely set a very large number. (Prior to BIND 9.10, in some contexts, including the `max-cache-size` option, it may mean the largest possible 32-bit unsigned integer, 0xffffffff.)

`default` uses the limit that was in force when the server was started.

`size_or_percent`

`size_spec` or integer value followed by '%' to represent percents.

The behavior is exactly the same as `size_spec`, but `size_or_percent` allows also to specify a positive integer value followed by '%' sign to represent percents.

This percent element was introduced in BIND 9.11.

`yes_or_no`

Either **yes** or **no**. The words **true** and **false** are also accepted, as are the numbers **1** and **0**.

`dialup_option`

One of **yes**, **no**, **notify**, **notify-passive**, **refresh** or **passive**. When used in a zone, **notify-passive**, **refresh**, and **passive** are restricted to slave and stub zones.

5.2 Address Match Lists

Syntax

```
address_match_list = address_match_list_element ;
  address_match_list_element; ...
address_match_list_element = ! (ip_address /length |
  key key_id | acl_name | { address_match_list } )
```

Definition and Usage

Address (or security key) match lists are primarily used to determine access control for various server operations. They are also used in the **listen-on** and **sortlist** statements. The elements which constitute an address match list can be any of the following:

- an IP address (IPv4 or IPv6)

- an IP prefix (in `/' notation)

- a key ID, as defined by the **key** statement

- the name of an address match list defined with the **acl** statement

- a nested address match list enclosed in braces

Elements can be negated with a leading exclamation mark (`!'), and the match list names "any", "none", "localhost", and "localnets" are predefined. More information on those names can be found in the description of the **acl** statement in Section 6.1.

The addition of the key clause made the name of this syntactic element something of a misnomer, since security keys can be used to validate access without regard to a host or network address.

When a given IP address or prefix is compared to an address match list, the comparison takes place in approximately O(1) time. However, key comparisons require that the list of keys be traversed until a matching key is found, and therefore may be somewhat slower.

The interpretation of a match depends on whether the list is being used for access control, defining **listen-on** ports, or in a **sortlist**, and whether the element was negated.

When used as an access control list, a non-negated match allows access and a negated match denies access. If there is no match, access is denied. The clauses **allow-notify**, **allow-recursion**, **allow-recursion-on**, **allow-query**, **allow-query-on**, **allow-query-cache**, **allow-query-cache-on**, **allow-transfer**, **allow-update**, **allow-update-forwarding**, **blackhole**, and **keep-response-order** all use address match lists. Similarly, the **listen-on** option will cause the server to refuse queries on any of the machine's addresses which do not match the list.

Order of insertion is significant. If more than one element in an ACL is found to match a given IP address or prefix, preference will be given to the one that came *first* in the ACL definition. Because of this first-match behavior, an element that defines a subset of another element in the list should come before the broader element, regardless of whether either is negated. For example, in **1.2.3/24; ! 1.2.3.13;** the 1.2.3.13 element is completely useless because the algorithm will match any lookup for 1.2.3.13 to the 1.2.3/24 element. Using **! 1.2.3.13; 1.2.3/24** fixes that problem by having 1.2.3.13 blocked by the negation, but all other 1.2.3.* hosts fall through.

5.3 Comment Syntax

The BIND 9 comment syntax allows for comments to appear anywhere that whitespace may appear in a BIND configuration file. To appeal to programmers of all kinds, they can be written in the C, C++, or shell/perl style.

Syntax

```
/* This is a BIND comment as in C */
```

```
// This is a BIND comment as in C++

# This is a BIND comment as in common UNIX shells
# and perl
```

Definition and Usage

Comments may appear anywhere that whitespace may appear in a BIND configuration file.

C-style comments start with the two characters /* (slash, star) and end with */ (star, slash). Because they are completely delimited with these characters, they can be used to comment only a portion of a line or to span multiple lines.

C-style comments cannot be nested. For example, the following is not valid because the entire comment ends with the first */:

```
/* This is the start of a comment.
   This is still part of the comment.
/* This is an incorrect attempt at nesting a comment. */
   This is no longer in any comment. */
```

C++-style comments start with the two characters // (slash, slash) and continue to the end of the physical line. They cannot be continued across multiple physical lines; to have one logical comment span multiple lines, each line must use the // pair. For example:

```
// This is the start of a comment.  The next line
// is a new comment, even though it is logically
// part of the previous comment.
```

Shell-style (or perl-style, if you prefer) comments start with the character # (number sign) and continue to the end of the physical line, as in C++ comments. For example:

```
# This is the start of a comment.  The next line
# is a new comment, even though it is logically
# part of the previous comment.
```

Warning
You cannot use the semicolon (`;`) character to start a comment such as you would in a zone file. The semicolon indicates the end of a configuration statement.

5.4 Configuration File Grammar

A BIND 9 configuration consists of statements and comments. Statements end with a semicolon. Statements and comments are the only elements that can appear without enclosing braces. Many statements contain a block of sub-statements, which are also terminated with a semicolon.

The following statements are supported:

acl

>   defines a named IP address matching list, for access control and other uses.

controls

>   declares control channels to be used by the **rndc** utility.

include

>   includes a file.

key

>   specifies key information for use in authentication and authorization using TSIG.

logging

>   specifies what the server logs, and where the log messages are sent.

lwres

>   configures **named** to also act as a light-weight resolver daemon (**lwresd**).

masters

>   defines a named masters list for inclusion in stub and slave zones' **masters** or **also-notify** lists.

options

>   controls global server configuration options and sets defaults for other statements.

server

>   sets certain configuration options on a per-server basis.

statistics-channels

>   declares communication channels to get access to **named** statistics.

trusted-keys

>   defines trusted DNSSEC keys.

managed-keys

>   lists DNSSEC keys to be kept up to date using RFC 5011 trust anchor maintenance.

view

>   defines a view.

zone

>   defines a zone.

The **logging** and **options** statements may only occur once per configuration.

These statements are documented in detail in the following chapters.

5.5 Sample Configurations

A Caching-only Name Server

The following sample configuration is appropriate for a caching-only name server for use by clients internal to a corporation. All queries from outside clients are refused using the **allow-query** option. Alternatively, the same effect could be achieved using suitable firewall rules.

```
// Two corporate subnets we wish to allow queries from.
acl corpnets { 192.168.4.0/24; 192.168.7.0/24; };
options {
    // Working directory
    directory "/etc/namedb";

    allow-query { corpnets; };
};
// Provide a reverse mapping for the loopback
// address 127.0.0.1
zone "0.0.127.in-addr.arpa" {
    type master;
    file "localhost.rev";
    notify no;
};
```

An Authoritative-only Name Server

This sample configuration is for an authoritative-only server that is the master server for "example. com" and a slave for the subdomain "eng.example.com".

```
options {
    // Working directory
    directory "/etc/namedb";
    // Do not allow access to cache
    allow-query-cache { none; };
    // This is the default
    allow-query { any; };
    // Do not provide recursive service
    recursion no;
};

// Provide a reverse mapping for the loopback
// address 127.0.0.1
zone "0.0.127.in-addr.arpa" {
    type master;
    file "localhost.rev";
    notify no;
};
// We are the master server for example.com
zone "example.com" {
```

```
    type master;
    file "example.com.db";
    // IP addresses of slave servers allowed to
    // transfer example.com
    allow-transfer {
  192.168.4.14;
  192.168.5.53;
    };
};
// We are a slave server for eng.example.com
zone "eng.example.com" {
    type slave;
    file "eng.example.com.bk";
    // IP address of eng.example.com master server
    masters { 192.168.4.12; };
};
```

5.6   named-checkconf — named configuration file syntax checker

Synopsis

```
named-checkconf [-h] [-v] [-j] [-t directory] filename [-p] [-x] [-z]
```

named-checkconf Description

named-checkconf checks the syntax, but not the semantics, of a **named** configuration file. The file is parsed and checked for syntax errors, along with all files included by it. If no file is specified, /etc/named.conf is read by default.

Note

Files that **named** reads in separate parser contexts, such as rndc.key and bind.keys, are not automatically read by **named-checkconf**. Configuration errors in these files may cause **named** to fail to run, even if **named-checkconf** was successful. **named-checkconf** can be run on these files explicitly, however.

---

named-checkconf Options

-h

  Print the usage summary and exit.

-t *directory*

  Chroot to directory so that include directives in the configuration file are processed as if run by a similarly chrooted **named**.

-v

Print the version of the **named-checkconf** program and exit.

-p

Print out the `named.conf` and included files in canonical form if no errors were detected.

-x

When printing the configuration files in canonical form, obscure shared secrets by replacing them with strings of question marks ('?'). This allows the contents of `named.conf` and related files to be shared — for example, when submitting bug reports — without compromising private data. This option cannot be used without -p.

-z

Perform a test load of all master zones found in `named.conf`.

-j

When loading a zonefile read the journal if it exists.

filename

The name of the configuration file to be checked. If not specified, it defaults to `/etc/named.conf`.

named-checkconf Return Values

named-checkconf returns an exit status of 1 if errors were detected and 0 otherwise.

Note

If you get error messages like "named.conf:99: unexpected end of input" where 99 is the last line of the file, the `named.conf` may have unbalanced quotes or missing an end of line marker. Some text editors (like Notepad and Wordpad) fail to put a line title indication (e.g. CR/LF) on the last line of a text file. This can be fixed by "adding" a blank line to the end of the file. **named** expects to see EOF immediately after EOL and treats text files where this is not met as truncated.

---

6 Name Server Configuration Reference

The **named** server recognizes over 250 keywords. This chapter provides the definitive documentation for the `named.conf` configuration organized by the different statements. The "Grammar" sections highlight the accepted format as entered into the configuration. The "Definition and Usage" sections describe the different options and explain their applicability. Reasonable values for certain option settings are also suggested. Note that some options are available for different statements, but are only documented once within this book.

6.1 acl Statement

acl Statement Grammar

```
acl acl-name {
    address_match_list
};
```

acl Statement Definition and Usage

The **acl** assigns a symbolic name to an address match list. It gets its name from a primary use of address match lists: Access Control Lists (ACLs).

Access Control Lists are address match lists that you can set up and nickname for future use in **allow-notify**, **allow-query**, **allow-query-on**, **allow-recursion**, **blackhole**, **allow-transfer**, **match-clients**, etc.

Using ACLs allows you to have finer control over who can access your name server, without cluttering up your config files with huge lists of IP addresses.

It is a *good idea* to use ACLs, and to control access to your server. Limiting access to your server by outside parties can help prevent spoofing and denial of service (DoS) attacks against your server.

ACLs match clients on the basis of up to three characteristics: 1) The client's IP address; 2) the TSIG or SIG(0) key that was used to sign the request, if any; and 3) an address prefix encoded in an EDNS Client Subnet option, if any.

The following ACLs are built-in:

73

any

> Matches all hosts.

none

> Matches no hosts.

localhost

> Matches the IPv4 and IPv6 addresses of all network interfaces on the system. When addresses are added or removed, the **localhost** ACL element is updated to reflect the changes.

localnets

> Matches any host on an IPv4 or IPv6 network for which the system has an interface. When addresses are added or removed, the **localnets** ACL element is updated to reflect the changes. Some systems do not provide a way to determine the prefix lengths of local IPv6 addresses. In such a case, **localnets** only matches the local IPv6 addresses, just like **localhost**.

Here is an example of ACLs based on client addresses:

```
// Set up an ACL named "bogusnets" that will block
// RFC1918 space and some reserved space, which is
// commonly used in spoofing attacks.
acl bogusnets {
  0.0.0.0/8;  192.0.2.0/24; 224.0.0.0/3;
  10.0.0.0/8; 172.16.0.0/12; 192.168.0.0/16;
};

// Set up an ACL called our-nets. Replace this with the
// real IP numbers.
acl our-nets { x.x.x.x/24; x.x.x.x/21; };
options {
  ...
  ...
  allow-query { our-nets; };
  allow-recursion { our-nets; };
  ...
  blackhole { bogusnets; };
  ...
};

zone "example.com" {
  type master;
  file "m/example.com";
  allow-query { any; };
};
```

This allows authoritative queries for "example.com" from any address, but recursive queries only from the networks specified in "our-nets", and no queries at all from the networks specified in "bogusnets".

ACLs use a "first-match" logic rather than "best-match": if an address prefix matches an ACL element, then that ACL is considered to have matched even if a later element would have matched more specifically. For example, the ACL **{ 10/8; !10.0.0.1; }** would actually match a query from 10.0.0.1, because the first element indicated that the query should be accepted, and the second element is ignored.

When using "nested" ACLs (that is, ACLs included or referenced within other ACLs), a negative match of a nested ACL will the containing ACL to continue looking for matches. This enables complex ACLs to be constructed, in which multiple client characteristics can be checked at the same time. For example, to construct an ACL which allows queries only when it originates from a particular network *and* only when it is signed with a particular key, use:

```
allow-query { !{ !10/8; any; }; key example; };
```

Within the nested ACL, any address that is *not* in the 10/8 network prefix will be rejected, and this will terminate processing of the ACL. Any address that *is* in the 10/8 network prefix will be accepted, but this causes a negative match of the nested ACL, so the containing ACL continues processing. The query will then be accepted if it is signed by the key "example", and rejected otherwise. The ACL, then, will only matches when *both* conditions are true.

EDNS Client Subnet (ECS)

In addition to network addresses and prefixes, which are matched against the source address of the DNS request, ACLs may include `key` elements, which specify the name of a TSIG or SIG(0) key, or, in BIND 9.11, `ecs` elements, which specify a network prefix but are only matched if that prefix matches an EDNS client subnet option included in the request.

The EDNS Client Subnet (ECS) option, introduced in BIND 9.11, is used by a recursive resolver to inform an authoritative name server of the network address block from which the original query was received, enabling authoritative servers to give different answers to the same resolver for different resolver clients. An ACL containing an element of the form **ecs *prefix*** will match if a request arrives in containing an ECS option encoding an address within that prefix. If the request has no ECS option, then "ecs" elements are simply ignored. Addresses in ACLs that are not prefixed with "ecs" are matched only against the source address.

GeoIP

When BIND 9 is built with GeoIP support, ACLs can also be used for geographic access restrictions. This is done by specifying an ACL element of the form: **geoip [db *database*] *field value***

GeoIP support was introduced in BIND 9.10. (For building with support for GeoIP, see Section 3.3.)

The `field` indicates which field to search for a match. Available fields are "country", "region", "city", "continent", "postal" (postal code), "metro" (metro code), "area" (area code), "tz" (timezone), "isp", "org", "asnum", "domain" and "netspeed".

`value` is the value to search for within the database. A string may be quoted if it contains spaces or other special characters. If this is an "asnum" search, then the leading "ASNNNN" string can be used, otherwise the full description must be used (e.g. "ASNNNN Example Company Name"). If this is a "country" search and the string is two characters long, then it must be a standard ISO-3166-1 two-letter country code, and if it is three characters long then it must be an ISO-3166-1 three-letter country code; otherwise it is the full name of the country. Similarly, if this is a "region" search and the string is two characters long, then it must be a standard two-letter state or province abbreviation; otherwise it is the full name of the state or province.

The `database` field indicates which GeoIP database to search for a match. In most cases this is unnecessary, because most search fields can only be found in a single database. However, searches for country can be answered from the "city", "region", or "country" databases, and searches for region (i.e., state or province) can be answered from the "city" or "region" databases. For these search types, specifying a `database` will force the query to be answered from that database and no other. If `database` is not specified, then these queries will be answered from the "city" database if it is installed, or the "region" database if it is installed, or the "country" database, in that order.

By default, if a DNS query includes an EDNS Client Subnet (ECS) option which encodes a non-zero address prefix, then GeoIP ACLs will be matched against that address prefix. Otherwise, they are matched against the source address of the query. To prevent GeoIP ACLs from matching against ECS options, set the **geoip-use-ecs** to `no`.

The following are some example GeoIP ACLs:

```
geoip country US;
geoip country JAP;
geoip db country country Canada;
geoip db region region WA;
geoip city "San Francisco";
geoip region Oklahoma;
geoip postal 95062;
geoip tz "America/Los_Angeles";
geoip org "Internet Systems Consortium";
```

6.2   controls Statement

controls Statement Grammar

```
controls {
   [ inet ( ip_addr | * ) [ port ip_port ]
     allow { address_match_list }
     keys { key_list }; ]
   [ inet ...; ]
   [ unix path perm number owner number group number
     keys { key_list }; ]
   [ unix ...; ]
};
```

controls Statement Definition and Usage

The **controls** statement declares control channels to be used by system administrators to control the operation of the name server. These control channels are used by the **rndc** utility to send commands to and retrieve non-DNS results from a name server. (The **rndc** program is covered in Chapter 4.)

An **inet** control channel is a TCP socket listening at the specified **ip_port** on the specified **ip_addr**, which can be an IPv4 or IPv6 address. An **ip_addr** of * (asterisk) is interpreted as the IPv4 wildcard address; connections will be accepted on any of the system's IPv4 addresses. To listen on the IPv6 wildcard address, use an **ip_addr** of : :. If you will only use **rndc** on the local host, using the loopback address (127.0.0.1 or : :1) is recommended for maximum security.

If no port is specified, port 953 is used. The asterisk "*" cannot be used for **ip_port**.

The ability to issue commands over the control channel is restricted by the **allow** and **keys** clauses. Connections to the control channel are permitted based on the **address_match_list**. This is for simple IP address based filtering only; any **key_id** elements of the **address_match_list** are ignored.

A **unix** control channel is a UNIX domain socket listening at the specified path in the file system. Access to the socket is specified by the **perm**, **owner** and **group** clauses. Note on some platforms (SunOS and Solaris) the permissions (**perm**) are applied to the parent directory as the permissions on the socket itself are ignored.

The primary authorization mechanism of the command channel is the **key_list**, which contains a list of **key_id**s. Each **key_id** in the **key_list** is authorized to execute commands over the control channel. See Chapter 4) for information about configuring keys in **rndc**.

If no **controls** statement is present, **named** will set up a default control channel listening on the loopback address 127.0.0.1 and its IPv6 counterpart ::1. In this case, and also when the **controls** statement is present but does not have a **keys** clause, **named** will attempt to load the command channel key from the file rndc.key in /etc (or whatever sysconfdir was specified as when BIND was built. (For details on sysconfdir, see Section 3.3.) To create a rndc.key file, run:

rndc-confgen -a

(The **rndc-confgen** tool is covered in Chapter 4.)

The rndc.key feature was created to ease the transition of systems from BIND 8, which did not have digital signatures on its command channel messages and thus did not have a **keys** clause. It makes it possible to use an existing BIND 8 configuration file in BIND 9 unchanged, and still have **rndc** work the same way **ndc** worked in BIND 8, simply by executing the command **rndc-confgen -a** after BIND 9 is installed.

Since the rndc.key feature is only intended to allow the backward-compatible usage of BIND 8 configuration files, this feature does not have a high degree of configurability. You cannot easily change the key name or the size of the secret, so you should make a rndc.conf with your own key if you wish to change those things. The rndc.key file also has its permissions set such that only the owner of the file (the user that **named** is running as) can access it. If you desire greater flexibility in allowing other users to access **rndc** commands, then you need to create a rndc.conf file and make it group readable by a group that contains the users who should have access.

To disable the command channel, use an empty **controls** statement:

controls { };

6.3 include Statement

include Statement Grammar

```
include filename;
```

include Statement Definition and Usage

The **include** inserts the specified file at the point where the **include** statement is encountered. The **include** statement facilitates the administration of configuration files by permitting the reading or writing of some things but not others. For example, the statement could include private keys that are readable only by the name server.

6.4   key Statement

key Statement Grammar

```
key key_id {
    algorithm algorithm_id;
    secret secret_string;
};
```

key Statement Definition and Usage

The **key** defines a shared secret key for use with TSIG (see Section 9.3) or the command channel (see Section 6.2).

The **key** can occur at the top level of the configuration file or inside a **view** statement. Keys defined in top-level **key** statements can be used in all views. Keys intended for use in a **controls** statement (see Section 6.2) must be defined at the top level.

The `key_id`, also known as the key name, is a domain name uniquely identifying the key. It can be used in a **server** statement to cause requests sent to that server to be signed with this key, or in address match lists to verify that incoming requests have been signed with a key matching this name, algorithm, and secret.

The `algorithm_id` is a string that specifies a security/authentication algorithm. The **named** server supports hmac-md5, hmac-sha1, hmac-sha224, hmac-sha256, hmac-sha384 and hmac-sha512 TSIG authentication. Truncated hashes are supported by appending the minimum number of required bits preceded by a dash, e.g. hmac-sha1-80. The `secret_string` is the secret to be used by the algorithm, and is treated as a base-64 encoded string.

6.5   logging Statement

logging Statement Grammar

```
logging {
    [ channel channel_name {
    ( file path_name
    [ versions ( number | unlimited ) ]
    [ size size_spec ]
        | syslog syslog_facility
        | stderr
        | null );
    [ severity (critical | error | warning | notice |
    info | debug [ level ] | dynamic ); ]
    [ print-category yes or no; ]
    [ print-severity yes or no; ]
    [ print-time yes or no; ]
    [ buffered yes or no; ]
    }; ]
    [ category category_name {
    channel_name ; [ channel_name ; ... ]
    }; ]
    ...
};
```

logging Statement Definition and Usage

The **logging** configures a wide variety of logging options for the name server. Its **channel** phrase associates output methods, format options and severity levels with a name that can then be used with the **category** phrase to select how various classes of messages are logged.

Only one **logging** statement is used to define as many channels and categories as are wanted. If there is no **logging** statement, the logging configuration will be:

```
logging {
    category default { default_syslog; default_debug; };
    category unmatched { null; };
};
```

If **named** is started with the −L option, it logs to the specified file at startup, instead of using syslog. (This option was introduced in BIND 9.11.) In this case the logging configuration will be:

```
logging {
    category default { default_logfile; default_debug; };
    category unmatched { null; };
};
```

In BIND 9, the logging configuration is only established when the entire configuration file has been parsed. In BIND 8, it was established as soon as the **logging** statement was parsed. When the server is starting up, all logging messages regarding syntax errors in the configuration file go to the default channels, or to standard error if the −g option was specified.

The channel Phrase

All log output goes to one or more *channels*; you can make as many of them as you want.

Every channel definition must include a destination clause that says whether messages selected for the channel go to a file, to a particular syslog facility, to the standard error stream, or are discarded. It can optionally also limit the message severity level that will be accepted by the channel (the default is **info**), and whether to include a **named**-generated time stamp, the category name and/or severity level (the default is not to include any).

The **null** destination clause causes all messages sent to the channel to be discarded; in that case, other options for the channel are meaningless.

The **file** destination clause directs the channel to a disk file. It can include limitations both on how large the file is allowed to become, and how many versions of the file will be saved each time the file is opened.

If you use the **versions** log file option, then **named** will retain that many backup versions of the file by renaming them when opening. For example, if you choose to keep three old versions of the file `lamers.log`, then just before it is opened `lamers.log.1` is renamed to `lamers.log.2`, `lamers.log.0` is renamed to `lamers.log.1`, and `lamers.log` is renamed to `lamers.log.0`. You can say **versions unlimited** to not limit the number of versions. If a **size** option is associated with the log file, then renaming is only done when the file being opened exceeds the indicated size. No backup versions are kept by default; any existing log file is simply appended.

The **size** option for files is used to limit log growth. If the file ever exceeds the size, then **named** will stop writing to the file unless it has a **versions** option associated with it. If backup versions are kept, the files are rolled as described above and a new one begun. If there is no **versions** option, no more data will be written to the log until some out-of-band mechanism removes or truncates the log to less than the maximum size. The default behavior is not to limit the size of the file.

Example usage of the **size** and **versions** options:

```
channel an_example_channel {
    file "example.log" versions 3 size 20m;
    print-time yes;
    print-category yes;
};
```

The **syslog** destination clause directs the channel to the system log. Its argument is a syslog facility as described in the **syslog** man page. Known facilities are **kern**, **user**, **mail**, **daemon**, **auth**, **syslog**, **lpr**, **news**, **uucp**, **cron**, **authpriv**, **ftp**, **local0**, **local1**, **local2**, **local3**, **local4**, **local5**, **local6** and **local7**, however not all facilities are supported on all operating systems. How **syslog** will handle messages sent to this facility is described in the **syslog.conf** man page. If you have a system which uses a very old version of **syslog** that only uses two arguments to the **openlog()** function, then this clause is silently ignored.

On Windows machines syslog messages are directed to the EventViewer.

The **severity** clause works like **syslog**'s "priorities", except that they can also be used if you are writing straight to a file rather than using **syslog**. Messages which are not at least of the severity level given will not be selected for the channel; messages of higher severity levels will be accepted.

If you are using **syslog**, then the **syslog.conf** priorities will also determine what eventually passes through. For example, defining a channel facility and severity as **daemon** and **debug** but only logging **daemon.warning** via **syslog.conf** will cause messages of severity **info** and **notice** to be dropped. If the situation were reversed, with **named** writing messages of only **warning** or higher, then **syslogd** would print all messages it received from the channel.

The **stderr** destination clause directs the channel to the server's standard error stream. This is intended for use when the server is running as a foreground process, for example when debugging a configuration.

The server can supply extensive debugging information when it is in debugging mode. If the server's global debug level is greater than zero, then debugging mode will be active. The global debug level is set either by starting the **named** server with the −d flag followed by a positive integer, or by running:

```
rndc trace
```

The global debug level can be set to zero, and debugging mode turned off, by running:

```
rndc notrace
```

All debugging messages in the server have a debug level, and higher debug levels give more detailed output. Channels that specify a specific debug severity, for example:

```
channel specific_debug_level {
    file "foo";
    severity debug 3;
};
```

will get debugging output of level 3 or less any time the server is in debugging mode, regardless of the global debugging level. Channels with **dynamic** severity use the server's global debug level to determine what messages to print.

If **print-time** has been turned on, then the date and time will be logged. **print-time** may be specified for a **syslog** channel, but is usually pointless since **syslog** also logs the date and time. If **print-category** is requested, then the category of the message will be logged as well. Finally, if **print-severity** is on, then the severity level of the message will be logged. The **print-** options may be used in any combination, and will always be printed in the following order: time, category, severity. Here is an example where all three **print-** options are on:

```
28-Feb-2000 15:05:32.863 general:notice:running
```

If **buffered** has been turned on the output to files will not be flushed after each log entry. By default all log messages are flushed. The **buffered** logging option was introduced in BIND 9.11.

There are four predefined channels that are used for **named**'s default logging as follows. If **named** is started with the −L then a fifth channel **default_logfile** is added. (This option was introduced in BIND 9.11.) How they are used is described in Section 6.5.

```
channel default_syslog {
    // send to syslog's daemon facility
    syslog daemon;
    // only send priority info and higher
    severity info;
```

```
channel default_debug {
    // write to named.run in the working directory
    // Note: stderr is used instead of "named.run" if
    // the server is started with the '-g' option.
    file "named.run";
    // log at the server's current debug level
    severity dynamic;
};

channel default_stderr {
    // writes to stderr
    stderr;
    // only send priority info and higher
    severity info;
};

channel null {
    // toss anything sent to this channel
    null;
};

channel default_logfile {
    // this channel is only present if named is
    // started with the -L option, whose argument
    // provides the file name
    file "...";
    // log at the server's current debug level
    severity dynamic;
};
```

The **default_debug** channel has the special property that it only produces output when the server's debug level is nonzero. It normally writes to a file called `named.run` in the server's working directory.

For security reasons, when the `-u` command line option is used, the `named.run` file is created only after **named** has changed to the new UID, and any debug output generated while **named** is starting up and still running as root is discarded. If you need to capture this output, you must run the server with the `-L` option (since BIND 9.11) to specify a default logfile, or the `-g` option to log to standard error which you can redirect to a file.

Once a channel is defined, it cannot be redefined. Thus you cannot alter the built-in channels directly, but you can modify the default logging by pointing categories at channels you have defined.

The category Phrase

There are many categories, so you can send the logs you want to see wherever you want, without seeing logs you don't want. If you don't specify a list of channels for a category, then log messages in that category will be sent to the **default** category instead. If you don't specify a **default** category, the following "default default" is used:

```
category default { default_syslog; default_debug; };
```

If you start **named** with the −L option (in BIND 9.11) then the default category is:

```
category default { default_logfile; default_debug; };
```

As an example, let's say you want to log security events to a file, but you also want keep the default logging behavior. You'd specify the following:

```
channel my_security_channel {
    file "my_security_file";
    severity info;
};
category security {
    my_security_channel;
    default_syslog;
    default_debug;
};
```

To discard all messages in a category, specify the **null** channel:

```
category xfer-out { null; };
category notify { null; };
```

Following are the available categories and brief descriptions of the types of log information they contain. More categories may be added in future BIND releases.

client
> Processing of client requests.

cname
> Logs nameservers that are skipped due to them being a CNAME rather than A / AAAA records. The **cname** logging category was introduced in BIND 9.11.

config
> Configuration file parsing and processing.

database
> Messages relating to the databases used internally by the name server to store zone and cache data.

default
> The default category defines the logging options for those categories where no specific configuration has been defined.

delegation-only
> Delegation only. Logs queries that have been forced to NXDOMAIN as the result of a delegation-only zone or a **delegation-only** in a forward, hint or stub zone declaration.

dispatch
> Dispatching of incoming packets to the server modules where they are to be processed.

dnssec

DNSSEC and TSIG protocol processing.

dnstap

The "dnstap" DNS traffic capture system.

edns-disabled

Log queries that have been forced to use plain DNS due to timeouts. This is often due to the remote servers not being RFC 1034 compliant (not always returning FORMERR or similar to EDNS queries and other extensions to the DNS when they are not understood). In other words, this is targeted at servers that fail to respond to DNS queries that they don't understand.

Note

The log message can also be due to packet loss. Before reporting servers for non-RFC 1034 compliance they should be re-tested to determine the nature of the non-compliance. This testing should prevent or reduce the number of false-positive reports.

Eventually **named** will have to stop treating such timeouts as due to RFC 1034 non compliance and start treating it as plain packet loss. Falsely classifying packet loss as due to RFC 1034 non compliance impacts on DNSSEC validation which requires EDNS for the DNSSEC records to be returned.

general

The catch-all. Many things still aren't classified into categories, and they all end up here.

lame-servers

Lame servers. These are misconfigurations in remote servers, discovered by BIND 9 when trying to query those servers during resolution.

network

Network operations.

notify

The NOTIFY protocol.

queries

Specify where queries should be logged to. At startup, specifying the category **queries** will also enable query logging unless **querylog** option has been specified. The query log entry reports the client's IP address and port number, and the query name, class and type. Next it reports whether the Recursion Desired flag was set (+ if set, - if not set), if the query was signed (S), EDNS was in used along with the EDNS version number (E(#)), if TCP was used (T), if DO (DNSSEC Ok) was set (D), if CD (Checking Disabled) was set (C), if a valid DNS Server COOKIE was received (V), or if a DNS COOKIE option without a valid Server COOKIE was present (K). After this the destination address the query was sent to is reported. `client 127.0.0.1#62536 (www.example.com):query:www.exam` `ple.com IN AAAA +SE client ::1#62537 (www.example.net):query:www.` `example.net IN AAAA -SE` (The first part of this log message, showing the client address/port number and query name, is repeated in all subsequent log messages related to the same query. Versions prior to BIND 9.9 did not report the query name.)

query-errors

> Information about queries that resulted in some failure. (See Section 6.5 for details.)

rate-limit

> The start, periodic, and final notices of the rate limiting of a stream of responses are logged at **info** severity in this category. These messages include a hash value of the domain name of the response and the name itself, except when there is insufficient memory to record the name for the final notice The final notice is normally delayed until about one minute after rate limit stops. A lack of memory can hurry the final notice, in which case it starts with an asterisk (*). Various internal events are logged at debug 1 level and higher. The **rate-limit** logging category was introduced in BIND 9.9. With BIND 9.9, it is available when BIND is configured with the **--enable-rrl** option at compile time. The code is built by default with BIND 9.10. Rate limiting of individual requests is logged in the **query-errors** category.

resolver

> DNS resolution, such as the recursive lookups performed on behalf of clients by a caching name server.

rpz

> Information about errors in response policy zone files, rewritten responses, and at the highest **debug** levels, mere rewriting attempts.

security

> Approval and denial of requests.

spill

> Logs queries that have been terminated, either by dropping or responding with SERVFAIL, as a result of a fetchlimit quota being exceeded.

unmatched

> Messages that **named** was unable to determine the class of or for which there was no matching **view**. A one line summary is also logged to the **client** category. This category is best sent to a file or stderr, by default it is sent to the **null** channel.

update

> Dynamic updates.

update-security

> Approval and denial of update requests.

xfer-in

> Zone transfers the server is receiving.

xfer-out

> Zone transfers the server is sending.

The query-errors Category

The **query-errors** category is specifically intended for debugging purposes: To identify why and how specific queries result in responses which indicate an error. Messages of this category are therefore only logged with **debug** levels.

At the debug levels of 1 or higher, each response with the rcode of SERVFAIL is logged as follows:

```
client 127.0.0.1#61502: query failed (SERVFAIL) for www.example.com/IN/ ←
    AAAA at query.c:3880
```

This means an error resulting in SERVFAIL was detected at line 3880 of source file `query.c`. Log messages of this level will particularly help identify the cause of SERVFAIL for an authoritative server.

At the debug levels of 2 or higher, detailed context information of recursive resolutions that resulted in SERVFAIL is logged. The log message will look like as follows:

```
fetch completed at resolver.c:2970 for www.example.com/A in 30.000183: ←
    timed out/success [domain:example.com, referral:2,restart:7,qrysent ←
    :8,timeout:5,lame:0,neterr:0, badresp:1,adberr:0,findfail:0,valfail ←
    :0]
```

The first part before the colon shows that a recursive resolution for AAAA records of www.example.com completed in 30.000183 seconds and the final result that led to the SERVFAIL was determined at line 2970 of source file `resolver.c`.

The following part shows the detected final result and the latest result of DNSSEC validation. The latter is always success when no validation attempt is made. In this example, this query resulted in SERVFAIL probably because all name servers are down or unreachable, leading to a timeout in 30 seconds. DNSSEC validation was probably not attempted.

The last part enclosed in square brackets shows statistics information collected for this particular resolution attempt. The `domain` field shows the deepest zone that the resolver reached; it is the zone where the error was finally detected. The meaning of the other fields is summarized in the following list.

referral
> The number of referrals the resolver received throughout the resolution process. In the above example this is 2, which are most likely com and example.com.

restart
> The number of cycles that the resolver tried remote servers at the `domain` zone. In each cycle the resolver sends one query (possibly resending it, depending on the response) to each known name server of the `domain` zone.

qrysent
> The number of queries the resolver sent at the `domain` zone.

timeout
> The number of timeouts since the resolver received the last response.

lame
> The number of lame servers the resolver detected at the `domain` zone. A server is detected to be lame either by an invalid response or as a result of lookup in BIND9's address database (ADB), where lame servers are cached.

neterr
> The number of erroneous results that the resolver encountered in sending queries at the `dom ain` zone. One common case is the remote server is unreachable and the resolver receives an ICMP unreachable error message.

badresp
> The number of unexpected responses (other than `lame`) to queries sent by the resolver at the `domain` zone.

adberr
> Failures in finding remote server addresses of the `domain` zone in the ADB. One common case of this is that the remote server's name does not have any address records.

findfail
> Failures of resolving remote server addresses. This is a total number of failures throughout the resolution process.

valfail
> Failures of DNSSEC validation. Validation failures are counted throughout the resolution process (not limited to the `domain` zone), but should only happen in `domain`.

At the debug levels of 3 or higher, the same messages as those at the debug 1 level are logged for other errors than SERVFAIL. Note that negative responses such as NXDOMAIN are not regarded as errors here.

At the debug levels of 4 or higher, the same messages as those at the debug 2 level are logged for other errors than SERVFAIL. Unlike the above case of level 3, messages are logged for negative responses. This is because any unexpected results can be difficult to debug in the recursion case.

6.6 masters Statement

masters Statement Grammar

```
masters name port ip_port dscp ip_dscp { ( masters_list |
    ip_addr port ip_port key key ) ; ... };
```

masters Statement Definition and Usage

masters lists allow for a common set of masters to be easily used by multiple stub and slave zones in their **masters** or **also-notify** lists.

6.7 options Statement

options Statement Grammar

This is the grammar of the **options** statement in the `named.conf` file:

```
options {
     attach-cache cache_name;
     version version_string;
     hostname hostname_string;
     server-id server_id_string;
     directory path_name;
     geoip-directory path_name;
     key-directory path_name;
     managed-keys-directory path_name;
     named-xfer path_name;
     tkey-gssapi-keytab path_name;
     tkey-gssapi-credential principal;
     tkey-domain domainname;
     tkey-dhkey key_name key_tag;
     cache-file path_name;
     dump-file path_name;
     bindkeys-file path_name;
     lock-file path_name;
     secroots-file path_name;
     session-keyfile path_name;
     session-keyname key_name;
     session-keyalg algorithm_id;
     memstatistics yes_or_no;
     memstatistics-file path_name;
     pid-file path_name;
     recursing-file path_name;
     statistics-file path_name;
     zone-statistics full | terse | none;
     auth-nxdomain yes_or_no;
     nxdomain-redirect string;
     deallocate-on-exit yes_or_no;
     dialup dialup_option;
     fake-iquery yes_or_no;
     fetch-glue yes_or_no;
     flush-zones-on-shutdown yes_or_no;
     has-old-clients yes_or_no;
     host-statistics yes_or_no;
     host-statistics-max number;
     minimal-responses yes_or_no;
     multiple-cnames yes_or_no;
     notify yes_or_no | explicit | master-only;
     recursion yes_or_no;
     send-cookie yes_or_no;
     require-server-cookie yes_or_no;
     cookie-algorithm secret_string;
     cookie-secret secret_string;
     nocookie-udp-size number ;
     request-nsid yes_or_no;
     rfc2308-type1 yes_or_no;
     use-id-pool yes_or_no;
     maintain-ixfr-base yes_or_no;
```

```
ixfr-from-differences (yes_or_no | master | slave);
auto-dnssec allow|maintain|off;
dnssec-enable yes_or_no;
dnssec-validation (yes_or_no | auto);
dnssec-lookaside ( auto |
        no |
        domain trust-anchor domain );
dnssec-must-be-secure domain yes_or_no;
dnssec-accept-expired yes_or_no;
forward ( only | first );
forwarders {  ip_addr port ip_port dscp ip_dscp ; ...  };
dual-stack-servers port ip_port dscp ip_dscp {
  ( domain_name port ip_port dscp ip_dscp |
    ip_addr port ip_port dscp ip_dscp) ;
  ... };
check-names ( master | slave | response )
   ( warn | fail | ignore );
check-dup-records ( warn | fail | ignore );
check-mx ( warn | fail | ignore );
check-wildcard yes_or_no;
check-integrity yes_or_no;
check-mx-cname ( warn | fail | ignore );
check-srv-cname ( warn | fail | ignore );
check-sibling yes_or_no;
check-spf ( warn | ignore );
allow-new-zones { yes_or_no };
allow-notify { address_match_list };
allow-query { address_match_list };
allow-query-on { address_match_list };
allow-query-cache { address_match_list };
allow-query-cache-on { address_match_list };
allow-transfer { address_match_list };
allow-recursion { address_match_list };
allow-recursion-on { address_match_list };
allow-update { address_match_list };
allow-update-forwarding { address_match_list };
automatic-interface-scan { yes_or_no };
geoip-use-ecs yes_or_no;
update-check-ksk yes_or_no;
dnssec-update-mode ( maintain | no-resign );
dnssec-dnskey-kskonly yes_or_no;
dnssec-loadkeys-interval number;
dnssec-secure-to-insecure yes_or_no ;
try-tcp-refresh yes_or_no;
allow-v6-synthesis { address_match_list };
blackhole { address_match_list };
keep-response-order { address_match_list };
no-case-compress { address_match_list };
use-v4-udp-ports { port_list };
avoid-v4-udp-ports { port_list };
use-v6-udp-ports { port_list };
```

```
avoid-v6-udp-ports { port_list };
listen-on  port ip_port  dscp ip_dscp { address_match_list };
listen-on-v6  port ip_port dscp ip_dscp { address_match_list };
query-source ( ( ip4_addr | * )
    port ( ip_port | * )   dscp ip_dscp |
    address ( ip4_addr | * )
    port ( ip_port | * )  )  dscp ip_dscp ;
query-source-v6 ( ( ip6_addr | * )
    port ( ip_port | * )   dscp ip_dscp |
    address ( ip6_addr | * )
    port ( ip_port | * )  )  dscp ip_dscp ;
use-queryport-pool yes_or_no;
queryport-pool-ports number;
queryport-pool-updateinterval number;
max-transfer-time-in number;
max-transfer-time-out number;
max-transfer-idle-in number;
max-transfer-idle-out number;
reserved-sockets number;
recursive-clients number;
tcp-clients number;
fetches-per-server number (drop | fail);
fetch-quota-params number fixedpoint fixedpoint fixedpoint ;
fetches-per-zone number (drop | fail);
notify-rate number;
startup-notify-rate number;
serial-query-rate number;
serial-queries number;
tcp-listen-queue number;
transfer-format ( one-answer | many-answers );
transfers-in   number;
transfers-out number;
transfers-per-ns number;
transfer-source (ip4_addr | *) port ip_port dscp ip_dscp ;
transfer-source-v6 (ip6_addr | *) port ip_port dscp ip_dscp ;
alt-transfer-source (ip4_addr | *) port ip_port dscp ip_dscp ;
alt-transfer-source-v6 (ip6_addr | *) port ip_port dscp ip_dscp ;
use-alt-transfer-source yes_or_no;
notify-delay seconds ;
notify-source (ip4_addr | *) port ip_port dscp ip_dscp ;
notify-source-v6 (ip6_addr | *) port ip_port dscp ip_dscp ;
notify-to-soa yes_or_no ;
also-notify { ip_addr
        port ip_port dscp ip_dscp key keyname ;
        ip_addr port ip_port dscp ip_dscp key keyname ; ...  };
max-ixfr-log-size number;
max-journal-size size_spec;
coresize size_spec ;
datasize size_spec ;
files size_spec ;
stacksize size_spec ;
```

```
cleaning-interval number;
heartbeat-interval number;
interface-interval number;
statistics-interval number;
topology { address_match_list };
sortlist { address_match_list };
rrset-order { order_spec ; order_spec ; ...   };
lame-ttl number;
max-ncache-ttl number;
max-cache-ttl number;
max-zone-ttl ( unlimited | number ;
serial-update-method increment|unixtime|date;
servfail-ttl number;
sig-validity-interval number number ;
sig-signing-nodes number ;
sig-signing-signatures number ;
sig-signing-type number ;
min-roots number;
use-ixfr yes_or_no ;
provide-ixfr yes_or_no;
request-ixfr yes_or_no;
request-expire yes_or_no;
treat-cr-as-space yes_or_no ;
min-refresh-time number ;
max-refresh-time number ;
min-retry-time number ;
max-retry-time number ;
nta-lifetime duration ;
nta-recheck duration ;
port ip_port;
dscp ip_dscp ;
additional-from-auth yes_or_no ;
additional-from-cache yes_or_no ;
random-device path_name ;
max-cache-size size_or_percent ;
match-mapped-addresses yes_or_no;
filter-aaaa-on-v4 ( yes_or_no | break-dnssec );
filter-aaaa-on-v6 ( yes_or_no | break-dnssec );
filter-aaaa { address_match_list };
dns64 ipv6-prefix {
    clients { address_match_list };
    mapped { address_match_list };
    exclude { address_match_list };
    suffix IPv6-address;
    recursive-only yes_or_no;
    break-dnssec yes_or_no;
    }; ;
dns64-server name
dns64-contact name
preferred-glue ( A | AAAA | NONE );
edns-udp-size number;
```

```
max-udp-size number;
max-rsa-exponent-size number;
root-delegation-only  exclude { namelist }  ;
querylog yes_or_no ;
disable-algorithms domain { algorithm;
        algorithm;  };
disable-ds-digests domain { digest_type;
        digest_type;  };
acache-enable yes_or_no ;
acache-cleaning-interval number;
max-acache-size size_spec ;
clients-per-query number ;
max-clients-per-query number ;
max-recursion-depth number ;
max-recursion-queries number ;
masterfile-format (text|raw|map) ;
masterfile-style (relative|full) ;
empty-server name ;
empty-contact name ;
empty-zones-enable yes_or_no ;
disable-empty-zone zone_name ;
zero-no-soa-ttl yes_or_no ;
zero-no-soa-ttl-cache yes_or_no ;
resolver-query-timeout number ;
deny-answer-addresses { address_match_list }
  except-from { namelist } ;
deny-answer-aliases { namelist }  except-from { namelist } ;
prefetch number number ;
rate-limit {
        responses-per-second number ;
        referrals-per-second number ;
        nodata-per-second number ;
        nxdomains-per-second number ;
        errors-per-second number ;
        all-per-second number ;
        window number ;
        log-only yes_or_no ;
        qps-scale number ;
        ipv4-prefix-length number ;
        ipv6-prefix-length number ;
        slip number ;
        exempt-clients  { address_match_list } ;
        max-table-size number ;
        min-table-size number ;
} ;
response-policy {
        zone zone_name
        policy (given | disabled | passthru | drop |
            tcp-only | nxdomain | nodata | cname domain)
        recursive-only yes_or_no
        log yes_or_no
```

```
              max-policy-ttl number
      ; ...
      }  recursive-only yes_or_no
         max-policy-ttl number
         break-dnssec yes_or_no
         min-ns-dots number
         qname-wait-recurse yes_or_no
         ;
      v6-bias number ;
};
```

options Statement Definition and Usage

The **options** sets up global options to be used by BIND. This statement may appear only once in a configuration file. If there is no **options** statement, an options block with each option set to its default will be used.

attach-cache

Allows multiple views to share a single cache database. Each view has its own cache database by default, but if multiple views have the same operational policy for name resolution and caching, those views can share a single cache to save memory and possibly improve resolution efficiency by using this option.

The **attach-cache** option may also be specified in **view** statements, in which case it overrides the global **attach-cache** option.

The *cache_name* specifies the cache to be shared. When the **named** server configures views which are supposed to share a cache, it creates a cache with the specified name for the first view of these sharing views. The rest of the views will simply refer to the already created cache.

One common configuration to share a cache would be to allow all views to share a single cache. This can be done by specifying the **attach-cache** as a global option with an arbitrary name.

Another possible operation is to allow a subset of all views to share a cache while the others to retain their own caches. For example, if there are three views A, B, and C, and only A and B should share a cache, specify the **attach-cache** option as a view A (or B)'s option, referring to the other view name:

```
view "A" {
  // this view has its own cache
  ...
};
view "B" {
  // this view refers to A's cache
  attach-cache "A";
};
view "C" {
  // this view has its own cache
  ...
};
```

Views that share a cache must have the same policy on configurable parameters that may affect caching. The following configurable options are required to be consistent among these views: **check-names**, **cleaning-interval**, **dnssec-accept-expired**, **dnssec-validation**, **max-cache-ttl**, **max-ncache-ttl**, **max-cache-size**, and **zero-no-soa-ttl**.

Note that there may be other parameters that may cause confusion if they are inconsistent for different views that share a single cache. For example, if these views define different sets of forwarders that can return different answers for the same question, sharing the answer does not make sense or could even be harmful. It is administrator's responsibility to ensure configuration differences in different views do not cause disruption with a shared cache.

directory

The working directory of the server. Any non-absolute pathnames in the configuration file will be taken as relative to this directory. The default location for most server output files (e.g. `named.run`) is this directory. If a directory is not specified, the working directory defaults to `` `.' ``, the directory from which the server was started. The directory specified should be an absolute path.

geoip-directory

Specifies the directory containing GeoIP `.dat` database files for GeoIP initialization. By default, this option is unset and the GeoIP support will use libGeoIP's built-in directory. (The **geoip-directory** option was introduced in BIND 9.10. For details about the **geoip** ACL, see Section 6.1.)

key-directory

When performing dynamic update of secure zones, the directory where the public and private DNSSEC key files should be found, if different than the current working directory. (Note that this option has no effect on the paths for files containing non-DNSSEC keys such as `bind.keys`, `rndc.key` or `session.key`.)

managed-keys-directory

Specifies the directory in which to store the files that track managed DNSSEC keys. By default, this is the working directory.

If **named** is not configured to use views, then managed keys for the server will be tracked in a single file called `managed-keys.bind`. Otherwise, managed keys will be tracked in separate files, one file per view; each file name will be the view name (or, if it contains characters that are incompatible with use as a file name, the SHA256 hash of the view name), followed by the extension `.mkeys`.

(Note: in releases previous to BIND 9.11, file names for views always used the SHA256 hash of the view name. To ensure compatibility after upgrade, if a file using the old name format is found to exist, it will be used instead of the new format.)

named-xfer

This option is obsolete. It was used in BIND 8 to specify the pathname to the **named-xfer** program. In BIND 9, no separate **named-xfer** program is needed; its functionality is built into the name server.

tkey-gssapi-keytab

The KRB5 keytab file to use for GSS-TSIG updates. If this option is set and tkey-gssapi-credential is not set, then updates will be allowed with any key matching a principal in the specified keytab.

tkey-gssapi-credential

The security credential with which the server should authenticate keys requested by the GSS-TSIG protocol. Currently only Kerberos 5 authentication is available and the credential is a Kerberos principal which the server can acquire through the default system key file, normally `/etc/krb5.keytab`. The location keytab file can be overridden using the **tkey-gssapi-keytab** option. Normally this principal is of the form `"DNS/server.domain"`. To use GSS-TSIG, **tkey-domain** must also be set if a specific keytab is not set with the **tkey-gssapi-keytab** option.

tkey-domain

The domain appended to the names of all shared keys generated with **TKEY**. When a client requests a **TKEY** exchange, it may or may not specify the desired name for the key. If present, the name of the shared key will be `client specified part + tkey-domain`. Otherwise, the name of the shared key will be `random hex digits + tkey-domain`. In most cases, the **domainname** should be the server's domain name, or an otherwise non-existent subdomain like `"_tkey.domainname"`. If you are using GSS-TSIG, this variable must be defined, unless you specify a specific keytab using **tkey-gssapi-keytab**.

tkey-dhkey

The Diffie-Hellman key used by the server to generate shared keys with clients using the Diffie-Hellman mode of **TKEY**. The server must be able to load the public and private keys from files in the working directory. In most cases, the keyname should be the server's host name.

cache-file

This is for testing only. Do not use.

dump-file

The pathname of the file the server dumps the database to when instructed to do so with:
rndc dumpdb

If not specified, the default is `named_dump.db`.

memstatistics-file

The pathname of the file the server writes memory usage statistics to on exit. If not specified, the default is `named.memstats`. (See the **memstatistics** option on page 103 for more details.)

lock-file

The pathname of a file on which **named** will attempt to acquire a file lock when starting up for the first time; if unsuccessful, the server will will terminate, under the assumption that another server is already running. If not specified, the default is `/var/run/named/named.lock`. The **lock-file** option was introduced in BIND 9.11.

Specifying **lock-file none** disables the use of a lock file. **lock-file** is ignored if **named** was run using the `-X` option, which overrides it. Changes to **lock-file** are ignored if **named** is being reloaded or reconfigured; it is only effective when the server is first started up.

pid-file

The pathname of the file the server writes its process ID in. If not specified, the default is `/var/run/named/named.pid`. The PID file is used by programs that want to send signals to the running name server. Specifying **pid-file none** disables the use of a PID file — no file will be written and any existing one will be removed. Note that **none** is a keyword, not a filename, and therefore is not enclosed in double quotes.

Q: *Why do see a log messages like "couldn't open pid file '/var/run/named.pid': Permission denied"?*

A: You are most likely running named as a non-root user, and that user does not have permission to write in `/var/run`. The common ways of fixing this are to create a `/var/run/named` directory owned by the named user and set pid-file to `"/var/run/named/named.pid"`, or set **pid-file** to `"named.pid"`, which will put the file in the directory specified by the directory option (which, in this case, must be writable by the user named is running as).

recursing-file

The pathname of the file the server dumps the queries that are currently recursing when instructed to do so with:

rndc recursing If not specified, the default is `named.recursing`.

statistics-file

The pathname of the file the server appends statistics to when instructed to do so using:

rndc stats If not specified, the default is `named.stats` in the server's current directory.

The statistics dump can be triggered by the **rndc stats** command.

The text format statistics dump begins with a line, like:

+++ Statistics Dump +++ (973798949)

The number in parentheses is a standard Unix-style (epoch) timestamp, measured as seconds since January 1, 1970. Following that line is a set of statistics information for a a specific category. Each section begins with a line, like:

++ Name Server Statistics ++

Each section consists of lines, each containing the statistics counter value followed by its textual description. For brevity, counters that have a value of 0 are not shown in the statistics file.

The statistics dump ends with the line where the number is identical to the number in the beginning line; for example:

--- Statistics Dump --- (973798949)

The numbers can be converted to human-readable format using BSD **date -r** or Coreutils **date -d** or Perl, for example:

```
$ date -d @973798949
Thu Nov  9 13:42:29 CST 2000
$ date -r 973798949
Thu Nov  9 13:42:29 CST 2000
$ perl -le "print scalar localtime 973798949"
Thu Nov  9 13:42:29 2000
```

For the interface to the statistics in JSON or XML formats instead, see Section 6.9.

bindkeys-file

The pathname of a file to override the built-in trusted keys provided by **named**. See the discussion of **dnssec-lookaside** and **dnssec-validation** for details. If not specified, the default is `/etc/bind.keys`.

secroots-file

The pathname of the file the server dumps security roots to when instructed to do so with **rndc secroots**. If not specified, the default is `named.secroots`.

session-keyfile

The pathname of the file into which to write a TSIG session key generated by **named** for use by **nsupdate -l**. If not specified, the default is `/var/run/named/session.key`. (See Section 9.2, and in particular the discussion of the **update-policy** statement's `local` option for more information about this feature.)

session-keyname

The key name to use for the TSIG session key. If not specified, the default is "local-ddns".

session-keyalg

The algorithm to use for the TSIG session key. Valid values are hmac-sha1, hmac-sha224, hmac-sha256, hmac-sha384, hmac-sha512 and hmac-md5. If not specified, the default is hmac-sha256.

port

The UDP/TCP port number the server uses for receiving and sending DNS protocol traffic. The default is 53. This option is mainly intended for server testing; a server using a port other than 53 will not be able to communicate with the global DNS.

dscp

The global Differentiated Services Code Point (DSCP) value to classify outgoing DNS traffic on operating systems that support DSCP. DSCP is used to identify traffic classification for quality of service. Valid values are 0 through 63. It is not configured by default. Most configuration options which take a `port` option (e.g., **listen-on**, **forwarders**, **also-notify**, **masters**, **notify-source**, etc.) can now also take a `dscp` option which may override this global default. (DSCP support was introduced in BIND 9.10.)

 Warning
Some network routes may incorrectly drop packets with some DSCP values set.

---

random-device

The source of entropy to be used by the server. Entropy is primarily needed for DNSSEC operations, such as TKEY transactions and dynamic update of signed zones. This options specifies the device (or file such as generated using the BIND **genrandom** tool) from which to read entropy. If this is a file, operations requiring entropy will fail when the file has been exhausted. If not specified, the default value is `/dev/random` (or equivalent) when present, and none otherwise. The **random-device** option takes effect during the initial configuration load at server startup time and is ignored on subsequent reloads.

Q: *What do "no source of entropy found" or "could not open entropy source foo" mean?*

A: The server requires a source of entropy to perform certain operations, mostly DNSSEC related. These messages indicate that you have no source of entropy. On systems with /dev/random or an equivalent, it is used by default. A source of entropy can also be defined using the random-device option in named.conf.

preferred-glue

If specified, the listed type (A or AAAA) will be emitted before other glue in the additional section of a query response. The default is to prefer A records when responding to queries that arrived via IPv4 and AAAA when responding to queries that arrived via IPv6.

root-delegation-only

Turn on enforcement of delegation-only in TLDs (top level domains) and root zones with an optional exclude list.

DS queries are expected to be made to and be answered by delegation only zones. Such queries and responses are treated as an exception to delegation-only processing and are not converted to NXDOMAIN responses provided a CNAME is not discovered at the query name.

If a delegation only zone server also serves a child zone it is not always possible to determine whether an answer comes from the delegation only zone or the child zone. SOA NS and DNSKEY records are apex only records and a matching response that contains these records or DS is treated as coming from a child zone. RRSIG records are also examined to see if they are signed by a child zone or not. The authority section is also examined to see if there is evidence that the answer is from the child zone. Answers that are determined to be from a child zone are not converted to NXDOMAIN responses. Despite all these checks there is still a possibility of false negatives when a child zone is being served.

Similarly false positives can arise from empty nodes (no records at the name) in the delegation only zone when the query type is not ANY.

Note some TLDs are not delegation only (e.g. "DE", "LV", "US" and "MUSEUM"). This list is not exhaustive.

```
options {
  root-delegation-only exclude { "de"; "lv"; "us"; "museum"; };
};
```

disable-algorithms

Disable the specified DNSSEC algorithms at and below the specified name. Multiple **disable-algorithms** statements are allowed. Only the best match **disable-algorithms** clause will be used to determine which algorithms are used.

If all supported algorithms are disabled, the zones covered by the **disable-algorithms** will be treated as insecure.

disable-ds-digests

Disable the specified DS/DLV digest types at and below the specified name. (The **disable-ds-digests** option was introduced in BIND 9.10.) Multiple **disable-ds-digests** statements are allowed. Only the best match **disable-ds-digests** clause will be used to determine which digest types are used.

If all supported digest types are disabled, the zones covered by the **disable-ds-digests** will be treated as insecure.

dnssec-lookaside

When set, **dnssec-lookaside** provides the validator with an alternate method to validate DNSKEY records at the top of a zone. When a DNSKEY is at or below a domain specified by the deepest **dnssec-lookaside**, and the normal DNSSEC validation has left the key untrusted, the trust-anchor will be appended to the key name and a DLV (DNSSEC Lookaside Validation) record will be looked up to see if it can validate the key. If the DLV record validates a DNSKEY (similarly to the way a DS record does) the DNSKEY RRset is deemed to be trusted.

If **dnssec-lookaside** is set to `auto`, then built-in default values for the DLV domain and trust anchor will be used, along with a built-in key for validation.

If **dnssec-lookaside** is set to `no`, then dnssec-lookaside is not used.

The default DLV key is stored in the file `bind.keys`; **named** will load that key at startup if **dnssec-lookaside** is set to `auto`. A copy of the file is installed along with BIND 9, and is current as of the release date. If the DLV key expires, a new copy of `bind.keys` can be downloaded from https://www.isc.org/solutions/dlv/.

(To prevent problems if `bind.keys` is not found, the current key is also compiled in to **named**. Relying on this is not recommended, however, as it requires **named** to be recompiled with a new key when the DLV key expires.)

Note

named only loads certain specific keys from `bind.keys`: those for the DLV zone and for the DNS root zone. The file cannot be used to store keys for other zones.

---

dnssec-must-be-secure

Specify hierarchies which must be or may not be secure (signed and validated). If **yes**, then **named** will only accept answers if they are secure. If **no**, then normal DNSSEC validation applies allowing for insecure answers to be accepted. The specified domain must be under a **trusted-keys** or **managed-keys** statement, or **dnssec-lookaside** must be active.

dns64

This directive instructs **named** to return mapped IPv4 addresses to AAAA queries when there are no AAAA records. It is intended to be used in conjunction with a NAT64. Each **dns64** defines one DNS64 prefix. Multiple DNS64 prefixes can be defined.

Compatible IPv6 prefixes have lengths of 32, 40, 48, 56, 64 and 96 as per RFC 6052.

Additionally a reverse IP6.ARPA zone will be created for the prefix to provide a mapping from the IP6.ARPA names to the corresponding IN-ADDR.ARPA names using synthesized CNAMEs. **dns64-server** and **dns64-contact** can be used to specify the name of the server and contact for the zones. These are settable at the view / options level. These are not settable on a per-prefix basis.

Each **dns64** supports an optional **clients** ACL that determines which clients are affected by this directive. If not defined, it defaults to **any;**.

Each **dns64** supports an optional **mapped** ACL that selects which IPv4 addresses are to be mapped in the corresponding A RRset. If not defined it defaults to **any;**.

Normally, DNS64 won't apply to a domain name that owns one or more AAAA records; these records will simply be returned. The optional **exclude** ACL allows specification of a list of IPv6 addresses that will be ignored if they appear in a domain name's AAAA records, and DNS64 will be applied to any A records the domain name owns. If not defined, **exclude** defaults to none.

A optional **suffix** can also be defined to set the bits trailing the mapped IPv4 address bits. By default these bits are set to : :. The bits matching the prefix and mapped IPv4 address must be zero.

If **recursive-only** is set to **yes** the DNS64 synthesis will only happen for recursive queries. The default is **no**.

If **break-dnssec** is set to **yes** the DNS64 synthesis will happen even if the result, if validated, would cause a DNSSEC validation failure. If this option is set to **no** (the default), the DO is set on the incoming query, and there are RRSIGs on the applicable records, then synthesis will not happen.

```
acl rfc1918 { 10/8; 192.168/16; 172.16/12; };

dns64 64:FF9B::/96 {
  clients { any; };
  mapped { !rfc1918; any; };
  exclude { 64:FF9B::/96; ::ffff:0000:0000/96; };
  suffix ::;
};
```

dnssec-loadkeys-interval

When a zone is configured with **auto-dnssec maintain;** its key repository must be checked periodically to see if any new keys have been added or any existing keys' timing metadata has been updated (see dnssec-keygen(8) and dnssec-settime(8)). The **dnssec-loadkeys-interval** option sets the frequency of automatic repository checks, in minutes. The default is 60 (1 hour), the minimum is 1 (1 minute), and the maximum is 1440 (24 hours); any higher value is silently reduced. (The **dnssec-loadkeys-interval** option was introduced in BIND 9.9.)

dnssec-update-mode

If this option is set to its default value of maintain in a zone of type master which is DNSSEC-signed and configured to allow dynamic updates (see Section 9.2), and if **named** has access to the private signing key(s) for the zone, then **named** will automatically sign all new or changed records and maintain signatures for the zone by regenerating RRSIG records whenever they approach their expiration date.

If the option is changed to no-resign, then **named** will sign all new or changed records, but scheduled maintenance of signatures is disabled.

With either of these settings, **named** will reject updates to a DNSSEC-signed zone when the signing keys are inactive or unavailable to **named**. (The **dnssec-update-mode** option was introduced in BIND 9.9. A planned third option, external, will disable all automatic signing and allow DNSSEC data to be submitted into a zone via dynamic update; this is not yet implemented.)

nta-lifetime

> Species the default lifetime, in seconds, that will be used for negative trust anchors added via **rndc nta**.
>
> A negative trust anchor selectively disables DNSSEC validation for zones that are known to be failing because of misconfiguration rather than an attack. When data to be validated is at or below an active NTA (and above any other configured trust anchors), **named** will abort the DNSSEC validation process and treat the data as insecure rather than bogus. This continues until the NTA's lifetime is elapsed. NTAs persist across **named** restarts.
>
> For convenience, TTL-style time unit suffixes can be used to specify the NTA lifetime in seconds, minutes or hours. `nta-lifetime` defaults to one hour. It cannot exceed one week.
>
> The negative trust anchors support was introduced in BIND 9.11. For more details, see the **rndc nta** command on page 53.

nta-recheck

> Species how often to check whether negative trust anchors added via **rndc nta** are still necessary.
>
> A negative trust anchor is normally used when a domain has stopped validating due to operator error; it temporarily disables DNSSEC validation for that domain. In the interest of ensuring that DNSSEC validation is turned back on as soon as possible, **named** will periodically send a query to the domain, ignoring negative trust anchors, to find out whether it can now be validated. If so, the negative trust anchor is allowed to expire early.
>
> Validity checks can be disabled for an individual NTA by using **rndc nta -f**, or for all NTAs by setting `nta-recheck` to zero.
>
> For convenience, TTL-style time unit suffixes can be used to specify the NTA recheck interval in seconds, minutes or hours. The default is five minutes. It cannot be longer than `nta-lifetime` (which cannot be longer than a week).
>
> The negative trust anchors support was introduced in BIND 9.11. For more details, see the **rndc nta** command on page 53.

max-zone-ttl

> Specifies a maximum permissible TTL value in seconds. For convenience, TTL-style time unit suffixes may be used to specify the maximum value. When loading a zone file using a `masterfile-format` of `text` or `raw`, any record encountered with a TTL higher than `max-zone-ttl` will cause the zone to be rejected. (The **max-zone-ttl** option was introduced in BIND 9.10.)
>
> This is useful in DNSSEC-signed zones because when rolling to a new DNSKEY, the old key needs to remain available until RRSIG records have expired from caches. The `max-zone-ttl` option guarantees that the largest TTL in the zone will be no higher than the set value.
>
> ---
>
> **Note**
> Because `map`-format files load directly into memory, this option cannot be used with them.
>
> ---
>
> The default value is `unlimited`. A `max-zone-ttl` of zero is treated as `unlimited`.

serial-update-method

> Zones configured for dynamic DNS may use this option to set the update method that will be used for the zone serial number in the SOA record. (The **serial-update-method** feature was introduced in BIND 9.9.)
>
> With the default setting of **serial-update-method increment;**, the SOA serial number will be incremented by one each time the zone is updated.
>
> When set to **serial-update-method unixtime;**, the SOA serial number will be set to the number of seconds since the UNIX epoch, unless the serial number is already greater than or equal to that value, in which case it is simply incremented by one.
>
> When set to **serial-update-method date;**, the new SOA serial number will be the current date in the form "YYYYMMDD", followed by two zeroes, unless the existing serial number is already greater than or equal to that value, in which case it is incremented by one. (This `date` method was introduced in BIND 9.11.)

zone-statistics

> If `full`, the server will collect statistical data on all zones (unless specifically turned off on a per-zone basis by specifying **zone-statistics terse** or **zone-statistics none** in the **zone** statement). The default is `terse`, providing minimal statistics on zones (including name and current serial number, but not query type counters).
>
> These statistics may be accessed via the **statistics-channel** or using **rndc stats**, which will dump them to the file listed in the **statistics-file**. See also page 96.
>
> For backward compatibility with earlier versions of BIND 9, the **zone-statistics** option can also accept **yes** or **no**; **yes** has the same meaning as `full`. As of BIND 9.10, **no** has the same meaning as **none**; previously, it was the same as `terse`.

Boolean Options

automatic-interface-scan

> If **yes** and supported by the OS, automatically rescan network interfaces when the interface addresses are added or removed. The default is **yes**. (The **automatic-interface-scan** option was introduced in BIND 9.10.)
>
> Currently the OS needs to support routing sockets (like OS X, *BSD, or Linux) for **automatic-interface-scan** to be supported. Scans can be done on a timed interval or manually triggered; see page 125 about the **interface-interval** option or the **rndc scan** command on page 54 for information.

allow-new-zones

> If **yes**, then zones can be added at runtime via **rndc addzone**. The default is **no**.

auth-nxdomain

> If **yes**, then the **AA** bit is always set on NXDOMAIN responses, even if the server is not actually authoritative. The default is **no**; this is a change from BIND 8. If you are using very old DNS software, you may need to set it to **yes**.

deallocate-on-exit

> This option was used in BIND 8 to enable checking for memory leaks on exit. BIND 9 ignores the option and always performs the checks.

memstatistics

Write memory statistics to the file specified by **memstatistics-file** at exit. The default is **no** unless '-m record' is specified on the command line in which case it is **yes**.

dialup

If **yes**, then the server treats all zones as if they are doing zone transfers across a dial-on-demand dialup link, which can be brought up by traffic originating from this server. This has different effects according to zone type and concentrates the zone maintenance so that it all happens in a short interval, once every **heartbeat-interval** and hopefully during the one call. It also suppresses some of the normal zone maintenance traffic. The default is **no**.

The **dialup** option may also be specified in the **view** and **zone** statements, in which case it overrides the global **dialup** option.

If the zone is a master zone, then the server will send out a NOTIFY request to all the slaves (default). This should trigger the zone serial number check in the slave (providing it supports NOTIFY) allowing the slave to verify the zone while the connection is active. The set of servers to which NOTIFY is sent can be controlled by **notify** and **also-notify**.

If the zone is a slave or stub zone, then the server will suppress the regular "zone up to date" (refresh) queries and only perform them when the **heartbeat-interval** expires in addition to sending NOTIFY requests.

Finer control can be achieved by using `notify` which only sends NOTIFY messages, `notify-passive` which sends NOTIFY messages and suppresses the normal refresh queries, `refresh` which suppresses normal refresh processing and sends refresh queries when the **heartbeat-interval** expires, and `passive` which just disables normal refresh processing.

dialup mode	normal refresh	heart-beat refresh	heart-beat notify
no (default)	yes	no	no
yes	no	yes	yes
notify	yes	no	yes
refresh	no	yes	no
passive	no	no	no
notify-passive	no	no	yes

Note
Normal NOTIFY processing is not affected by the **dialup** option.

fake-iquery

In BIND 8, this option enabled simulating the obsolete DNS query type IQUERY. BIND 9 never does IQUERY simulation.

fetch-glue

This option is obsolete. In BIND 8, `fetch-glue yes` caused the server to attempt to fetch glue resource records it didn't have when constructing the additional data section of a response. This is now considered a bad idea and BIND 9 never does it.

flush-zones-on-shutdown

When the nameserver exits due receiving SIGTERM, flush or do not flush any pending zone writes. The default is **flush-zones-on-shutdown no**.

geoip-use-ecs

When BIND is compiled with GeoIP support and configured with "geoip" ACL elements, this option indicates whether the EDNS Client Subnet option, if present in a request, should be used for matching against the GeoIP database. The default is **geoip-use-ecs yes**. (This option was introduced in BIND 9.11.)

has-old-clients

This option was incorrectly implemented in BIND 8, and is ignored by BIND 9. To achieve the intended effect of **has-old-clients yes**, specify **auth-nxdomain yes** instead.

host-statistics

In BIND 8, this enabled keeping of statistics for every host that the name server interacts with. This is not implemented in BIND 9.

maintain-ixfr-base

This option is obsolete. It was used in BIND 8 to determine whether a transaction log was kept for Incremental Zone Transfer. BIND 9 maintains a transaction log whenever possible. If you need to disable outgoing incremental zone transfers, use **provide-ixfr no**.

minimal-responses

If **yes**, then when generating responses the server will only add records to the authority and additional data sections when they are required (e.g. delegations, negative responses). This may improve the performance of the server. The default is **no**.

multiple-cnames

This option was used in BIND 8 to allow a domain name to have multiple CNAME records in violation of the DNS standards. BIND 9.2 onwards always strictly enforces the CNAME rules both in master files and dynamic updates.

notify

If **yes** (the default), DNS NOTIFY messages are sent when a zone the server is authoritative for changes. For details, see Section 7.5. The messages are sent to the servers listed in the zone's NS records (except the master server identified in the SOA MNAME field), and to any servers listed in the **also-notify** option.

If `master-only`, notifies are only sent for master zones. If `explicit`, notifies are sent only to servers explicitly listed using **also-notify**. If **no**, no notifies are sent.

The **notify** option may also be specified in the **zone** statement, in which case it overrides the **options notify** statement. It would only be necessary to turn off this option if it caused slaves to crash.

notify-to-soa

If **yes** do not check the nameservers in the NS RRset against the SOA MNAME. Normally a NOTIFY message is not sent to the SOA MNAME (SOA ORIGIN) as it is supposed to contain the name of the ultimate master. Sometimes, however, a slave is listed as the SOA MNAME in hidden master configurations and in that case you would want the ultimate master to still send NOTIFY messages to all the nameservers listed in the NS RRset.

recursion

If **yes**, and a DNS query requests recursion, then the server will attempt to do all the work required to answer the query. If recursion is off and the server does not already know the answer, it will return a referral response. The default is **yes**.

Note

Setting **recursion no** does not prevent clients from getting data from the server's cache; it only prevents new data from being cached as an effect of client queries.

Caching may still occur as an effect the server's internal operation, such as NOTIFY address lookups. Also see the **allow-recursion** ACL on page 113.)

request-nsid

If **yes**, then an empty EDNS(0) NSID (Name Server Identifier) option is sent with all queries to authoritative name servers during iterative resolution. If the authoritative server returns an NSID option in its response, then its contents are logged in the **resolver** category at level **info**. The default is **no**.

request-sit

If **yes**, then a SIT (Source Identity Token) EDNS option is sent along with the query. If the resolver has previously talked to the server, the SIT returned in the previous transaction is sent. This is used by the server to determine whether the resolver has talked to it before. A resolver sending the correct SIT is assumed not to be an off-path attacker sending a spoofed-source query; the query is therefore unlikely to be part of a reflection/amplification attack, so resolvers sending a correct SIT option are not subject to response rate limiting (RRL). Resolvers which do not send a correct SIT option may be limited to receiving smaller responses via the **nosit-udp-size** option.

This experimental option was introduced in BIND 9.10 and is obsolete in BIND 9.11; see its replacement **send-cookie** option instead.

require-server-cookie

Require a valid server cookie before sending a full response to a UDP request from a cookie aware client. BADCOOKIE is sent if there is a bad or no existent server cookie. (This option was introduced in BIND 9.11.)

send-cookie

If **yes**, then a COOKIE EDNS option is sent along with the query. If the resolver has previously talked to the server, the COOKIE returned in the previous transaction is sent. This is used by the server to determine whether the resolver has talked to it before. A resolver sending the correct COOKIE is assumed not to be an off-path attacker sending a spoofed-source query; the query is therefore unlikely to be part of a reflection/amplification attack, so resolvers sending a correct COOKIE option are not subject to response rate limiting (RRL). Resolvers which do not send a correct COOKIE option may be limited to receiving smaller responses via the **nocookie-udp-size** option. (The **send-cookie** option was introduced in BIND 9.11.)

nocookie-udp-size

Sets the maximum size of UDP responses that will be sent to queries without a valid server COOKIE. A value below 128 will be silently raised to 128. The default value is 4096, but the **max-udp-size** option may further limit the response size. (The **nocookie-udp-size** option was introduced in BIND 9.11.)

nosit-udp-size

Sets the maximum size of UDP responses that will be sent to queries without a valid Source Identity Token (SIT). A value below 128 will be silently raised to 128. The default value is 4096, but the **max-udp-size** option may further limit the response size.

This experimental option was introduced in BIND 9.10 and is obsolete in BIND 9.11; see its replacement **nocookie-udp-size** option instead.

sit-secret

If set, this is a shared secret used for generating and verifying Source Identity Token EDNS options within an Anycast cluster. If not set the system will generate a random secret at startup. The shared secret is encoded as a hex string and needs to be 128 bits for AES128, 160 bits for SHA1, and 256 bits for SHA256.

The experimental **sit-secret** option was introduced in BIND 9.10 and is obsoleted in BIND 9.11; see its replacement **cookie-secret** option instead.

cookie-algorithm

Set the algorithm to be used when generating the server cookie. One of "aes", "sha1" or "sha256". The default is "aes" if supported by the cryptographic library or otherwise "sha256". (This option was introduced in BIND 9.11.)

cookie-secret

If set, this is a shared secret used for generating and verifying COOKIE EDNS options within an Anycast cluster. If not set, the system will generate a random secret at startup. The shared secret is encoded as a hex string and needs to be 128 bits for AES128, 160 bits for SHA1 and 256 bits for SHA256.

The **cookie-secret** option was introduced in BIND 9.11.

rfc2308-type1

This is not yet implemented in BIND 9. The plan is setting this to **yes** will cause the server to send NS records along with the SOA record for negative answers.

use-id-pool

This option is obsolete. BIND 9 always allocates query IDs from a pool.

use-ixfr

This option is obsolete. If you need to disable IXFR to a particular server or servers, see the information on the **provide-ixfr** option in Section 6.8. See also Section 7.6.

provide-ixfr

See the description of **provide-ixfr** in Section 6.8.

request-ixfr

See the description of **request-ixfr** in Section 6.8.

request-expire

See the description of **request-expire** in Section 6.8.

treat-cr-as-space

This option was used in BIND 8 to make the server treat carriage return ("\r") characters the same way as a space or tab character, to facilitate loading of zone files on a UNIX system that were generated on an NT or DOS machine. In BIND 9, both UNIX "\n" and NT/DOS "\r\n" newlines are always accepted, and the option is ignored.

additional-from-auth, additional-from-cache

These options control the behavior of an authoritative server when answering queries which have additional data, or when following CNAME and DNAME chains.

When both of these options are set to **yes** (the default) and a query is being answered from authoritative data (a zone configured into the server), the additional data section of the reply will be filled in using data from other authoritative zones and from the cache. In some situations this is undesirable, such as when there is concern over the correctness of the cache, or in servers where slave zones may be added and modified by untrusted third parties. Also, avoiding the search for this additional data will speed up server operations at the possible expense of additional queries to resolve what would otherwise be provided in the additional section.

For example, if a query asks for an MX record for host `foo.example.com`, and the record found is "`MX 10 mail.example.net`", normally the address records (A and AAAA) for `mail.example.net` will be provided as well, if known, even though they are not in the example.com zone. Setting these options to **no** disables this behavior and makes the server only search for additional data in the zone it answers from.

These options are intended for use in authoritative-only servers, or in authoritative-only views. Attempts to set them to **no** without also specifying **recursion no** will cause the server to ignore the options and log a warning message.

Specifying **additional-from-cache no** actually disables the use of the cache not only for additional data lookups but also when looking up the answer. This is usually the desired behavior in an authoritative-only server where the correctness of the cached data is an issue.

When a name server is non-recursively queried for a name that is not below the apex of any served zone, it normally answers with an "upwards referral" to the root servers or the servers of some other known parent of the query name. Since the data in an upwards referral comes from the cache, the server will not be able to provide upwards referrals when **additional-from-cache no** has been specified. Instead, it will respond to such queries with REFUSED. This should not cause any problems since upwards referrals are not required for the resolution process.

match-mapped-addresses

If **yes**, then an IPv4-mapped IPv6 address will match any address match list entries that match the corresponding IPv4 address.

This option was introduced to work around a kernel quirk in some operating systems that causes IPv4 TCP connections, such as zone transfers, to be accepted on an IPv6 socket using mapped addresses. This caused address match lists designed for IPv4 to fail to match. However, **named** now solves this problem internally. The use of this option is discouraged.

filter-aaaa-on-v4

This option is only available when BIND 9 is compiled with the `--enable-filter-aaaa` option on the "configure" command line. It is intended to help the transition from IPv4 to IPv6 by not giving IPv6 addresses to DNS clients unless they have connections to the IPv6 Internet. This is not recommended unless absolutely necessary. The default is **no**. The **filter-aaaa-on-v4** option may also be specified in **view** statements to override the global **filter-aaaa-on-v4** option.

If **yes**, the DNS client is at an IPv4 address, in **filter-aaaa**, and if the response does not include DNSSEC signatures, then all AAAA records are deleted from the response. This filtering applies to all responses and not only authoritative responses.

If **break-dnssec**, then AAAA records are deleted even when DNSSEC is enabled. As suggested by the name, this makes the response not verify, because the DNSSEC protocol is designed detect deletions.

This mechanism can erroneously cause other servers to not give AAAA records to their clients. A recursing server with both IPv6 and IPv4 network connections that queries an authoritative server using this mechanism via IPv4 will be denied AAAA records even if its client is using IPv6.

This mechanism is applied to authoritative as well as non-authoritative records. A client using IPv4 that is not allowed recursion can erroneously be given AAAA records because the server is not allowed to check for A records.

Some AAAA records are given to IPv4 clients in glue records. IPv4 clients that are servers can then erroneously answer requests for AAAA records received via IPv4.

filter-aaaa-on-v6

Identical to **filter-aaaa-on-v4**, except it filters AAAA responses to queries from IPv6 clients instead of IPv4 clients. To filter all responses, set both options to **yes**. (The **filter-aaaa-on-v6** option was introduced in BIND 9.10.)

ixfr-from-differences

When **yes** and the server loads a new version of a master zone from its zone file or receives a new version of a slave file via zone transfer, it will compare the new version to the previous one and calculate a set of differences. The differences are then logged in the zone's journal file such that the changes can be transmitted to downstream slaves as an incremental zone transfer.

By allowing incremental zone transfers to be used for non-dynamic zones, this option saves bandwidth at the expense of increased CPU and memory consumption at the master. In particular, if the new version of a zone is completely different from the previous one, the set of differences will be of a size comparable to the combined size of the old and new zone version, and the server will need to temporarily allocate memory to hold this complete difference set.

ixfr-from-differences also accepts **master** and **slave** at the view and options levels which causes **ixfr-from-differences** to be enabled for all **master** or **slave** zones respectively. It is off by default.

multi-master

This should be set when you have multiple masters for a zone and the addresses refer to different machines. If **yes**, **named** will not log when the serial number on the master is less than what **named** currently has. The default is **no**.

auto-dnssec

Zones configured for dynamic DNS may use this option to allow varying levels of automatic DNSSEC key management. There are three possible settings:

auto-dnssec allow; permits keys to be updated and the zone fully re-signed whenever the user issues the command **rndc sign** `zonename`.

auto-dnssec maintain; includes the above, but also automatically adjusts the zone's DNSSEC keys on schedule, according to the keys' timing metadata (see dnssec-keygen(8) and dnssec-settime(8) in Chapter 10.) The command **rndc sign** `zonename` causes **named** to load keys from the key repository and sign the zone with all keys that are active. **rndc loadkeys** `zonename` causes **named** to load keys from the key repository and schedule key maintenance events to occur in the future, but it does not sign the full zone immediately. Note: once keys have been loaded for a zone the first time, the repository will be searched for changes periodically, regardless of whether **rndc loadkeys** is used. The recheck interval is defined by **dnssec-loadkeys-interval**.)

The default setting is **auto-dnssec off**.

dnssec-enable

This indicates whether DNSSEC-related resource records are to be returned by **named**. If set to **no**, **named** will not return DNSSEC-related resource records unless specifically queried for. The default is **yes**.

dnssec-validation

Enable DNSSEC validation in **named**. Note **dnssec-enable** also needs to be set to **yes** to be effective. If set to **no**, DNSSEC validation is disabled. If set to **auto**, DNSSEC validation is enabled, and a default trust-anchor for the DNS root zone is used. If set to **yes**, DNSSEC validation is enabled, but a trust anchor must be manually configured using a **trusted-keys** or **managed-keys** statement. The default is **yes**.

Note

Whenever the resolver sends out queries to an EDNS-compliant server, it always sets the DO bit indicating it can support DNSSEC responses even if **dnssec-validation** is off.

---

dnssec-accept-expired

Accept expired signatures when verifying DNSSEC signatures. The default is **no**. Setting this option to **yes** leaves **named** vulnerable to replay attacks (a once valid response is fraudulently repeated later).

querylog

Specify whether query logging should be started when **named** starts. If **querylog** is not specified, then the query logging is determined by the presence of the logging category **queries**.

check-names

This option is used to restrict the character set and syntax of certain domain names in master files and/or DNS responses received from the network. The default varies according to usage area. For **master** zones the default is **fail**. For **slave** zones the default is **warn**. For answers received from the network (**response**) the default is **ignore**.

The rules for legal hostnames and mail domains are derived from RFC 952 and RFC 821 as modified by RFC 1123.

check-names applies to the owner names of A, AAAA and MX records. It also applies to the domain names in the RDATA of NS, SOA, MX, and SRV records. It also applies to the RDATA of PTR records where the owner name indicated that it is a reverse lookup of a hostname (the owner name ends in IN-ADDR.ARPA, IP6.ARPA, or IP6.INT).

check-dup-records

Check master zones for records that are treated as different by DNSSEC but are semantically equal in plain DNS. The default is to **warn**. Other possible values are **fail** and **ignore**.

Note
named automatically eliminates some duplicate records so they won't be recognized by **check-dup-records**.

---

check-mx

Check whether the MX record appears to refer to a IP address. The default is to **warn**. Other possible values are **fail** and **ignore**.

check-wildcard

This option is used to check for non-terminal wildcards. The use of non-terminal wildcards is almost always as a result of a failure to understand the wildcard matching algorithm (RFC 1034). This option affects master zones. The default (**yes**) is to check for non-terminal wildcards and issue a warning.

check-integrity

Perform post load zone integrity checks on master zones. This checks that MX and SRV records refer to address (A or AAAA) records and that glue address records exist for delegated zones. For MX and SRV records only in-zone hostnames are checked (for out-of-zone hostnames use **named-checkzone**). For NS records only names below top of zone are checked (for out-of-zone names and glue consistency checks use **named-checkzone**). The default is **yes**.

The use of the SPF record for publishing Sender Policy Framework is deprecated as the migration from using TXT records to SPF records was abandoned. Enabling this option also checks that a TXT Sender Policy Framework record exists (starts with "v=spf1") if there is an SPF record. Warnings are emitted if the TXT record does not exist and can be suppressed with **check-spf**.

check-mx-cname

If **check-integrity** is set then fail, warn or ignore MX records that refer to CNAMES. The default is to **warn**.

check-srv-cname

If **check-integrity** is set then fail, warn or ignore SRV records that refer to CNAMES. The default is to **warn**.

check-sibling

When performing integrity checks, also check that sibling glue exists. The default is **yes**.

check-spf

If **check-integrity** is set then check that there is a TXT Sender Policy Framework record present (starts with "v=spf1") if there is an SPF record present. The default is **warn**.

zero-no-soa-ttl

When returning authoritative negative responses to SOA queries set the TTL of the SOA record returned in the authority section to zero. The default is **yes**.

zero-no-soa-ttl-cache

When caching a negative response to a SOA query set the TTL to zero. The default is **no**.

update-check-ksk

When set to the default value of yes, check the KSK bit in each key to determine how the key should be used when generating RRSIGs for a secure zone. (As of BIND 9.9, this option is also allowed in slave zones as long as inline-signing is in use.)

Ordinarily, zone-signing keys (that is, keys without the KSK bit set) are used to sign the entire zone, while key-signing keys (keys with the KSK bit set) are only used to sign the DNSKEY RRset at the zone apex. However, if this option is set to no, then the KSK bit is ignored; KSKs are treated as if they were ZSKs and are used to sign the entire zone. This is similar to the **dnssec-signzone -z** command line option.

When this option is set to yes, there must be at least two active keys for every algorithm represented in the DNSKEY RRset: at least one KSK and one ZSK per algorithm. If there is any algorithm for which this requirement is not met, this option will be ignored for that algorithm.

dnssec-dnskey-kskonly

When this option and **update-check-ksk** are both set to yes, only key-signing keys (that is, keys with the KSK bit set) will be used to sign the DNSKEY RRset at the zone apex. Zone-signing keys (keys without the KSK bit set) will be used to sign the remainder of the zone, but not the DNSKEY RRset. This is similar to the **dnssec-signzone -x** command line option. (As of BIND 9.9, this option is also allowed in slave zones as long as inline-signing is in use.)

The default is **no**. If **update-check-ksk** is set to no, this option is ignored.

try-tcp-refresh

Try to refresh the zone using TCP if UDP queries fail. For BIND 8 compatibility, the default is **yes**.

dnssec-secure-to-insecure

Allow a dynamic zone to transition from secure to insecure (i.e., signed to unsigned) by deleting all of the DNSKEY records. The default is **no**. If set to **yes**, and if the DNSKEY RRset at the zone apex is deleted, all RRSIG and NSEC records will be removed from the zone as well.

If the zone uses NSEC3, then it is also necessary to delete the NSEC3PARAM RRset from the zone apex; this will cause the removal of all corresponding NSEC3 records. (It is expected that this requirement will be eliminated in a future release.)

Note that if a zone has been configured with **auto-dnssec maintain** and the private keys remain accessible in the key repository, then the zone will be automatically signed again the next time **named** is started.

Forwarding

The forwarding facility can be used to create a large site-wide cache on a few servers, reducing traffic over links to external name servers. It can also be used to allow queries by servers that do not have direct access to the Internet, but wish to look up exterior names anyway. Forwarding occurs only on those queries for which the server is not authoritative and does not have the answer in its cache.

forward
> This option is only meaningful if the forwarders list is not empty. A value of `first`, the default, causes the server to query the forwarders first — and if that doesn't answer the question, the server will then look for the answer itself. If `only` is specified, the server will only query the forwarders.

forwarders
> Specifies the IP addresses to be used for forwarding. The default is the empty list (no forwarding).

Forwarding can also be configured on a per-domain basis, allowing for the global forwarding options to be overridden in a variety of ways. You can set particular domains to use different forwarders, or have a different **forward only/first** behavior, or not forward at all. For further details, see Section 7.2.

Dual-stack Servers

Dual-stack servers are used as servers of last resort to work around problems in reachability due the lack of support for either IPv4 or IPv6 on the host machine.

dual-stack-servers
> Specifies host names or addresses of machines with access to both IPv4 and IPv6 transports. If a hostname is used, the server must be able to resolve the name using only the transport it has. If the machine is dual stacked, then the **dual-stack-servers** have no effect unless access to a transport has been disabled on the command line (e.g. **named -4**).

Access Control

Access to the server can be restricted based on the IP address of the requesting system. See Section 5.2 for details on how to specify IP address lists.

allow-notify
> Specifies which hosts are allowed to notify this server, a slave, of zone changes in addition to the zone masters. **allow-notify** may also be specified in the **zone** statement, in which case it overrides the **options allow-notify** statement. It is only meaningful for a slave zone. If not specified, the default is to process notify messages only from a zone's master.

allow-query

Specifies which hosts are allowed to ask ordinary DNS questions. **allow-query** may also be specified in the **zone** statement, in which case it overrides the **options allow-query** statement. If not specified, the default is to allow queries from all hosts.

Note
allow-query-cache is used to specify access to the cache.

---

allow-query-on

Specifies which local addresses can accept ordinary DNS questions. This makes it possible, for instance, to allow queries on internal-facing interfaces but disallow them on external-facing ones, without necessarily knowing the internal network's addresses.

Note
Note that **allow-query-on** is only checked for queries that are permitted by **allow-query**. A query must be allowed by both ACLs, or it will be refused.

---

allow-query-on may also be specified in the **zone** statement, in which case it overrides the **options allow-query-on** statement.

If not specified, the default is to allow queries on all addresses.

Note
allow-query-cache is used to specify access to the cache.

---

allow-query-cache

Specifies which hosts are allowed to get answers from the cache. If **allow-query-cache** is not set then **allow-recursion** is used if set, otherwise **allow-query** is used if set unless **recursion no;** is set in which case **none;** is used, otherwise the default (**localnets; localhost;**) is used.

allow-query-cache-on

Specifies which local addresses can give answers from the cache. If not specified, the default is to allow cache queries on any address, **localnets** and **localhost**.

allow-recursion

Specifies which hosts are allowed to make recursive queries through this server. If **allow-recursion** is not set then **allow-query-cache** is used if set, otherwise **allow-query** is used if set, otherwise the default (**localnets; localhost;**) is used. (Also see the **recursion** option on page 105.)

allow-recursion-on

Specifies which local addresses can accept recursive queries. If not specified, the default is to allow recursive queries on all addresses.

allow-update

Specifies which hosts are allowed to submit Dynamic DNS updates for master zones. The default is to deny updates from all hosts.

 Warning

Allowing updates based on the requestor's IP address is insecure; see Section 9.2 for details.

---

allow-update-forwarding

Specifies which hosts are allowed to submit Dynamic DNS updates to slave zones to be forwarded to the master. The default is `{ none; }`, which means that no update forwarding will be performed. To enable update forwarding, specify `allow-update-forwarding { any; };`. Specifying values other than `{ none; }` or `{ any; }` is usually counterproductive, since the responsibility for update access control should rest with the master server, not the slaves.

 Warning

Enabling the update forwarding feature on a slave server may expose master servers relying on insecure IP address based access control to attacks; see Section 9.2 for more details.

---

allow-v6-synthesis

This option was introduced for the smooth transition from AAAA to A6 and from "nibble labels" to binary labels. However, since both A6 and binary labels were then deprecated, this option was also deprecated. It is now ignored with some warning messages.

allow-transfer

Specifies which hosts are allowed to receive zone transfers from the server. **allow-transfer** may also be specified in the **zone** statement, in which case it overrides the **options allow-transfer** statement. If not specified, the default is to allow transfers to all hosts.

blackhole

Specifies a list of addresses that the server will not accept queries from or use to resolve a query. Queries from these addresses will not be responded to. The default is **none**.

filter-aaaa

Specifies a list of addresses to which **filter-aaaa-on-v4** is applies. The default is **any**.

keep-response-order

Specifies a list of addresses to which the server will send responses to TCP queries in the same order in which they were received. This disables the processing of TCP queries in parallel. The default is **none**. The **keep-response-order** option was introduced in BIND 9.11.

no-case-compress

Specifies a list of addresses which require responses to use case-insensitive compression. This

ACL can be used when **named** needs to work with clients that do not comply with the requirement in RFC 1034 to use case-insensitive name comparisons when checking for matching domain names.

If left undefined, the ACL defaults to **none**: case-insensitive compression will be used for all clients. If the ACL is defined and matches a client, then case will be ignored when compressing domain names in DNS responses sent to that client.

This can result in slightly smaller responses: if a response contains the names "example.com" and "example.COM", case-insensitive compression would treat the second one as a duplicate. It also ensures that the case of the query name exactly matches the case of the owner names of returned records, rather than matching the case of the records entered in the zone file. This allows responses to exactly match the query, which is required by some clients due to incorrect use of case-sensitive comparisons.

Case-insensitive compression is *always* used in AXFR and IXFR responses, regardless of whether the client matches this ACL.

There are circumstances in which **named** will not preserve the case of owner names of records: if a zone file defines records of different types with the same name, but the capitalization of the name is different (e.g., "www.example.com/A" and "WWW.EXAMPLE.COM/AAAA"), then all responses for that name will use the *first* version of the name that was used in the zone file. This limitation may be addressed in a future release. However, domain names specified in the rdata of resource records (i.e., records of type NS, MX, CNAME, etc) will always have their case preserved unless the client matches this ACL.

resolver-query-timeout
The amount of time in seconds that the resolver will spend attempting to resolve a recursive query before failing. The default and minimum is 10 and the maximum is 30. Setting it to 0 will result in the default being used.

Interfaces

The interfaces and ports that the server will answer queries from may be specified using the **listen-on** option. **listen-on** takes an optional port and an `address_match_list` of IPv4 addresses. (IPv6 addresses are ignored, with a logged warning.) The server will listen on all interfaces allowed by the address match list. If a port is not specified, port 53 will be used.

Multiple **listen-on** statements are allowed. For example,

```
listen-on { 5.6.7.8; };
listen-on port 1234 { !1.2.3.4; 1.2/16; };
```

will enable the name server on port 53 for the IP address 5.6.7.8, and on port 1234 of an address on the machine in net 1.2 that is not 1.2.3.4.

If no **listen-on** is specified, the server will listen on port 53 on all IPv4 interfaces.

The **listen-on-v6** option is used to specify the interfaces and the ports on which the server will listen for incoming queries sent using IPv6. If not specified, the server will listen on port 53 on all IPv6 interfaces. (Prior to BIND 9.10, the server previously only listened on IPv4 interfaces by default unless **named** was running in IPv6-only mode. For more information, see the **named** -4 and -6 options in Chapter 4.)

When { any; } is specified as the address_match_list for the **listen-on-v6** option, the server does not bind a separate socket to each IPv6 interface address as it does for IPv4 if the operating system has enough API support for IPv6 (specifically if it conforms to RFC 3493 and RFC 3542). Instead, it listens on the IPv6 wildcard address. If the system only has incomplete API support for IPv6, however, the behavior is the same as that for IPv4.

A list of particular IPv6 addresses can also be specified, in which case the server listens on a separate socket for each specified address, regardless of whether the desired API is supported by the system. IPv4 addresses specified in **listen-on-v6** will be ignored, with a logged warning.

Multiple **listen-on-v6** options can be used. For example,

```
listen-on-v6 { any; };
listen-on-v6 port 1234 { !2001:db8::/32; any; };
```

will enable the name server on port 53 for any IPv6 addresses (with a single wildcard socket), and on port 1234 of IPv6 addresses that is not in the prefix 2001:db8::/32 (with separate sockets for each matched address.)

To make the server not listen on any IPv6 address, use:

```
listen-on-v6 { none; };
```

Query Address

If the server doesn't know the answer to a question, it will query other name servers. **optionquery-source** specifies the address and port used for such queries. For queries sent over IPv6, there is a separate **query-source-v6** option. If **address** is * (asterisk) or is omitted, a wildcard IP address (**INADDR_ANY**) will be used.

If **port** is * or is omitted, a random port number from a pre-configured range is picked up and will be used for each query. The port range(s) is that specified in the **use-v4-udp-ports** (for IPv4) and **use-v6-udp-ports** (for IPv6) options, excluding the ranges specified in the **avoid-v4-udp-ports** and **avoid-v6-udp-ports** options, respectively.

The defaults of the **query-source** and **query-source-v6** options are:

```
query-source address * port *;
query-source-v6 address * port *;
```

Note

The address specified in the **query-source** option is used for both UDP and TCP queries, but the port applies only to UDP queries. TCP queries always use a random unprivileged port.

Also see the **transfer-source** and **notify-source** options.

If **use-v4-udp-ports** or **use-v6-udp-ports** is unspecified, **named** will check if the operating system provides a programming interface to retrieve the system's default range for ephemeral ports. If such an interface is available, **named** will use the corresponding system default range; otherwise, it will use its own defaults:

```
use-v4-udp-ports { range 1024 65535; };
use-v6-udp-ports { range 1024 65535; };
```

Make sure the ranges be sufficiently large for security. A desirable size depends on various parameters, but it is generally recommended to contain at least 16384 ports (14 bits of entropy). Note also that the system's default range when used may be too small for this purpose, and that the range may even be changed while **named** is running; the new range will automatically be applied when **named** is reloaded. It is encouraged to configure **use-v4-udp-ports** and **use-v6-udp-ports** explicitly so that the ranges are sufficiently large and are reasonably independent from the ranges used by other applications.

The operational configuration where **named** runs may prohibit the use of some ports. For example, UNIX systems will not allow **named** running without a root privilege to use ports less than 1024. If such ports are included in the specified (or detected) set of query ports, the corresponding query attempts will fail, resulting in resolution failures or delay. It is therefore important to configure the set of ports that can be safely used in the expected operational environment.

The defaults of the **avoid-v4-udp-ports** and **avoid-v6-udp-ports** options are:

```
avoid-v4-udp-ports {};
avoid-v6-udp-ports {};
```

BIND 9.5.0 introduced the **use-queryport-pool** option to support a pool of such random ports, but this option is now obsolete because reusing the same ports in the pool may not be sufficiently secure. For the same reason, it is generally strongly discouraged to specify a particular port for the **query-source** or **query-source-v6** options; it implicitly disables the use of randomized port numbers.

use-queryport-pool
> This option is obsolete.

queryport-pool-ports
> This option is obsolete.

queryport-pool-updateinterval
> This option is obsolete.

Zone Transfers

BIND has mechanisms in place to facilitate zone transfers and set limits on the amount of load that transfers place on the system. The following options apply to zone transfers.

also-notify
> Defines a global list of IP addresses of name servers that are also sent NOTIFY messages

whenever a fresh copy of the zone is loaded, in addition to the servers listed in the zone's NS records. This helps to ensure that copies of the zones will quickly converge on stealth servers. Optionally, a port may be specified with each **also-notify** address to send the notify messages to a port other than the default of 53. Since BIND 9.9, an optional TSIG key can also be specified with each address to cause the notify messages to be signed; this can be useful when sending notifies to multiple views. In place of explicit addresses, one or more named **masters** lists can be used.

If an **also-notify** list is given in a **zone** statement, it will override the **options also-notify** statement. When a **zone notify** statement is set to **no**, the IP addresses in the global **also-notify** list will not be sent NOTIFY messages for that zone. The default is the empty list (no global notification list).

max-transfer-time-in

Inbound zone transfers running longer than this many minutes will be terminated. The default is 120 minutes (2 hours). The maximum value is 28 days (40320 minutes).

max-transfer-idle-in

Inbound zone transfers making no progress in this many minutes will be terminated. The default is 60 minutes (1 hour). The maximum value is 28 days (40320 minutes).

max-transfer-time-out

Outbound zone transfers running longer than this many minutes will be terminated. The default is 120 minutes (2 hours). The maximum value is 28 days (40320 minutes).

max-transfer-idle-out

Outbound zone transfers making no progress in this many minutes will be terminated. The default is 60 minutes (1 hour). The maximum value is 28 days (40320 minutes).

notify-rate

The rate at which NOTIFY requests will be sent during normal zone maintenance operations. (NOTIFY requests due to initial zone loading are subject to a separate rate limit; see below.) The default is 20 per second. The lowest possible rate is one per second; when set to zero, it will be silently raised to one. The **notify-rate** option was introduced in BIND 9.11.

startup-notify-rate

The rate at which NOTIFY requests will be sent when the name server is first starting up, or when zones have been newly added to the nameserver. The default is 20 per second. The lowest possible rate is one per second; when set to zero, it will be silently raised to one. The **startup-notify-rate** option was introduced in BIND 9.11.

serial-query-rate

Slave servers will periodically query master servers to find out if zone serial numbers have changed. Each such query uses a minute amount of the slave server's network bandwidth. To limit the amount of bandwidth used, BIND 9 limits the rate at which queries are sent. The value of the **serial-query-rate** option, an integer, is the maximum number of queries sent per second. The default is 20 per second. The lowest possible rate is one per second; when set to zero, it will be silently raised to one.

In BIND versions prior to 9.11, **serial-query-rate** also controls the rate at which NOTIFY messages are sent from both master and slave zones. (For BIND 9.11, see the **notify-rate** and **startup-notify-rate** options.)

serial-queries

In BIND 8, the **serial-queries** option set the maximum number of concurrent serial number queries allowed to be outstanding at any given time. BIND 9 does not limit the number of outstanding serial queries and ignores the **serial-queries** option. Instead, it limits the rate at which the queries are sent as defined using the **serial-query-rate** option.

suppress-initial-notify

This is not yet implemented in BIND 9. The plan is to stop **named** from sending NOTIFY messages when it starts.

transfer-format

Zone transfers can be sent using two different formats, **one-answer** and **many-answers**. The **transfer-format** option is used on the master server to determine which format it sends. **one-answer** uses one DNS message per resource record transferred. **many-answers** packs as many resource records as possible into a message. **many-answers** is more efficient, but is only supported by relatively new slave servers, such as BIND 9, BIND 8.x and BIND 4.9.5 onwards. The **many-answers** format is also supported by recent Microsoft Windows nameservers. The default is **many-answers**. **transfer-format** may be overridden on a per-server basis by using the **server** statement.

transfers-in

The maximum number of inbound zone transfers that can be running concurrently. The default value is 10. Increasing **transfers-in** may speed up the convergence of slave zones, but it also may increase the load on the local system.

transfers-out

The maximum number of outbound zone transfers that can be running concurrently. Zone transfer requests in excess of the limit will be refused. The default value is 10.

transfers-per-ns

The maximum number of inbound zone transfers that can be concurrently transferring from a given remote name server. The default value is 2. Increasing **transfers-per-ns** may speed up the convergence of slave zones, but it also may increase the load on the remote name server. **transfers-per-ns** may be overridden on a per-server basis by using the **transfers** phrase of the **server** statement.

transfer-source

transfer-source determines which local address will be bound to IPv4 TCP connections used to fetch zones transferred inbound by the server. It also determines the source IPv4 address, and optionally the UDP port, used for the refresh queries and forwarded dynamic updates. If not set, it defaults to a system controlled value which will usually be the address of the interface "closest to" the remote end. This address must appear in the remote end's **allow-transfer** option for the zone being transferred, if one is specified. This statement sets the **transfer-source** for all zones, but can be overridden on a per-view or per-zone basis by including a **transfer-source** statement within the **view** or **zone** block in the configuration file.

Note
Solaris 2.5.1 and earlier do not support setting the source address for TCP sockets.

---

transfer-source-v6

    The same as **transfer-source**, except zone transfers are performed using IPv6.

alt-transfer-source

    An alternate transfer source if the one listed in **transfer-source** fails and **use-alt-transfer-source** is set.

Note

If you do not wish the alternate transfer source to be used, you should set **use-alt-transfer-source** appropriately and you should not depend upon getting an answer back to the first refresh query.

---

alt-transfer-source-v6

    An alternate transfer source if the one listed in **transfer-source-v6** fails and **use-alt-transfer-source** is set.

use-alt-transfer-source

    Use the alternate transfer sources or not. If views are specified this defaults to **no** otherwise it defaults to **yes** (for BIND 8 compatibility).

notify-source

    notify-source determines which local source address, and optionally UDP port, will be used to send NOTIFY messages. This address must appear in the slave server's **masters** zone clause or in an **allow-notify** clause. This statement sets the **notify-source** for all zones, but can be overridden on a per-zone or per-view basis by including a **notify-source** statement within the **zone** or **view** block in the configuration file.

Note

Solaris 2.5.1 and earlier do not support setting the source address for TCP sockets.

---

notify-source-v6

    Like **notify-source**, but applies to notify messages sent to IPv6 addresses.

UDP Port Lists

use-v4-udp-ports, **avoid-v4-udp-ports**, **use-v6-udp-ports**, and **avoid-v6-udp-ports** specify a list of IPv4 and IPv6 UDP ports that will be used or not used as source ports for UDP messages. See Section 6.7 about how the available ports are determined. For example, with the following configuration:

```
use-v6-udp-ports { range 32768 65535; };
avoid-v6-udp-ports { 40000; range 50000 60000; };
```

UDP ports of IPv6 messages sent from **named** will be in one of the following ranges: 32768 to 39999, 40001 to 49999, and 60001 to 65535.

avoid-v4-udp-ports and **avoid-v6-udp-ports** can be used to prevent **named** from choosing as its random source port a port that is blocked by your firewall or a port that is used by other applications; if a query went out with a source port blocked by a firewall, the answer would not get by the firewall and the name server would have to query again. Note: the desired range can also be represented only with **use-v4-udp-ports** and **use-v6-udp-ports**, and the **avoid-** options are redundant in that sense; they are provided for backward compatibility and to possibly simplify the port specification.

Operating System Resource Limits

The server's usage of many system resources can be limited. Scaled values are allowed when specifying resource limits. For example, **1G** can be used instead of **1073741824** to specify a limit of one gigabyte. **unlimited** requests unlimited use, or the maximum available amount. **default** uses the limit that was in force when the server was started. See the description of **size_spec** in Section 5.1.

The following options set operating system resource limits for the name server process. Some operating systems don't support some or any of the limits. On such systems, a warning will be issued if the unsupported limit is used.

coresize
> The maximum size of a core dump. The default is `default`.

datasize
> The maximum amount of data memory the server may use. The default is `default`. This is a hard limit on server memory usage. If the server attempts to allocate memory in excess of this limit, the allocation will fail, which may in turn leave the server unable to perform DNS service. Therefore, this option is rarely useful as a way of limiting the amount of memory used by the server, but it can be used to raise an operating system data size limit that is too small by default. If you wish to limit the amount of memory used by the server, use the **max-cache-size** and **recursive-clients** options instead.

files
> The maximum number of files the server may have open concurrently. The default is `unlimi ted`.

stacksize
> The maximum amount of stack memory the server may use. The default is `default`.

Server Resource Limits

The following options set limits on the server's resource consumption that are enforced internally by the server rather than the operating system.

max-ixfr-log-size
> This option is obsolete; it is accepted and ignored for BIND 8 compatibility. The option **max-journal-size** performs a similar function in BIND 9.

max-journal-size

> Sets a maximum size for each journal file (see Section 9.1). When the journal file approaches the specified size, some of the oldest transactions in the journal will be automatically removed. The largest permitted value is 2 gigabytes. The default is `unlimited`, which also means 2 gigabytes. This may also be set on a per-zone basis.

host-statistics-max

> In BIND 8, this specified the maximum number of host statistics entries to be kept. This is not implemented in BIND 9.

recursive-clients

> The maximum number ("hard quota") of simultaneous recursive lookups the server will perform on behalf of clients. The default is `1000`. Because each recursing client uses a fair bit of memory (on the order of 20 kilobytes), the value of the **recursive-clients** option may have to be decreased on hosts with limited memory.

> `recursive-clients` defines a "hard quota" limit for pending recursive clients: when more clients than this are pending, new incoming requests will not be accepted, and for each incoming request a previous pending request will also be dropped.

> A "soft quota" is also set. When this lower quota is exceeded, incoming requests are accepted, but for each one, a pending request will be dropped. If `recursive-clients` is greater than 1000, the soft quota is set to `recursive-clients` minus 100; otherwise it is set to 90% of `recursive-clients`.

tcp-clients

> The maximum number of simultaneous client TCP connections that the server will accept. The default is `100`.

clients-per-query, max-clients-per-query

> These set the initial value (minimum) and maximum number of recursive simultaneous clients for any given query (<qname,qtype,qclass>) that the server will accept before dropping additional clients. **named** will attempt to self tune this value and changes will be logged. The default values are 10 and 100.

> This value should reflect how many queries come in for a given name in the time it takes to resolve that name. If the number of queries exceed this value, **named** will assume that it is dealing with a non-responsive zone and will drop additional queries. If it gets a response after dropping queries, it will raise the estimate. The estimate will then be lowered in 20 minutes if it has remained unchanged.

> If **clients-per-query** is set to zero, then there is no limit on the number of clients per query and no queries will be dropped.

> If **max-clients-per-query** is set to zero, then there is no upper bound other than imposed by **recursive-clients**.

fetches-per-zone

> The maximum number of simultaneous iterative queries to any one domain that the server will permit before blocking new queries for data in or beneath that zone. This value should reflect how many fetches would normally be sent to any one zone in the time it would take to resolve them. It should be smaller than `recursive-clients`.

When many clients simultaneously query for the same name and type, the clients will all be attached to the same fetch, up to the `max-clients-per-query` limit, and only one iterative query will be sent. However, when clients are simultaneously querying for *different* names or types, multiple queries will be sent and `max-clients-per-query` is not effective as a limit.

Optionally, this value may be followed by the keyword `drop` or `fail`, indicating whether queries which exceed the fetch quota for a zone will be dropped with no response, or answered with SERVFAIL. The default is `drop`.

If **fetches-per-zone** is set to zero, then there is no limit on the number of fetches per query and no queries will be dropped. The default is zero.

The current list of active fetches can be dumped by running **rndc recursing**. The list includes the number of active fetches for each domain and the number of queries that have been passed or dropped as a result of the `fetches-per-zone` limit.

These counters are not cumulative over time; whenever the number of active fetches for a domain drops to zero, the counter for that domain is deleted, and the next time a fetch is sent to that domain, it is recreated with the counters set to zero.

For BIND 9.9 and 9.10, this DoS attack mitigation option is only available when BIND 9.9 or 9.10 is compiled with the **--enable-fetchlimit** option on the "configure" command line as introduced in Section 3.3.

fetches-per-server

The maximum number of simultaneous iterative queries that the server will allow to be sent to a single upstream name server before blocking additional queries. This value should reflect how many fetches would normally be sent to any one server in the time it would take to resolve them. It should be smaller than `recursive-clients`.

Optionally, this value may be followed by the keyword `drop` or `fail`, indicating whether queries will be dropped with no response, or answered with SERVFAIL, when all of the servers authoritative for a zone are found to have exceeded the per-server quota. The default is `fail`.

If **fetches-per-server** is set to zero, then there is no limit on the number of fetches per query and no queries will be dropped. The default is zero.

The **fetches-per-server** quota is dynamically adjusted in response to detected congestion. As queries are sent to a server and are either answered or time out, an exponentially weighted moving average is calculated of the ratio of timeouts to responses. If the current average timeout ratio rises above a "high" threshold, then **fetches-per-server** is reduced for that server. If the timeout ratio drops below a "low" threshold, then **fetches-per-server** is increased. The **fetch-quota-params** options can be used to adjust the parameters for this calculation. (For BIND 9.9 and 9.10, this DoS attack mitigation option is only available when BIND 9.9 or 9.10 is compiled with the **--enable-fetchlimit** option on the "configure" command line as introduced in Section 3.3.)

fetch-quota-params

Sets the parameters to use for dynamic resizing of the `fetches-per-server` quota in response to detected congestion.

The first argument is an integer value indicating how frequently to recalculate the moving average of the ratio of timeouts to responses for each server. The default is 100, meaning we recalculate the average ratio after every 100 queries have either been answered or timed out.

The remaining three arguments represent the "low" threshold (defaulting to a timeout ratio of 0.1), the "high" threshold (defaulting to a timeout ratio of 0.3), and the discount rate for the moving average (defaulting to 0.7). A higher discount rate causes recent events to weigh more heavily when calculating the moving average; a lower discount rate causes past events to weigh more heavily, smoothing out short-term blips in the timeout ratio. These arguments are all fixed-point numbers with precision of 1/100: at most two places after the decimal point are significant. (For BIND 9.9 and 9.10, this DoS attack mitigation option is only available when BIND 9.9 or 9.10 is compiled with the **--enable-fetchlimit** option on the "configure" command line as introduced in Section 3.3.)

reserved-sockets

The number of file descriptors reserved for TCP, stdio, etc. This needs to be big enough to cover the number of interfaces **named** listens on, **tcp-clients** as well as to provide room for outgoing TCP queries and incoming zone transfers. The default is `512`. The minimum value is `128` and the maximum value is `128` less than maxsockets (-S). This option may be removed in the future.

This option has little effect on Windows.

max-cache-size

The maximum amount of memory to use for the server's cache, in bytes or, in BIND 9.11, the percent (`%`) of total physical memory. When the amount of data in the cache reaches this limit, the server will cause records to expire prematurely based on an LRU based strategy so that the limit is not exceeded. The keyword **unlimited**, or the value 0, will place no limit on cache size; records will be purged from the cache only when their TTLs expire. Any positive values less than 2MB will be ignored and reset to 2MB. In a server with multiple views, the limit applies separately to the cache of each view.

Prior to BIND 9.10, the default is **0** and the keyword **unlimited** means the maximum value of 32-bit unsigned integers, 0xffffffff, which may not have the same effect as 0 on machines that support more than 32 bits of memory space.

In BIND 9.10, the default is **unlimited**.

In BIND 9.11, the default is **90%**. On systems where detection of amount of physical memory is not supported values represented as % fall back to unlimited. Note that the detection of physical memory is done only once at startup, so **named** will not adjust the cache size if the amount of physical memory is changed during runtime.

tcp-listen-queue

The listen queue depth. The default and minimum is 10. If the kernel supports the accept filter "dataready" this also controls how many TCP connections that will be queued in kernel space waiting for some data before being passed to accept. Nonzero values less than 10 will be silently raised. A value of 0 may also be used; on most platforms this sets the listen queue length to a system-defined default value.

Periodic Task Intervals

cleaning-interval

> This interval is effectively obsolete. Previously, the server would remove expired resource records from the cache every **cleaning-interval** minutes. BIND 9 now manages cache memory in a more sophisticated manner and does not rely on the periodic cleaning any more. Specifying this option therefore has no effect on the server's behavior.

heartbeat-interval

> The server will perform zone maintenance tasks for all zones marked as **dialup** whenever this interval expires. The default is 60 minutes. Reasonable values are up to 1 day (1440 minutes). The maximum value is 28 days (40320 minutes). If set to 0, no zone maintenance for these zones will occur.

interface-interval

> The server will scan the network interface list every **interface-interval** minutes. The default is 60 minutes. The maximum value is 28 days (40320 minutes). If set to 0, interface scanning will only occur when the configuration file is loaded. After the scan, the server will begin listening for queries on any newly discovered interfaces (provided they are allowed by the **listen-on** configuration), and will stop listening on interfaces that have gone away.

> On operating systems that support it, see the **automatic-interface-scan** option on page 102 for automatically updating the interface information.

statistics-interval

> This is not yet implemented in BIND 9. The plan is that name server statistics will be logged every **statistics-interval** minutes.

Topology

The **topology** option is not implemented in BIND 9. The plan is for it to define the order of preferring networks for choosing name servers to query.

All other things being equal, when the server chooses a name server to query from a list of name servers, it prefers the one that is topologically closest to itself.

The sortlist Statement

The response to a DNS query may consist of multiple resource records (RRs) forming a resource records set (RRset). The name server will normally return the RRs within the RRset in an indeterminate order (but see the **rrset-order** statement in Section 6.7). The client resolver code should rearrange the RRs as appropriate, that is, using any addresses on the local net in preference to other addresses. However, not all resolvers can do this or are correctly configured. When a client is using a local server, the sorting can be performed in the server, based on the client's address. This only requires configuring the name servers, not all the clients.

The **sortlist** (see below) takes an **address_match_list** and interprets it to return the RRs within the RRset in a determined order. Each top level statement in the **sortlist** must itself be an explicit **address_match_list** with one or two elements. The first element (which may be an IP address, an IP prefix, an ACL name or a nested **address_match_list**) of each top level list is checked against the source address of the query until a match is found.

Once the source address of the query has been matched, if the top level statement contains only one element, the actual primitive element that matched the source address is used to select the address in the response to move to the beginning of the response. If the statement is a list of two elements, then each top level element is assigned a distance and the address in the response with the minimum distance is moved to the beginning of the response.

In the following example, any queries received from any of the addresses of the host itself will get responses preferring addresses on any of the locally connected networks. Next most preferred are addresses on the 192.168.1/24 network, and after that either the 192.168.2/24 or 192.168.3/24 network with no preference shown between these two networks. Queries received from a host on the 192.168.1/24 network will prefer other addresses on that network to the 192.168.2/24 and 192.168.3/24 networks. Queries received from a host on the 192.168.4/24 or the 192.168.5/24 network will only prefer other addresses on their directly connected networks.

```
sortlist {
    // IF the local host
    // THEN first fit on the following nets
    { localhost;
  { localnets;
      192.168.1/24;
        { 192.168.2/24; 192.168.3/24; }; }; };
    // IF on class C 192.168.1 THEN use .1, or .2 or .3
    { 192.168.1/24;
  { 192.168.1/24;
        { 192.168.2/24; 192.168.3/24; }; }; };
    // IF on class C 192.168.2 THEN use .2, or .1 or .3
    { 192.168.2/24;
  { 192.168.2/24;
        { 192.168.1/24; 192.168.3/24; }; }; };
    // IF on class C 192.168.3 THEN use .3, or .1 or .2
    { 192.168.3/24;
  { 192.168.3/24;
        { 192.168.1/24; 192.168.2/24; }; }; };
    // IF .4 or .5 THEN prefer that net
    { { 192.168.4/24; 192.168.5/24; };
    };
};
```

The following example will give reasonable behavior for the local host and hosts on directly connected networks. It is similar to the behavior of the address sort in BIND 4.9.x. Responses sent to queries from the local host will favor any of the directly connected networks. Responses sent to queries from any other hosts on a directly connected network will prefer addresses on that same network. Responses to other queries will not be sorted.

```
sortlist {
      { localhost; localnets; };
      { localnets; };
};
```

RRset Ordering

When multiple records are returned in an answer it may be useful to configure the order of the records placed into the response. The **rrset-order** permits configuration of the ordering of the records in a multiple record response. See also the **sortlist** statement, Section 6.7.

An **order_spec** is defined as follows:

[class *class_name*] [type *type_name*] [name *"domain_name"*] order *ordering*

If no class is specified, the default is **ANY**. If no type is specified, the default is **ANY**. If no name is specified, the default is "*" (asterisk).

The legal values for **ordering** are:

fixed
> Records are returned in the order they are defined in the zone file.

random
> Records are returned in some random order.

cyclic
> Records are returned in a cyclic round-robin order. If BIND is configured with the "--enable-fixed-rrset" option at compile time, then the initial ordering of the RRset will match the one specified in the zone file.

For example:

```
rrset-order {
    class IN type A name "host.example.com" order random;
    order cyclic;
};
```

will cause any responses for type A records in class IN that have "host.example.com" as a suffix, to always be returned in random order. All other records are returned in cyclic order.

If multiple **rrset-order** statements appear, they are not combined — the last one applies.

By default, all records are returned in random order.

Note

The **rrset-order** statement does not support "fixed" ordering by default. Fixed ordering can be enabled at compile time by specifying "--enable-fixed-rrset" on the "configure" command line as introduced in Section 3.3.)

Tuning

lame-ttl
> Sets the number of seconds to cache a lame server indication. 0 disables caching. (This is not recommended.) The default is 600 (10 minutes) and the maximum value is 1800 (30 minutes).

servfail-ttl

Sets the number of seconds to cache a SERVFAIL response due to DNSSEC validation failure or other general server failure. If set to 0, SERVFAIL caching is disabled. The SERVFAIL cache is not consulted if a query has the CD (Checking Disabled) bit set; this allows a query that failed due to DNSSEC validation to be retried without waiting for the SERVFAIL TTL to expire.

The maximum value is 30 seconds; any higher value will be silently reduced. The default is 1 second. The **servfail-ttl** option was introduced in BIND 9.11.

max-ncache-ttl

To reduce network traffic and increase performance, the server stores negative answers. **max-ncache-ttl** is used to set a maximum retention time for these answers in the server in seconds. The default **max-ncache-ttl** is 10800 seconds (3 hours). **max-ncache-ttl** cannot exceed 7 days and will be silently truncated to 7 days if set to a greater value.

max-cache-ttl

Sets the maximum time (in seconds) for which the server will cache ordinary (positive) answers in seconds. The default is 604800 (one week). A value of zero may cause all queries to return SERVFAIL, because of lost caches of intermediate RRsets (such as NS and glue AAAA/A records) in the resolution process.

min-roots

This is not implemented in BIND 9. The plan is that this will set the minimum number of root servers required for a request for the root servers to be accepted.

sig-validity-interval

Specifies the number of days into the future when DNSSEC signatures automatically generated as a result of dynamic updates (Section 9.1) will expire. There is an optional second field which specifies how long before expiry that the signatures will be regenerated. If not specified, the signatures will be regenerated at 1/4 of base interval. The second field is specified in days if the base interval is greater than 7 days otherwise it is specified in hours. The default base interval is 30 days giving a re-signing interval of 7 1/2 days. The maximum values are 10 years (3660 days).

The signature inception time is unconditionally set to one hour before the current time to allow for a limited amount of clock skew.

The **sig-validity-interval** should be, at least, several multiples of the SOA expire interval to allow for reasonable interaction between the various timer and expiry dates.

sig-signing-nodes

Specify the maximum number of nodes to be examined in each quantum when signing a zone with a new DNSKEY. The default is 100.

sig-signing-signatures

Specify a threshold number of signatures that will terminate processing a quantum when signing a zone with a new DNSKEY. The default is 10.

sig-signing-type

Specify a private RDATA type to be used when generating signing state records. The default is 65534.

It is expected that this parameter may be removed in a future version once there is a standard type.

Signing state records are used to internally by **named** to track the current state of a zone-signing process, i.e., whether it is still active or has been completed. The records can be inspected using the command **rndc signing -list** `zone`. Once **named** has finished signing a zone with a particular key, the signing state record associated with that key can be removed from the zone by running **rndc signing -clear** `keyid/algorithm zone`. To clear all of the completed signing state records for a zone, use **rndc signing -clear all** `zone`. (The **rndc signing** feature was introduced in BIND 9.9.)

min-refresh-time, max-refresh-time, min-retry-time, max-retry-time

These options control the server's behavior on refreshing a zone (querying for SOA changes) or retrying failed transfers. Usually the SOA values for the zone are used, but these values are set by the master, giving slave server administrators little control over their contents.

These options allow the administrator to set a minimum and maximum refresh and retry time in seconds per-zone, per-view, or globally. These options are valid for slave and stub zones, and clamp the SOA refresh and retry times to the specified values.

The following defaults apply. **min-refresh-time** 300 seconds, **max-refresh-time** 2419200 seconds (4 weeks), **min-retry-time** 500 seconds, and **max-retry-time** 1209600 seconds (2 weeks).

edns-udp-size

Sets the maximum advertised EDNS UDP buffer size in bytes, to control the size of packets received from authoritative servers in response to recursive queries. Valid values are 512 to 4096 (values outside this range will be silently adjusted to the nearest value within it). The default value is 4096.

The usual reason for setting **edns-udp-size** to a non-default value is to get UDP answers to pass through broken firewalls that block fragmented packets and/or block UDP DNS packets that are greater than 512 bytes.

When **named** first queries a remote server, it will advertise a UDP buffer size of 512, as this has the greatest chance of success on the first try.

If the initial response times out, **named** will try again with plain DNS, and if that is successful, it will be taken as evidence that the server does not support EDNS. After enough failures using EDNS and successes using plain DNS, **named** will default to plain DNS for future communications with that server. (Periodically, **named** will send an EDNS query to see if the situation has improved.)

However, if the initial query is successful with EDNS advertising a buffer size of 512, then **named** will advertise progressively larger buffer sizes on successive queries, until responses begin timing out or **edns-udp-size** is reached.

The default buffer sizes used by **named** are 512, 1232, 1432, and 4096, but never exceeding **edns-udp-size**. (The values 1232 and 1432 are chosen to allow for an IPv4/IPv6 encapsulated UDP message to be sent without fragmentation at the minimum MTU sizes for Ethernet and IPv6 networks.)

This behavior changed in BIND 9.10; prior versions of **named** will fallback to using 512 bytes if it gets a series of timeouts at the initial value.

max-udp-size

Sets the maximum EDNS UDP message size **named** will send in bytes. Valid values are 512 to 4096 (values outside this range will be silently adjusted to the nearest value within it). The default value is 4096.

This value applies to responses sent by a server; to set the advertised buffer size in queries, see **edns-udp-size**.

The usual reason for setting **max-udp-size** to a non-default value is to get UDP answers to pass through broken firewalls that block fragmented packets and/or block UDP packets that are greater than 512 bytes. This is independent of the advertised receive buffer (**edns-udp-size**).

Setting this to a low value will encourage additional TCP traffic to the nameserver.

masterfile-format

Specifies the file format of zone files (see Section 2.12). The default value is `text`, which is the standard textual representation, except for slave zones (as of BIND 9.9), in which the default value is `raw`. Files in other formats than `text` are typically expected to be generated by the **named-compilezone** tool (introduced on page 24), or dumped by **named**.

Note that when a zone file in a different format than `text` is loaded, **named** may omit some of the checks which would be performed for a file in the `text` format. In particular, **check-names** checks do not apply for the `raw` format.[1] This means a zone file in the `raw` format must be generated with the same check level as that specified in the **named** configuration file. Also, `map` format files are loaded directly into memory via memory mapping, with only minimal checking. (Support for the `map` format was introduced in BIND 9.10.)

This statement sets the **masterfile-format** for all zones, but can be overridden on a per-zone or per-view basis by including a **masterfile-format** statement within the **zone** or **view** block in the configuration file.

masterfile-style

Specifies the formatting of zone files during dump when the `masterfile-format` is `text`. (This option is ignored with any other `masterfile-format`.) The **masterfile-style** option was introduced in BIND 9.11.

When set to `relative`, records are printed in a multi-line format with owner names expressed relative to a shared origin. When set to `full`, records are printed in a single-line format with absolute owner names. The `full` format is most suitable when a zone file needs to be processed automatically by a script. The `relative` format is more human-readable, and is thus suitable when a zone is to be edited by hand. The default is `relative`.

max-recursion-depth

Sets the maximum number of levels of recursion that are permitted at any one time while servicing a recursive query. Resolving a name may require looking up a name server address, which in turn requires resolving another name, etc; if the number of indirections exceeds this value, the recursive query is terminated and returns SERVFAIL. The default is 7.

max-recursion-queries

Sets the maximum number of iterative queries that may be sent while servicing a recursive query. If more queries are sent, the recursive query is terminated and returns SERVFAIL.

---

[1] See page 109 about the **check-names** option for details.

Queries to look up top level domains such as "com" and "net" and the DNS root zone are exempt from this limitation. The default is 75. (For BIND 9.9, the default is 50.)

notify-delay

The delay, in seconds, between sending sets of notify messages for a zone. The default is 5 (five seconds).

The overall rate that NOTIFY messages are sent for all zones is controlled by **serial-query-rate**.

max-rsa-exponent-size

The maximum RSA exponent size, in bits, that will be accepted when validating. Valid values are 35 to 4096 bits. The default zero (0) is also accepted and is equivalent to 4096. (The **max-rsa-exponent-size** option was introduced in BIND 9.9.)

prefetch

When a query is received for cached data which is to expire shortly, **named** can refresh the data from the authoritative server immediately, ensuring that the cache always has an answer available.

The `prefetch` specifies the "trigger" TTL value at which prefetch of the current query will take place: when a cache record with a lower TTL value is encountered during query processing, it will be refreshed. Valid trigger TTL values are 1 to 10 seconds. Values larger than 10 seconds will be silently reduced to 10. Setting a trigger TTL to zero (0) causes prefetch to be disabled. The default trigger TTL is 2.

An optional second argument specifies the "eligibility" TTL: the smallest *original* TTL value that will be accepted for a record to be eligible for prefetching. The eligibility TTL must be at least six seconds longer than the trigger TTL; if it isn't, **named** will silently adjust it upward. The default eligibility TTL is 9.

The **prefetch** option was introduced in BIND 9.10.

v6-bias

When determining the next nameserver to try preference IPv6 nameservers by this many milliseconds. The default is 50 milliseconds. The **v6-bias** option was introduced in BIND 9.11.

Built-in server information zones

The server provides some helpful diagnostic information through a number of built-in zones under the pseudo-top-level-domain `bind` in the **CHAOS** class. These zones are part of a built-in view (see Section 7.1) of class **CHAOS** which is separate from the default view of class **IN**. Most global configuration options (**allow-query**, etc) will apply to this view, but some are locally overridden: **notify**, **recursion** and **allow-new-zones** are always set to **no**, and **rate-limit** is set to allow three responses per second.

If you need to disable these zones, use the options below, or hide the built-in **CHAOS** view by defining an explicit view of class **CHAOS** that matches all clients.

version

The version the server should report via a query of the name `version.bind` with type **TXT**, class **CHAOS**. The default is the real version number of this server. Specifying **version none** disables processing of the queries.

Q: *How do I restrict people from looking up the server version?*

A: Put a "version" option containing something other than the real version in the "options" section of named.conf. Note doing this will not prevent attacks and may impede people trying to diagnose problems with your server. Also it is possible to "fingerprint" nameservers to determine their version.

Q: *How do I restrict only remote users from looking up the server version?*

A: The following view statement will intercept lookups as the internal view that holds the version information will be matched last. The caveats of the previous answer still apply, of course.

```
view "chaos" chaos {
        match-clients { <those to be refused>; };
        allow-query { none; };
        zone "." {
                type hint;
                file "/dev/null";  // or any empty file
        };
};
```

hostname

> The hostname the server should report via a query of the name `hostname.bind` with type **TXT**, class **CHAOS**. This defaults to the hostname of the machine hosting the name server as found by the gethostname() function. The primary purpose of such queries is to identify which of a group of Anycast servers is actually answering your queries. Specifying **hostname none;** disables processing of the queries.

server-id

> The ID the server should report when receiving a Name Server Identifier (NSID) query, or a query of the name `ID.SERVER` with type **TXT**, class **CHAOS**. The primary purpose of such queries is to identify which of a group of Anycast servers is actually answering your queries. Specifying **server-id none;** disables processing of the queries. Specifying **server-id hostname;** will cause **named** to use the hostname as found by the gethostname() function. The default **server-id** is **none**.

Built-in Empty Zones

The **named** server has some built-in empty zones (SOA and NS records only). These are for zones that should normally be answered locally and which queries should not be sent to the Internet's root servers. The official servers which cover these namespaces return NXDOMAIN responses to these queries. In particular, these cover the reverse namespaces for addresses from RFC 1918, RFC 4193, RFC 5737 and RFC 6598. They also include the reverse namespace for IPv6 local address (locally assigned), IPv6 link local addresses, the IPv6 loopback address and the IPv6 unknown address.

The server will attempt to determine if a built-in zone already exists or is active (covered by a forward-only forwarding declaration) and will not create an empty zone in that case.

The current list of empty zones is:

- 10.IN-ADDR.ARPA

- 16.172.IN-ADDR.ARPA

- 17.172.IN-ADDR.ARPA

- 18.172.IN-ADDR.ARPA

- 19.172.IN-ADDR.ARPA

- 20.172.IN-ADDR.ARPA

- 21.172.IN-ADDR.ARPA

- 22.172.IN-ADDR.ARPA

- 23.172.IN-ADDR.ARPA

- 24.172.IN-ADDR.ARPA

- 25.172.IN-ADDR.ARPA

- 26.172.IN-ADDR.ARPA

- 27.172.IN-ADDR.ARPA

- 28.172.IN-ADDR.ARPA

- 29.172.IN-ADDR.ARPA

- 30.172.IN-ADDR.ARPA

- 31.172.IN-ADDR.ARPA

- 168.192.IN-ADDR.ARPA

- 64.100.IN-ADDR.ARPA

- 65.100.IN-ADDR.ARPA

- 66.100.IN-ADDR.ARPA

- 67.100.IN-ADDR.ARPA

- 68.100.IN-ADDR.ARPA

- 69.100.IN-ADDR.ARPA

- 70.100.IN-ADDR.ARPA

- 71.100.IN-ADDR.ARPA

- 72.100.IN-ADDR.ARPA

- 73.100.IN-ADDR.ARPA

- 74.100.IN-ADDR.ARPA

- 75.100.IN-ADDR.ARPA

- 76.100.IN-ADDR.ARPA

- 77.100.IN-ADDR.ARPA

- 78.100.IN-ADDR.ARPA

- 79.100.IN-ADDR.ARPA

- 80.100.IN-ADDR.ARPA

- 81.100.IN-ADDR.ARPA

- 82.100.IN-ADDR.ARPA

- 83.100.IN-ADDR.ARPA

- 84.100.IN-ADDR.ARPA

- 85.100.IN-ADDR.ARPA

- 86.100.IN-ADDR.ARPA

- 87.100.IN-ADDR.ARPA

- 88.100.IN-ADDR.ARPA

- 89.100.IN-ADDR.ARPA

- 90.100.IN-ADDR.ARPA

- 91.100.IN-ADDR.ARPA

- 92.100.IN-ADDR.ARPA

- 93.100.IN-ADDR.ARPA

- 94.100.IN-ADDR.ARPA

- 95.100.IN-ADDR.ARPA

- 96.100.IN-ADDR.ARPA

- 97.100.IN-ADDR.ARPA

- 98.100.IN-ADDR.ARPA

- 99.100.IN-ADDR.ARPA

- 100.100.IN-ADDR.ARPA

- 101.100.IN-ADDR.ARPA

- 102.100.IN-ADDR.ARPA

- 103.100.IN-ADDR.ARPA

- 104.100.IN-ADDR.ARPA

- 105.100.IN-ADDR.ARPA

- 106.100.IN-ADDR.ARPA

- 107.100.IN-ADDR.ARPA

- 108.100.IN-ADDR.ARPA

- 109.100.IN-ADDR.ARPA

- 110.100.IN-ADDR.ARPA

- 111.100.IN-ADDR.ARPA

- 112.100.IN-ADDR.ARPA

- 113.100.IN-ADDR.ARPA

- 114.100.IN-ADDR.ARPA

- 115.100.IN-ADDR.ARPA

- 116.100.IN-ADDR.ARPA

- 117.100.IN-ADDR.ARPA

- 118.100.IN-ADDR.ARPA

- 119.100.IN-ADDR.ARPA

- 120.100.IN-ADDR.ARPA

- 121.100.IN-ADDR.ARPA

- 122.100.IN-ADDR.ARPA

- 123.100.IN-ADDR.ARPA

- 124.100.IN-ADDR.ARPA

- 125.100.IN-ADDR.ARPA

- 126.100.IN-ADDR.ARPA

- 127.100.IN-ADDR.ARPA

- 0.IN-ADDR.ARPA

- 127.IN-ADDR.ARPA

- 254.169.IN-ADDR.ARPA

- 2.0.192.IN-ADDR.ARPA

- 100.51.198.IN-ADDR.ARPA

- 113.0.203.IN-ADDR.ARPA

- 255.255.255.255.IN-ADDR.ARPA

- 0.0.0.0.0.0.0.0.0.0.0.0.0.0.0.0.0.0.0.0.0.0.0.0.0.0.0.0.0.0.0.0.IP6.ARPA

- 1.0.0.0.0.0.0.0.0.0.0.0.0.0.0.0.0.0.0.0.0.0.0.0.0.0.0.0.0.0.0.0.IP6.ARPA

- 8.B.D.0.1.0.0.2.IP6.ARPA

- D.F.IP6.ARPA

- 8.E.F.IP6.ARPA

- 9.E.F.IP6.ARPA

- A.E.F.IP6.ARPA

- B.E.F.IP6.ARPA

Empty zones are settable at the view level and only apply to views of class IN. Disabled empty zones are only inherited from options if there are no disabled empty zones specified at the view level. To override the options list of disabled zones, you can disable the root zone at the view level, for example:

```
disable-empty-zone ".";
```

If you are using the address ranges covered here, you should already have reverse zones covering the addresses you use. In practice this appears to not be the case with many queries being made to the infrastructure servers for names in these spaces. So many in fact that sacrificial servers were needed to be deployed to channel the query load away from the infrastructure servers.

Note

The real parent servers for these zones should disable all empty zone under the parent zone they serve. For the real root servers, this is all built-in empty zones. This will enable them to return referrals to deeper in the tree.

---

empty-server

Specify what server name will appear in the returned SOA record for empty zones. If none is specified, then the zone's name will be used.

empty-contact

Specify what contact name will appear in the returned SOA record for empty zones. If none is specified, then "." will be used.

empty-zones-enable

Enable or disable all empty zones. By default, they are enabled.

disable-empty-zone

Disable individual empty zones. By default, none are disabled. This option can be specified multiple times.

Additional Section Caching

The additional section cache, also called *acache*, is an internal cache to improve the response performance of BIND 9. When additional section caching is enabled, BIND 9 will cache an internal short-cut to the additional section content for each answer RR.

Note
The additional section cache is an internal caching mechanism of BIND 9, and is not related to the DNS caching server function.

Additional section caching does not change the response content (except the RRsets ordering of the additional section, see below), but can improve the response performance significantly. It is particularly effective when BIND 9 acts as an authoritative server for a zone that has many delegations with many glue RRs.

In order to obtain the maximum performance improvement from additional section caching, setting **additional-from-cache** to **no** is recommended, since the current implementation of *acache* does not short-cut of additional section information from the DNS cache data.

One obvious disadvantage of *acache* is that it requires much more memory for the internal cached data. Thus, if the response performance does not matter and memory consumption is much more critical, the *acache* mechanism can be disabled by setting **acache-enable** to **no**. It is also possible to specify the upper limit of memory consumption for acache by using **max-acache-size**.

Additional section caching also has a minor effect on the RRset ordering in the additional section. Without *acache*, **cyclic** order is effective for the additional section as well as the answer and authority sections. However, additional section caching fixes the ordering when it first caches an RRset for the additional section, and the same ordering will be kept in succeeding responses, regardless of the setting of **rrset-order**. The effect of this should be minor, however, since an RRset in the additional section typically only contains a small number of RRs (and in many cases it only contains a single RR), in which case the ordering does not matter much.

The following is a summary of options related to *acache*.

acache-enable
> If **yes**, additional section caching is enabled. The default value is **no**.

acache-cleaning-interval
> The server will remove stale cache entries, based on an LRU based algorithm, every **acache-cleaning-interval** minutes. The default is 60 minutes. If set to 0, no periodic cleaning will occur.

max-acache-size
> The maximum amount of memory in bytes to use for the server's acache. When the amount of data in the acache reaches this limit, the server will clean more aggressively so that the limit is not exceeded. In a server with multiple views, the limit applies separately to the acache of each view. The keyword `unlimited` means the entries are purged from the acache only at the periodic cleaning time. The default is 16M. (It will silently raise to 2 MB if below.)

Content Filtering

BIND 9 provides the ability to filter out DNS responses from external DNS servers containing certain types of data in the answer section. Specifically, it can reject address (A or AAAA) records if the corresponding IPv4 or IPv6 addresses match the given `address_match_list` of the **deny-answer-addresses** option. It can also reject CNAME or DNAME records if the "alias" name (i.e., the CNAME alias or the substituted query name due to DNAME) matches the given `namelist` of the **deny-answer-aliases** option, where "match" means the alias name is a subdomain of one of the `name_list` elements. If the optional `namelist` is specified with **except-from**, records whose query name matches the list will be accepted regardless of the filter setting. Likewise, if the alias name is a subdomain of the corresponding zone, the **deny-answer-aliases** filter will not apply; for example, even if "example.com" is specified for **deny-answer-aliases**,

```
www.example.com. CNAME xxx.example.com.
```

returned by an "example.com" server will be accepted.

In the `address_match_list` of the **deny-answer-addresses** option, only `ip_addr` and `ip_p refix` are meaningful; any `key_id` will be silently ignored.

If a response message is rejected due to the filtering, the entire message is discarded without being cached, and a SERVFAIL error will be returned to the client.

This filtering is intended to prevent "DNS rebinding attacks," in which an attacker, in response to a query for a domain name the attacker controls, returns an IP address within your own network or an alias name within your own domain. A naive web browser or script could then serve as an unintended proxy, allowing the attacker to get access to an internal node of your local network that couldn't be externally accessed otherwise. See the paper available at http://portal.acm.org/-citation.cfm?id=1315245.1315298 for more details about the attacks.

For example, if you own a domain named "example.net" and your internal network uses an IPv4 prefix 192.0.2.0/24, you might specify the following rules:

```
deny-answer-addresses { 192.0.2.0/24; } except-from { "example.net"; };
deny-answer-aliases { "example.net"; };
```

If an external attacker lets a web browser in your local network look up an IPv4 address of "attacker.example.com", the attacker's DNS server would return a response like this:

```
attacker.example.com. A 192.0.2.1
```

in the answer section. Since the rdata of this record (the IPv4 address) matches the specified prefix 192.0.2.0/24, this response will be ignored.

On the other hand, if the browser looks up a legitimate internal web server "www.example.net" and the following response is returned to the BIND 9 server

```
www.example.net. A 192.0.2.2
```

it will be accepted since the owner name "www.example.net" matches the **except-from** element, "example.net".

Note that this is not really an attack on the DNS per se. In fact, there is nothing wrong for an "external" name to be mapped to your "internal" IP address or domain name from the DNS point of view. It might actually be provided for a legitimate purpose, such as for debugging. As long as the mapping is provided by the correct owner, it is not possible or does not make sense to detect whether the intent of the mapping is legitimate or not within the DNS. The "rebinding" attack must primarily be protected at the application that uses the DNS. For a large site, however, it may be difficult to protect all possible applications at once. This filtering feature is provided only to help such an operational environment; it is generally discouraged to turn it on unless you are very sure you have no other choice and the attack is a real threat for your applications.

Care should be particularly taken if you want to use this option for addresses within 127.0.0.0/8. These addresses are obviously "internal", but many applications conventionally rely on a DNS mapping from some name to such an address. Filtering out DNS records containing this address spuriously can break such applications.

Response Policy Zone (RPZ) Rewriting

BIND 9 includes a limited mechanism to modify DNS responses for requests analogous to email anti-spam DNS blacklists. Responses can be changed to deny the existence of domains (NXDOMAIN), deny the existence of IP addresses for domains (NODATA), or contain other IP addresses or data.

Response policy zones are named in the **response-policy** option for the view or among the global options if there is no response-policy option for the view. Response policy zones are ordinary DNS zones containing RRsets that can be queried normally if allowed. It is usually best to restrict those queries with something like **allow-query { localhost; };**.

As of BIND 9.10, the **response-policy** option can support multiple policy zones. To maximize performance, a radix tree is used to quickly identify response policy zones containing triggers that match the current query. This imposes an upper limit of 32 on the number of policy zones in a single **response-policy** option; more than that is a configuration error.

Five policy triggers can be encoded in RPZ records.

RPZ-CLIENT-IP

IP records are triggered by the IP address of the DNS client. This can be used, for example, to blacklist misbehaving recursive or stub resolvers. Client IP address triggers are encoded in records that have owner names that are subdomains of **rpz-client-ip** relativized to the policy zone origin name and encode an address or address block. IPv4 addresses are represented as `prefixlength.B4.B3.B2.B1.rpz-client-ip`. The IPv4 prefix length must be between 1 and 32. All four bytes, B4, B3, B2, and B1, must be present. B4 is the decimal value of the least significant byte of the IPv4 address as in IN-ADDR.ARPA. (Support for **rpz-client-ip** policy triggers was introduced in BIND 9.10.)

IPv6 addresses are encoded in a format similar to the standard IPv6 text representation:

`prefixlength.W8.W7.W6.W5.W4.W3.W2.W1.rpz-client-ip`

Each of W8,...,W1 is a one to four digit hexadecimal number representing 16 bits of the IPv6 address as in the standard text representation of IPv6 addresses, but reversed as in IP6.ARPA. (Note that this representation of IPv6 address is different from IP6.ARPA where each hex digit occupies a label.) All 8 words must be present except when one set of consecutive zero words is replaced with **.zz.** analogous to double colons (::) in standard IPv6 text encodings. The IPv6 prefix length must be between 1 and 128.

QNAME

QNAME policy records are triggered by query names of requests and targets of CNAME records resolved to generate the response. The owner name of a QNAME policy record is the query name relativized to the policy zone.

RPZ-IP

IP triggers are IP addresses in an A or AAAA record in the ANSWER section of a response. They are encoded like client-IP triggers except as subdomains of **rpz-ip**.

RPZ-NSDNAME

NSDNAME triggers match names of authoritative servers for the query name, a parent of the query name, a CNAME for query name, or a parent of a CNAME. They are encoded as subdomains of **rpz-nsdname** relativized to the RPZ origin name. NSIP triggers match IP addresses in A and AAAA RRsets for domains that can be checked against NSDNAME policy records.

RPZ-NSIP

NSIP triggers are encoded like IP triggers except as subdomains of **rpz-nsip**. NSDNAME and NSIP triggers are checked only for names with at least **min-ns-dots** dots. The default value of **min-ns-dots** is 1 to exclude top level domains.

The query response is checked against all response policy zones, so two or more policy records can be triggered by a response. Because DNS responses are rewritten according to at most one policy record, a single record encoding an action (other than **DISABLED** actions) must be chosen. Triggers or the records that encode them are chosen for the rewriting in the following order:

1. Choose the triggered record in the zone that appears first in the **response-policy** option.

2. Prefer CLIENT-IP to QNAME to IP to NSDNAME to NSIP triggers in a single zone.

3. Among NSDNAME triggers, prefer the trigger that matches the smallest name under the DNSSEC ordering.

4. Among IP or NSIP triggers, prefer the trigger with the longest prefix.

5. Among triggers with the same prefix length, prefer the IP or NSIP trigger that matches the smallest IP address.

When the processing of a response is restarted to resolve DNAME or CNAME records and a policy record set has not been triggered, all response policy zones are again consulted for the DNAME or CNAME names and addresses.

RPZ record sets are any types of DNS record except DNAME or DNSSEC that encode actions or responses to individual queries. Any of the policies can be used with any of the triggers. For example, while the **TCP-only** policy is commonly used with **client-IP** triggers, it can be used with any type of trigger to force the use of TCP for responses with owner names in a zone.

PASSTHRU

The whitelist policy is specified by a CNAME whose target is **rpz-passthru**. It causes the response to not be rewritten and is most often used to "poke holes" in policies for CIDR blocks.

DROP

The blacklist policy is specified by a CNAME whose target is **rpz-drop**. It causes the response to be discarded. Nothing is sent to the DNS client.

TCP-Only

The "slip" policy is specified by a CNAME whose target is **rpz-tcp-only**. It changes UDP responses to short, truncated DNS responses that require the DNS client to try again with TCP. It is used to mitigate distributed DNS reflection attacks.

NXDOMAIN

The domain undefined response is encoded by a CNAME whose target is the root domain (.)

NODATA

The empty set of resource records is specified by CNAME whose target is the wildcard top-level domain (*.). It rewrites the response to NODATA or ANCOUNT=1.

Local Data

A set of ordinary DNS records can be used to answer queries. Queries for record types not the set are answered with NODATA.

A special form of local data is a CNAME whose target is a wildcard such as *.example.com. It is used as if were an ordinary CNAME after the asterisk (*) has been replaced with the query name. The purpose for this special form is query logging in the walled garden's authority DNS server.

All of the actions specified in all of the individual records in a policy zone can be overridden with a **policy** clause in the **response-policy** option. An organization using a policy zone provided by another organization might use this mechanism to redirect domains to its own walled garden.

GIVEN

The placeholder policy says "do not override but perform the action specified in the zone."

DISABLED

The testing override policy causes policy zone records to do nothing but log what they would have done if the policy zone were not disabled. The response to the DNS query will be written (or not) according to any triggered policy records that are not disabled. Disabled policy zones should appear first, because they will often not be logged if a higher precedence trigger is found first.

PASSTHRU, DROP, TCP-Only, NXDOMAIN, NODATA

override with the corresponding per-record policy.

CNAME domain

causes all RPZ policy records to act as if they were "cname domain" records.

By default, the actions encoded in a response policy zone are applied only to queries that ask for recursion (RD=1). That default can be changed for a single policy zone or all response policy zones in a view with a **recursive-only no** clause. This feature is useful for serving the same zone files both inside and outside an RFC 1918 cloud and using RPZ to delete answers that would otherwise contain RFC 1918 values on the externally visible name server or view.

Also by default, RPZ actions are applied only to DNS requests that either do not request DNSSEC metadata (DO=0) or when no DNSSEC records are available for request name in the original zone (not the response policy zone). This default can be changed for all response policy zones in a view with a **break-dnssec yes** clause. In that case, RPZ actions are applied regardless of DNSSEC. The name of the clause option reflects the fact that results rewritten by RPZ actions cannot verify.

No DNS records are needed for a QNAME or Client-IP trigger. The name or IP address itself is sufficient, so in principle the query name need not be recursively resolved. However, not resolving the requested name can leak the fact that response policy rewriting is in use and that the name is listed in a policy zone to operators of servers for listed names. To prevent that information leak, by default any recursion needed for a request is done before any policy triggers are considered. Because listed domains often have slow authoritative servers, this default behavior can cost significant time. The **qname-wait-recurse no** option (introduced in BIND 9.10) overrides that default behavior when recursion cannot change a non-error response. The option does not affect QNAME or client-IP triggers in policy zones listed after other zones containing IP, NSIP and NSDNAME triggers, because those may depend on the A, AAAA, and NS records that would be found during recursive resolution. It also does not affect DNSSEC requests (DO=1) unless **break-dnssec yes** is in use, because the response would depend on whether or not RRSIG records were found during resolution. Using this option can cause error responses such as SERVFAIL to appear to be rewritten, since no recursion is being done to discover problems at the authoritative server.

The TTL of a record modified by RPZ policies is set from the TTL of the relevant record in policy zone. It is then limited to a maximum value. The **max-policy-ttl** clause changes the maximum seconds from its default of 5.

For example, you might use this option statement

```
response-policy { zone "badlist"; };
```

and this zone statement

```
zone "badlist" {type master; file "master/badlist"; allow-query {none ←
    ;}; };
```

with this zone file

```
$TTL 1H
@                       SOA LOCALHOST. named-mgr.example.com (1 1h 15m  ←
    30d 2h)
      NS  LOCALHOST.

; QNAME policy records.  There are no periods (.) after the owner names ←
    .
nxdomain.domain.com     CNAME   .              ; NXDOMAIN policy
*.nxdomain.domain.com   CNAME   .              ; NXDOMAIN policy
nodata.domain.com       CNAME   *.             ; NODATA policy
*.nodata.domain.com     CNAME   *.             ; NODATA policy
bad.domain.com          A       10.0.0.1       ; redirect to a walled  ←
    garden
        AAAA    2001:2::1
bzone.domain.com        CNAME   garden.example.com.
```

```
; do not rewrite (PASSTHRU) OK.DOMAIN.COM
ok.domain.com              CNAME   rpz-passthru.

; redirect x.bzone.domain.com to x.bzone.domain.com.garden.example.com
*.bzone.domain.com         CNAME   *.garden.example.com.


; IP policy records that rewrite all responses containing A records in  ←
   127/8
;        except 127.0.0.1
8.0.0.0.127.rpz-ip         CNAME   .
32.1.0.0.127.rpz-ip        CNAME   rpz-passthru.

; NSDNAME and NSIP policy records
ns.domain.com.rpz-nsdname  CNAME   .
48.zz.2.2001.rpz-nsip      CNAME   .

; blacklist and whitelist some DNS clients
112.zz.2001.rpz-client-ip   CNAME   rpz-drop.
8.0.0.0.127.rpz-client-ip   CNAME   rpz-drop.

; force some DNS clients and responses in the example.com zone to TCP
16.0.0.1.10.rpz-client-ip   CNAME   rpz-tcp-only.
example.com                 CNAME   rpz-tcp-only.
*.example.com               CNAME   rpz-tcp-only.
```

RPZ can affect server performance. Each configured response policy zone requires the server to perform one to four additional database lookups before a query can be answered. For example, a DNS server with four policy zones, each with all four kinds of response triggers, QNAME, IP, NSIP, and NSDNAME, requires a total of 17 times as many database lookups as a similar DNS server with no response policy zones. A BIND9 server with adequate memory and one response policy zone with QNAME and IP triggers might achieve a maximum queries-per-second rate about 20% lower. A server with four response policy zones with QNAME and IP triggers might have a maximum QPS rate about 50% lower.

Responses rewritten by RPZ are counted in the **RPZRewrites** statistics.

The **log** clause can be used to optionally turn off rewrite logging for a particular response policy zone. By default, all rewrites are logged. (This **log** feature was introduced in BIND 9.11.)

Warning
The Response Policy Zone feature in BIND 9.9 is considered experimental and may be unstable; also it may not properly parse new style RPZ zone syntax. It is recommended that BIND 9.10 or later be used for RPZ.

Response Rate Limiting

Excessive almost identical UDP *responses* can be controlled by configuring a **rate-limit** clause in an **options** or **view** statement. This mechanism keeps authoritative BIND 9 from being used in amplifying reflection denial of service (DoS) attacks. Short truncated (TC=1) responses can be sent to provide rate-limited responses to legitimate clients within a range of forged, attacked IP addresses. Legitimate clients react to dropped or truncated response by retrying with UDP or with TCP respectively.

The **rate-limit** feature was enabled by default in BIND 9.10. It was introduced in BIND 9.9 and is only available when BIND 9.9 is compiled with the `--enable-rrl` option on the "configure" command line as introduced in Section 3.3.)

This mechanism is intended for authoritative DNS servers. It can be used on recursive servers but can slow applications such as SMTP servers (mail receivers) and HTTP clients (web browsers) that repeatedly request the same domains. When possible, closing "open" recursive servers is better.

Response rate limiting uses a "credit" or "token bucket" scheme. Each combination of identical response and client has a conceptual account that earns a specified number of credits every second. A prospective response debits its account by one. Responses are dropped or truncated while the account is negative. Responses are tracked within a rolling window of time which defaults to 15 seconds, but can be configured with the **window** option to any value from 1 to 3600 seconds (1 hour). The account cannot become more positive than the per-second limit or more negative than **window** times the per-second limit. When the specified number of credits for a class of responses is set to 0, those responses are not rate limited.

The notions of "identical response" and "DNS client" for rate limiting are not simplistic. All responses to an address block are counted as if to a single client. The prefix lengths of addresses blocks are specified with **ipv4-prefix-length** (default 24) and **ipv6-prefix-length** (default 56).

All non-empty responses for a valid domain name (qname) and record type (qtype) are identical and have a limit specified with **responses-per-second** (default 0 or no limit). All empty (NODATA) responses for a valid domain, regardless of query type, are identical. Responses in the NODATA class are limited by **nodata-per-second** (default **responses-per-second**). Requests for any and all undefined subdomains of a given valid domain result in NXDOMAIN errors, and are identical regardless of query type. They are limited by **nxdomains-per-second** (default **responses-per-second**). This controls some attacks using random names, but can be relaxed or turned off (set to 0) on servers that expect many legitimate NXDOMAIN responses, such as from anti-spam blacklists. Referrals or delegations to the server of a given domain are identical and are limited by **referrals-per-second** (default **responses-per-second**).

Responses generated from local wildcards are counted and limited as if they were for the parent domain name. This controls flooding using random.wild.example.com.

All requests that result in DNS errors other than NXDOMAIN, such as SERVFAIL and FORMERR, are identical regardless of requested name (qname) or record type (qtype). This controls attacks using invalid requests or distant, broken authoritative servers. By default the limit on errors is the same as the **responses-per-second** value, but it can be set separately with **errors-per-second**.

Many attacks using DNS involve UDP requests with forged source addresses. Rate limiting prevents the use of BIND 9 to flood a network with responses to requests with forged source addresses, but could let a third party block responses to legitimate requests. There is a mechanism that can answer some legitimate requests from a client whose address is being forged in a flood. Setting **slip** to 2 (its default) causes every other UDP request to be answered with a small truncated (TC=1) response. The small size and reduced frequency, and so lack of amplification, of "slipped" responses make them unattractive for reflection DoS attacks. **slip** must be between 0 and 10. A value of 0 does not "slip": no truncated responses are sent due to rate limiting, all responses are dropped. A value of 1 causes every response to slip; values between 2 and 10 cause every n'th response to slip. Some error responses including REFUSED and SERVFAIL cannot be replaced with truncated responses and are instead leaked at the **slip** rate.

Note

Dropped responses from an authoritative server may reduce the difficulty of a third party success-fully forging a response to a recursive resolver. The best security against forged responses is for authoritative operators to sign their zones using DNSSEC and for resolver operators to validate the responses. When this is not an option, operators who are more concerned with response integrity than with flood mitigation may consider setting **slip** to 1, causing all rate-limited responses to be truncated rather than dropped. This reduces the effectiveness of rate-limiting against reflection attacks.

When the approximate query per second rate exceeds the **qps-scale** value, then the **responses-per-second**, **errors-per-second**, **nxdomains-per-second** and **all-per-second** values are reduced by the ratio of the current rate to the **qps-scale** value. This feature can tighten defenses during attacks. For example, with **qps-scale 250; responses-per-second 20;** and a total query rate of 1000 queries/second for all queries from all DNS clients including via TCP, then the effective responses/second limit changes to (250/1000)*20 or 5. Responses sent via TCP are not limited but are counted to compute the query per second rate.

Communities of DNS clients can be given their own parameters or no rate limiting by putting **rate-limit** statements in **view** statements instead of the global **option** statement. A **rate-limit** statement in a view replaces, rather than supplementing, a **rate-limit** statement among the main options. DNS clients within a view can be exempted from rate limits with the **exempt-clients** clause.

UDP responses of all kinds can be limited with the **all-per-second** phrase. This rate limiting is unlike the rate limiting provided by **responses-per-second**, **errors-per-second**, and **nxdomains-per-second** on a DNS server which are often invisible to the victim of a DNS reflection attack. Unless the forged requests of the attack are the same as the legitimate requests of the victim, the victim's requests are not affected. Responses affected by an **all-per-second** limit are always dropped; the **slip** value has no effect. An **all-per-second** limit should be at least 4 times as large as the other limits, because single DNS clients often send bursts of legitimate requests. For example, the receipt of a single mail message can prompt requests from an SMTP server for NS, PTR, A, and AAAA records as the incoming SMTP/TCP/IP connection is considered. The SMTP server can need additional NS, A, AAAA, MX, TXT, and SPF records as it considers the STMP **Mail From** command. Web browsers often repeatedly resolve the same names that are repeated in HTML <IMG> tags in a page. **all-per-second** is similar to the rate limiting offered by firewalls but often inferior. Attacks that justify ignoring the contents of DNS responses are likely to be attacks on the DNS server itself. They usually should be discarded before the DNS server spends resources make TCP connections or parsing DNS requests, but that rate limiting must be done before the DNS server sees the requests.

The maximum size of the table used to track requests and rate limit responses is set with **max-table-size**. Each entry in the table is between 40 and 80 bytes. The table needs approximately as many entries as the number of requests received per second. The default is 20,000. To reduce the cold start of growing the table, **min-table-size** (default 500) can set the minimum table size. Enable **rate-limit** category logging to monitor expansions of the table and inform choices for the initial and maximum table size.

Use **log-only yes** to test rate limiting parameters without actually dropping any requests.

Responses dropped by rate limits are included in the **RateDropped** and **QryDropped** statistics. Responses that truncated by rate limits are included in **RateSlipped** and **RespTruncated**.

NXDOMAIN Redirection

named supports NXDOMAIN redirection via two methods:

- Redirect zone (See Section 7.2)

- Redirect namespace

With both methods when named gets a NXDOMAIN response it examines a seperate namespace to see if the NXDOMAIN response should be replaced with a alternative response.

With a redirect zone (**zone "." { type redirect; };**), the data used to replace the NXDOMAIN is held in a single zone which is not part of the normal namespace. All the redirect information is contained in the zone; there are no delegations.

With a redirect namespace (**option { nxdomain-redirect <suffix> };**) the data used to replace the NXDOMAIN is part of the normal namespace and is looked up by appending the specified suffix to the original query name. This roughly doubles the cache required to process NXDOMAIN responses as you have the original NXDOMAIN response and the replacement data or a NXDOMAIN indicating that there is no replacement. (The `nxdomain-redirect` feature was introduced in BIND 9.11.)

If both a redirect zone and a redirect namespace are configured, the redirect zone is tried first.

6.8   server Statement

server Statement Grammar

```
server ip_addr[/prefixlen] {
    bogus yes_or_no ;
    provide-ixfr yes_or_no ;
    request-ixfr yes_or_no ;
    request-expire yes_or_no ;
    request-nsid yes_or_no ;
    send-cookie yes_or_no ;
    edns yes_or_no ;
    edns-udp-size number ;
    edns-version number ;
```

```
    max-udp-size number ;
    tcp-only yes_or_no ;
    transfers number ;
    transfer-format ( one-answer | many-answers ) ; ]
    keys { key_id };
    transfer-source (ip4_addr | *) port ip_port dscp ip_dscp ;
    transfer-source-v6 (ip6_addr | *) port ip_port dscp ip_dscp ;
    notify-source (ip4_addr | *) port ip_port dscp ip_dscp ;
    notify-source-v6 (ip6_addr | *) port ip_port dscp ip_dscp ;
    query-source  address ( ip_addr | * )
      port ( ip_port | * )  dscp ip_dscp ;
    query-source-v6  address ( ip_addr | * )
        port ( ip_port | * )  dscp ip_dscp ;
    use-queryport-pool yes_or_no;
    queryport-pool-ports number;
    queryport-pool-updateinterval number;
};
```

server Statement Definition and Usage

The **server** defines characteristics to be associated with a remote name server. If a prefix length is specified, then a range of servers is covered. Only the most specific server clause applies regardless of the order in `named.conf`.

The **server** can occur at the top level of the configuration file or inside a **view** statement. If a **view** statement contains one or more **server** statements, only those apply to the view and any top-level ones are ignored. If a view contains no **server** statements, any top-level **server** statements are used as defaults.

If you discover that a remote server is giving out bad data, marking it as bogus will prevent further queries to it. The default value of **bogus** is **no**.

The **provide-ixfr** clause determines whether the local server, acting as master, will respond with an incremental zone transfer when the given remote server, a slave, requests it. If set to **yes**, incremental transfer will be provided whenever possible. If set to **no**, all transfers to the remote server will be non-incremental. If not set, the value of the **provide-ixfr** option in the view or global options block is used as a default.

The **request-ixfr** clause determines whether the local server, acting as a slave, will request incremental zone transfers from the given remote server, a master. If not set, the value of the **request-ixfr** option in the view or global options block is used as a default. It may also be set in the zone block and, if set there, it will override the global or view setting for that zone. (The **request-ixfr** option was extended for specific use in zone settings in BIND 9.9.)

IXFR requests to servers that do not support IXFR will automatically fall back to AXFR. Therefore, there is no need to manually list which servers support IXFR and which ones do not; the global default of **yes** should always work. The purpose of the **provide-ixfr** and **request-ixfr** clauses is to make it possible to disable the use of IXFR even when both master and slave claim to support it, for example if one of the servers is buggy and crashes or corrupts data when IXFR is used.

The **request-expire** clause determines whether the local server, when acting as a slave, will request the EDNS EXPIRE value. The EDNS EXPIRE value indicates the remaining time before the zone data will expire and need to be be refreshed. This is used when a secondary server transfers a zone from another secondary server; when transferring from the primary, the expiration timer is set from the EXPIRE field of the SOA record instead. The default is **yes**. (The **request-expire** feature was introduced in BIND 9.11.)

The **edns** clause determines whether the local server will attempt to use Extension Mechanisms for DNS (EDNS) when communicating with the remote server. The default is **yes**.

The **edns-udp-size** option sets the EDNS UDP size that is advertised by **named** when querying the remote server. Valid values are 512 to 4096 bytes (values outside this range will be silently adjusted to the nearest value within it). This option is useful when you wish to advertise a different value to this server than the value you advertise globally, for example, when there is a firewall at the remote site that is blocking large replies.

Currently, this sets a single UDP size for all packets sent to the server; **named** will not deviate from this value. This differs from the behavior of **edns-udp-size** in **options** or **view** statements, where it specifies a maximum value. The **server** behavior may be brought into conformance with the **options/view** behavior in future releases.

The **edns-version** option sets the maximum EDNS VERSION that will be sent to the server(s) by the resolver. The actual EDNS version sent is still subject to normal EDNS version negotiation rules (see RFC 6891), the maximum EDNS version supported by the server, and any other heuristics that indicate that a lower version should be sent. This option is intended to be used when a remote server reacts badly to a given EDNS version or higher; it should be set to the highest version the remote server is known to support. Valid values are 0 to 255; higher values will be silently adjusted. This option will not be needed until higher EDNS versions than 0 are in use. (The **edns-version** option was introduced in BIND 9.11.)

The **max-udp-size** option sets the maximum EDNS UDP message size **named** will send. Valid values are 512 to 4096 bytes (values outside this range will be silently adjusted). This option is useful when you know that there is a firewall that is blocking large replies from **named**.

The **tcp-only** option sets the transport protocol to TCP. The default is to use the UDP transport and to fallback on TCP only when a truncated response is received. (The **tcp-only** option was introduced in BIND 9.11.)

The server supports two zone transfer methods. The first, **one-answer**, uses one DNS message per resource record transferred. **many-answers** packs as many resource records as possible into a message. **many-answers** is more efficient, but is only known to be understood by BIND 9, BIND 8.x, and patched versions of BIND 4.9.5. You can specify which method to use for a server with the **transfer-format** option. If **transfer-format** is not specified, the **transfer-format** specified by the **options** statement will be used. (See page 119 for details on the **transfer-format** option.)

transfers is used to limit the number of concurrent inbound zone transfers from the specified server. If no **transfers** clause is specified, the limit is set according to the **transfers-per-ns** option.

The **keys** clause identifies a **key_id** defined by the **key** statement, to be used for transaction security (TSIG) when talking to the remote server. When a request is sent to the remote server, a request signature will be generated using the key specified here and appended to the message. A request originating from the remote server is not required to be signed by this key. (See Section 9.3 for more information about TSIG.)

Only a single key per server is currently supported.

The **transfer-source** and **transfer-source-v6** clauses specify the IPv4 and IPv6 source address to be used for zone transfer with the remote server, respectively. For an IPv4 remote server, only **transfer-source** can be specified. Similarly, for an IPv6 remote server, only **transfer-source-v6** can be specified. For more details, see the description of **transfer-source** and **transfer-source-v6** in Section 6.7.

The **notify-source** and **notify-source-v6** clauses specify the IPv4 and IPv6 source address to be used for notify messages sent to remote servers, respectively. For an IPv4 remote server, only **notify-source** can be specified. Similarly, for an IPv6 remote server, only **notify-source-v6** can be specified. For more details, see page 120.

The **query-source** and **query-source-v6** clauses specify the IPv4 and IPv6 source address to be used for queries sent to remote servers, respectively. For an IPv4 remote server, only **query-source** can be specified. Similarly, for an IPv6 remote server, only **query-source-v6** can be specified.

The **request-nsid** clause determines whether the local server will add a NSID EDNS option to requests sent to the server. This overrides **request-nsid** set at the view or option level.

The **send-cookie** clause determines whether the local server will add a COOKIE EDNS option to requests sent to the server. This overrides **send-cookie** set at the view or option level. The **named** server may determine that COOKIE is not supported by the remote server and not add a COOKIE EDNS option to requests. (The **send-cookie** option was introduced in BIND 9.11. Note that the experimental **request-sit** option is now obsolete.)

6.9   statistics-channels Statement

statistics-channels Statement Grammar

```
statistics-channels {
    [ inet ( ip_addr | * ) [ port ip_port ]
    [ allow { address_match_list } ]; ]
    [ inet ...; ]
};
```

statistics-channels Statement Definition and Usage

The **statistics-channels** declares communication channels to be used by system administrators to get access to statistics information of the name server.

This statement intends to be flexible to support multiple communication protocols in the future, but currently only HTTP access is supported. It requires that BIND 9 be compiled with libxml2 and/or json-c (also known as libjson0); the **statistics-channels** statement is still accepted even if it is built without the library, but any HTTP access will fail with an error. (For details on building BIND, see Section 3.3.)

An **inet** control channel is a TCP socket listening at the specified **ip_port** on the specified **ip_addr**, which can be an IPv4 or IPv6 address. An **ip_addr** of * (asterisk) is interpreted as the IPv4 wildcard address; connections will be accepted on any of the system's IPv4 addresses. To listen on the IPv6 wildcard address, use an **ip_addr** of : :.

If no port is specified, port 80 is used for HTTP channels. The asterisk "*" cannot be used for **ip_port**.

The attempt of opening a statistics channel is restricted by the optional **allow** clause. Connections to the statistics channel are permitted based on the **address_match_list**. If no **allow** clause is present, **named** accepts connection attempts from any address; since the statistics may contain sensitive internal information, it is highly recommended to restrict the source of connection requests appropriately.

If no **statistics-channels** statement is present, **named** will not open any communication channels.

The statistics are available in various formats and views depending on the URI used to access them. For example, if the statistics channel is configured to listen on 127.0.0.1 port 8888, then the statistics are accessible in XML format at http://127.0.0.1:8888/ or http://127.0.0.1:8888/xml. A CSS file is included which can format the XML statistics into tables when viewed with a stylesheet-capable browser, and into charts and graphs using the Google Charts API when using a javascript-capable browser.

Applications that depend on a particular XML schema can request http://127.0.0.1:8888/xml/v2 for version 2 of the statistics XML schema or http://127.0.0.1:8888/xml/v3 for version 3. If the requested schema is supported by the server, then it will respond; if not, it will return a "page not found" error.

Broken-out subsets of the statistics can be viewed at:

- http://127.0.0.1:8888/xml/v3/status (server uptime and last reconfiguration time)

- http://127.0.0.1:8888/xml/v3/server (server and resolver statistics)

- http://127.0.0.1:8888/xml/v3/zones (zone statistics)

- http://127.0.0.1:8888/xml/v3/net (network status and socket statistics)

- http://127.0.0.1:8888/xml/v3/mem (memory manager statistics)

- http://127.0.0.1:8888/xml/v3/tasks (task manager statistics)

- http://127.0.0.1:8888/xml/v3/traffic (traffic sizes)

The new stats schema with the Google Charts API support was introduced in BIND 9.9 when BIND 9 is configured with "--enable-newstats". It was enabled by default in BIND 9.10 and the old XML schema was deprecated. The task manager statistics is introduced in BIND 9.11.

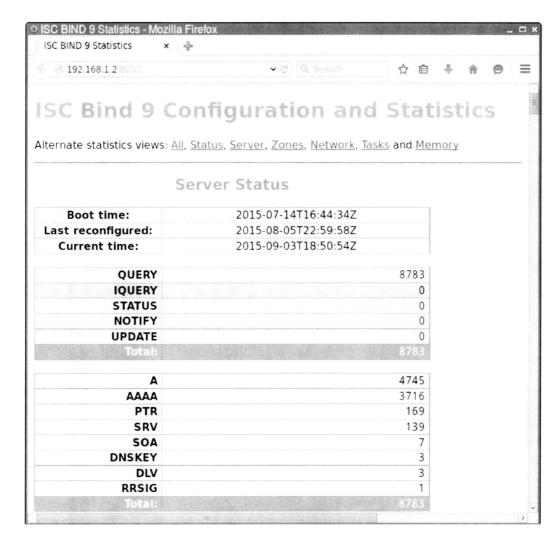

The full set of statistics can also be read in JSON format at http://127.0.0.1:8888/json, with the broken-out subsets at:

- http://127.0.0.1:8888/json/v1/status (server uptime and last reconfiguration time)

- http://127.0.0.1:8888/json/v1/server (server and resolver statistics)

- http://127.0.0.1:8888/json/v1/zones (zone statistics)

- http://127.0.0.1:8888/json/v1/net (network status and socket statistics)

- http://127.0.0.1:8888/json/v1/mem (memory manager statistics)

- http://127.0.0.1:8888/json/v1/tasks (task manager statistics)

- http://127.0.0.1:8888/json/v1/traffic (traffic sizes)

The JSON-based statistics supported was introduced in BIND 9.10. (The task manager statistics is introduced in BIND 9.11.)

An alternative interface to get access to the statistics in plain text format is via the **rndc stats** command which dumps to the file specified by the **statistics-file** configuration option.

6.10   trusted-keys Statement

trusted-keys Statement Grammar

```
trusted-keys {
    string number number number string ;
    string number number number string ; ...
};
```

trusted-keys Statement Definition and Usage

The **trusted-keys** defines DNSSEC security roots. DNSSEC is described in Chapter 10. A security root is defined when the public key for a non-authoritative zone is known, but cannot be securely obtained through DNS, either because it is the DNS root zone or because its parent zone is unsigned. Once a key has been configured as a trusted key, it is treated as if it had been validated and proven secure. The resolver attempts DNSSEC validation on all DNS data in subdomains of a security root.

All keys (and corresponding zones) listed in **trusted-keys** are deemed to exist regardless of what parent zones say. Similarly for all keys listed in **trusted-keys** only those keys are used to validate the DNSKEY RRset. The parent's DS RRset will not be used.

The **trusted-keys** can contain multiple key entries, each consisting of the key's domain name, flags, protocol, algorithm, and the Base-64 representation of the key data. Spaces, tabs, newlines and carriage returns are ignored in the key data, so the configuration may be split up into multiple lines.

trusted-keys may be set at the top level of `named.conf` or within a view. If it is set in both places, they are additive: keys defined at the top level are inherited by all views, but keys defined in a view are only used within that view.

Validation below specified names can be temporarily disabled by using **rndc nta** (as described on page 53). The negative trust anchors support was introduced in BIND 9.11.

6.11   managed-keys Statement

managed-keys Statement Grammar

```
managed-keys {
    name initial-key flags protocol algorithm key-data ;
    name initial-key flags protocol algorithm key-data ; ...
};
```

managed-keys Statement Definition and Usage

The **managed-keys**, like **trusted-keys**, defines DNSSEC security roots. The difference is that **managed-keys** can be kept up to date automatically, without intervention from the resolver operator.

Suppose, for example, that a zone's key-signing key was compromised, and the zone owner had to revoke and replace the key. A resolver which had the old key in a **trusted-keys** statement would be unable to validate this zone any longer; it would reply with a SERVFAIL response code. This would continue until the resolver operator had updated the **trusted-keys** statement with the new key.

If, however, the zone were listed in a **managed-keys** statement instead, then the zone owner could add a "stand-by" key to the zone in advance. **named** would store the stand-by key, and when the original key was revoked, **named** would be able to transition smoothly to the new key. It would also recognize that the old key had been revoked, and cease using that key to validate answers, minimizing the damage that the compromised key could do.

A **managed-keys** statement contains a list of the keys to be managed, along with information about how the keys are to be initialized for the first time. The only initialization method currently supported (as of BIND 9.7.0) is `initial-key`. This means the **managed-keys** statement must contain a copy of the initializing key. (Future releases may allow keys to be initialized by other methods, eliminating this requirement.)

Consequently, a **managed-keys** statement appears similar to a **trusted-keys**, differing in the presence of the second field, containing the keyword `initial-key`. The difference is, whereas the keys listed in a **trusted-keys** continue to be trusted until they are removed from `named.conf`, an initializing key listed in a **managed-keys** statement is only trusted *once*: for as long as it takes to load the managed key database and start the RFC 5011 key maintenance process.

The first time **named** runs with a managed key configured in `named.conf`, it fetches the DNSKEY RRset directly from the zone apex, and validates it using the key specified in the **managed-keys** statement. If the DNSKEY RRset is validly signed, then it is used as the basis for a new managed keys database.

From that point on, whenever **named** runs, it sees the **managed-keys** statement, checks to make sure RFC 5011 key maintenance has already been initialized for the specified domain, and if so, it simply moves on. The key specified in the **managed-keys** is not used to validate answers; it has been superseded by the key or keys stored in the managed keys database.

The next time **named** runs after a name has been *removed* from the **managed-keys** statement, the corresponding zone will be removed from the managed keys database, and RFC 5011 key maintenance will no longer be used for that domain.

named only maintains a single managed keys database; consequently, unlike **trusted-keys**, **managed-keys** may only be set at the top level of `named.conf`, not within a view.

The managed keys database is stored as a master-format zone file called `managed-keys.bind`. When the key database is changed, the zone is updated. As with any other dynamic zone, changes will be written into a journal file, `managed-keys.bind.jnl`. They are committed to the master file as soon as possible afterward; in the case of the managed key database, this will usually occur within 30 seconds. So, whenever **named** is using automatic key maintenance, those two files can be expected to exist in the working directory. (For this reason among others, the working directory should be always be writable by **named**.)

If the **dnssec-validation** option is set to `auto`, **named** will automatically initialize a managed key for the root zone. Similarly, if the **dnssec-lookaside** option is set to `auto`, **named** will automatically initialize a managed key for the zone `dlv.isc.org`. In both cases, the key that is used to initialize the key maintenance process is built into **named**, and can be overridden from **bindkeys-file**.

7 Views and Zones

The **view** is a powerful feature of BIND 9 that lets a name server answer a DNS query differently depending on who is asking. It is particularly useful for implementing split DNS setups without having to run multiple servers.

This chapter also introduces using multiple **named** servers instead of *views* and using an external database with Dynamically Loadable Zones (DLZ).

Zones are defined with the **zone** statement. The data can be stored locally or slaved from another server.

7.1 view Statement

view Statement Grammar

```
view view_name
     class {
     match-clients { address_match_list };
     match-destinations { address_match_list };
     match-recursive-only yes_or_no ;
      view_option; ...
      zone_statement; ...
};
```

view Statement Definition and Usage

Each **view** statement defines a view of the DNS namespace that will be seen by a subset of clients. A client matches a view if its source IP address matches the `address_match_list` of the view's **match-clients** clause and its destination IP address matches the `address_match_list` of the view's **match-destinations** clause. If not specified, both **match-clients** and **match-destinations** default to matching all addresses. In addition to checking IP addresses **match-clients** and **match-destinations** can also take **keys** which provide an mechanism for the client to select the view. A view can also be specified as **match-recursive-only**, which means that only recursive requests from matching clients will match that view. The order of the **view** statements is significant — a client request will be resolved in the context of the first **view** that it matches.

Zones defined within a **view** statement will only be accessible to clients that match the **view**. By defining a zone of the same name in multiple views, different zone data can be given to different clients, for example, "internal" and "external" clients in a split DNS setup.

Many of the options given in the **options** statement can also be used within a **view** statement, and then apply only when resolving queries with that view. When no view-specific value is given, the value in the **options** statement is used as a default. Also, zone options can have default values specified in the **view** statement; these view-specific defaults take precedence over those in the **options** statement.

Views are class specific. If no class is given, class IN is assumed. Note that all non-IN views must contain a hint zone, since only the IN class has compiled-in default hints.

If there are no **view** statements in the config file, a default view that matches any client is automatically created in class IN. Any **zone** statements specified on the top level of the configuration file are considered to be part of this default view, and the **options** statement will apply to the default view. If any explicit **view** statements are present, all **zone** statements must occur inside **view** statements.

Here is an example of a typical split DNS setup implemented using **view** statements:

```
view "internal" {
        // This should match our internal networks.
        match-clients { 10.0.0.0/8; };

        // Provide recursive service to internal
        // clients only.
        recursion yes;

        // Provide a complete view of the example.com
        // zone including addresses of internal hosts.
        zone "example.com" {
        type master;
        file "example-internal.db";
        };
};

view "external" {
        // Match all clients not matched by the
        // previous view.
        match-clients { any; };

        // Refuse recursive service to external clients.
        recursion no;

        // Provide a restricted view of the example.com
        // zone containing only publicly accessible hosts.
        zone "example.com" {
        type master;
        file "example-external.db";
        };
};
```

7.2 zone Statement

zone Statement Grammar

```
zone zone_name class {
    type master;
    allow-query { address_match_list };
    allow-query-on { address_match_list };
    allow-transfer { address_match_list };
    allow-update { address_match_list };
    update-check-ksk yes_or_no;
    dnssec-dnskey-kskonly yes_or_no;
    dnssec-loadkeys-interval number;
    update-policy local | { update_policy_rule ... };
    also-notify { ip_addr port ip_port dscp ip_dscp ;
      ip_addr port ip_port dscp ip_dscp ; ...  };
    check-names (warn|fail|ignore) ;
    check-mx (warn|fail|ignore) ;
    check-wildcard yes_or_no;
    check-spf ( warn | ignore );
    check-integrity yes_or_no ;
    dialup dialup_option ;
    file string ;
    masterfile-format (text|raw|map) ;
    journal string ;
    max-journal-size size_spec;
    forward (only|first) ;
    forwarders {  ip_addr port ip_port dscp ip_dscp ; ...  };
    ixfr-base string ;
    ixfr-from-differences yes_or_no;
    ixfr-tmp-file string ;
    request-ixfr yes_or_no ;
    maintain-ixfr-base yes_or_no ;
    max-ixfr-log-size number ;
    max-transfer-idle-out number ;
    max-transfer-time-out number ;
    notify yes_or_no | explicit | master-only ;
    notify-delay seconds ;
    notify-to-soa yes_or_no;
    pubkey number number number string ;
    notify-source (ip4_addr | *) port ip_port dscp ip_dscp ;
    notify-source-v6 (ip6_addr | *) port ip_port dscp ip_dscp ;
    zone-statistics full | terse | none;
    sig-validity-interval number number ;
    sig-signing-nodes number ;
    sig-signing-signatures number ;
    sig-signing-type number ;
    database string ;
    min-refresh-time number ;
    max-refresh-time number ;
```

```
        min-retry-time number ;
        max-retry-time number ;
        key-directory path_name;
        auto-dnssec allow|maintain|off;
        inline-signing yes_or_no;
        zero-no-soa-ttl yes_or_no ;
        serial-update-method increment|unixtime|date;
        max-zone-ttl number ;
};

zone zone_name class {
    type slave;
        allow-notify { address_match_list };
        allow-query { address_match_list };
        allow-query-on { address_match_list };
        allow-transfer { address_match_list };
        allow-update-forwarding { address_match_list };
        dnssec-update-mode ( maintain | no-resign );
        update-check-ksk yes_or_no;
        dnssec-dnskey-kskonly yes_or_no;
        dnssec-loadkeys-interval number;
        dnssec-secure-to-insecure yes_or_no ;
        try-tcp-refresh yes_or_no;
        also-notify port ip_port dscp ip_dscp { ( masters_list | ip_addr
                port ip_port
                dscp ip_dscp
                key key ) ; ... };
        check-names (warn|fail|ignore) ;
        dialup dialup_option ;
        file string ;
        masterfile-format (text|raw|map) ;
        journal string ;
        max-journal-size size_spec;
        forward (only|first) ;
        forwarders { ip_addr port ip_port dscp ip_dscp ; ... };
        ixfr-base string ;
        ixfr-from-differences yes_or_no;
        ixfr-tmp-file string ;
        maintain-ixfr-base yes_or_no ;
        masters port ip_port dscp ip_dscp { ( masters_list | ip_addr
                port ip_port
                dscp ip_dscp
                key key ) ; ... };
        max-ixfr-log-size number ;
        max-transfer-idle-in number ;
        max-transfer-idle-out number ;
        max-transfer-time-in number ;
        max-transfer-time-out number ;
        notify yes_or_no | explicit | master-only ;
        notify-delay seconds ;
        notify-to-soa yes_or_no;
```

```
        pubkey number number number string ;
        transfer-source (ip4_addr | *) port ip_port dscp ip_dscp ;
        transfer-source-v6 (ip6_addr | *) port ip_port dscp ip_dscp ;
        alt-transfer-source (ip4_addr | *) port ip_port dscp ip_dscp ;
        alt-transfer-source-v6 (ip6_addr | *)
            port ip_port
            dscp ip_dscp ;
        use-alt-transfer-source yes_or_no;
        notify-source (ip4_addr | *) port ip_port dscp ip_dscp ;
        notify-source-v6 (ip6_addr | *) port ip_port dscp ip_dscp ;
        zone-statistics full | terse | none;
        sig-validity-interval number number ;
        sig-signing-nodes number ;
        sig-signing-signatures number ;
        sig-signing-type number ;
        database string ;
        min-refresh-time number ;
        max-refresh-time number ;
        min-retry-time number ;
        max-retry-time number ;
        key-directory path_name;
        auto-dnssec allow|maintain|off;
        inline-signing yes_or_no;
        multi-master yes_or_no ;
        zero-no-soa-ttl yes_or_no ;
};

zone zone_name class {
    type hint;
    file string ;
    delegation-only yes_or_no ;

};

zone zone_name class {
    type stub;
    allow-query { address_match_list };
    allow-query-on { address_match_list };
    check-names (warn|fail|ignore) ;
    dialup dialup_option ;
    delegation-only yes_or_no ;
    file string ;
    masterfile-format (text|raw|map) ;
    forward (only|first) ;
    forwarders { ip_addr port ip_port dscp ip_dscp ; ... };
    masters port ip_port dscp ip_dscp { ( masters_list | ip_addr
            port ip_port
            dscp ip_dscp
            key key ) ; ... };
    max-transfer-idle-in number ;
    max-transfer-time-in number ;
```

```
        pubkey number number number string ;
        transfer-source (ip4_addr | *) port ip_port dscp ip_dscp ;
        transfer-source-v6 (ip6_addr | *)
          port ip_port dscp ip_dscp ;
        alt-transfer-source (ip4_addr | *) port ip_port dscp ip_dscp ;
        alt-transfer-source-v6 (ip6_addr | *)
            port ip_port dscp ip_dscp ;
        use-alt-transfer-source yes_or_no;
        zone-statistics full | terse | none;
        database string ;
        min-refresh-time number ;
        max-refresh-time number ;
        min-retry-time number ;
        max-retry-time number ;
        multi-master yes_or_no ;
};

zone zone_name class {
    type static-stub;
        allow-query { address_match_list };
        server-addresses {  ip_addr ; ...  };
        server-names {  namelist  };
        zone-statistics full | terse | none;
};

zone zone_name class {
    type forward;
        forward (only|first) ;
        forwarders {  ip_addr port ip_port dscp ip_dscp ; ...  };
        delegation-only yes_or_no ;
};

zone "." class {
    type redirect;
    file string ;
        masterfile-format (text|raw|map) ;
        allow-query { address_match_list };
        max-zone-ttl number ;
};

zone zone_name class {
    type delegation-only;
};

zone zone_name class {
        in-view string ;
};
```

zone Statement Definition and Usage

Zone Types

The **type** keyword is required for the **zone** configuration unless it is an **in-view** configuration. Its acceptable values include: `delegation-only`, `forward`, `hint`, `master`, `redirect`, `slave`, `static-stub`, and `stub`.

`master`

 The server has a master copy of the data for the zone and will be able to provide authoritative answers for it.

`slave`

 A slave zone is a replica of a master zone. The **masters** list specifies one or more IP addresses of master servers that the slave contacts to update its copy of the zone. Masters list elements can also be names of other masters lists. By default, transfers are made from port 53 on the servers; this can be changed for all servers by specifying a port number before the list of IP addresses, or on a per-server basis after the IP address. Authentication to the master can also be done with per-server TSIG keys.

 If a file is specified, then the replica will be written to this file whenever the zone is changed, and reloaded from this file on a server restart. Use of a file is recommended, since it often speeds server startup and eliminates a needless waste of bandwidth.

 Note that for large numbers (in the tens or hundreds of thousands) of zones per server, it is best to use a two-level naming scheme for zone filenames. For example, a slave server for the zone `example.com` might place the zone contents into a file called `ex/example.com` where `ex/` is just the first two letters of the zone name. (Most operating systems behave very slowly if you put 100000 files into a single directory.)

`stub`

 A stub zone is similar to a slave zone, except that it replicates only the NS records of a master zone instead of the entire zone. Stub zones are not a standard part of the DNS; they are a feature specific to the BIND implementation.

 Stub zones can be used to eliminate the need for glue NS record in a parent zone at the expense of maintaining a stub zone entry and a set of name server addresses in `named.conf`. This usage is not recommended for new configurations, and BIND 9 supports it only in a limited way. In BIND 4/8, zone transfers of a parent zone included the NS records from stub children of that zone. This meant that, in some cases, users could get away with configuring child stubs only in the master server for the parent zone. BIND 9 never mixes together zone data from different zones in this way. Therefore, if a BIND 9 master serving a parent zone has child stub zones configured, all the slave servers for the parent zone also need to have the same child stub zones configured. Stub zones can also be used as a way of forcing the resolution of a given domain to use a particular set of authoritative servers. For example, the caching name servers on a private network using RFC1918 addressing may be configured with stub zones for `10.in-addr.arpa` to use a set of internal name servers as the authoritative servers for that domain.

`static-stub`

 A static-stub zone is similar to a stub zone with the following exceptions: the zone data is statically configured, rather than transferred from a master server; when recursion is necessary for a query that matches a static-stub zone, the locally configured data (nameserver names and glue addresses) is always used even if different authoritative information is cached.

Zone data is configured via the **server-addresses** and **server-names** zone options.

The zone data is maintained in the form of NS and (if necessary) glue A or AAAA RRs internally, which can be seen by dumping zone databases by **rndc dumpdb -all**. The configured RRs are considered local configuration parameters rather than public data. Non recursive queries (i.e., those with the RD bit off) to a static-stub zone are therefore prohibited and will be responded with REFUSED.

Since the data is statically configured, no zone maintenance action takes place for a static-stub zone.

For example, there is no periodic refresh attempt, and an incoming notify message will be rejected with an rcode of NOTAUTH.

Each static-stub zone is configured with internally generated NS and (if necessary) glue A or AAAA RRs

forward

A "forward zone" is a way to configure forwarding on a per-domain basis. A **zone** statement of type **forward** can contain a **forward** and/or **forwarders** statement, which will apply to queries within the domain given by the zone name. If no **forwarders** statement is present or an empty list for **forwarders** is given, then no forwarding will be done for the domain, canceling the effects of any forwarders in the **options** statement. Thus if you want to use this type of zone to change the behavior of the global **forward** option (that is, "forward first" to, then "forward only", or vice versa, but want to use the same servers as set globally) you need to re-specify the global forwarders.

hint

The initial set of root name servers is specified using a "hint zone". When the server starts up, it uses the root hints to find a root name server and get the most recent list of root name servers. If no hint zone is specified for class IN, the server uses a compiled-in default set of root servers hints. Classes other than IN have no built-in defaults hints.

redirect

Redirect zones are used to provide answers to queries when normal resolution would result in NXDOMAIN being returned. (The `redirect` type was introduced in BIND 9.9.) Only one redirect zone is supported per view. **allow-query** can be used to restrict which clients see these answers.

If the client has requested DNSSEC records (DO=1) and the NXDOMAIN response is signed then no substitution will occur.

To redirect all NXDOMAIN responses to 100.100.100.2 and 2001:ffff:ffff::100.100.100.2, one would configure a type redirect zone named ".", with the zone file containing wildcard records that point to the desired addresses: `"*.IN A 100.100.100.2"` and `"*.IN AAAA 2 001:ffff:ffff::100.100.100.2"`.

To redirect all Spanish names (under .ES) one would use similar entries but with the names "*.ES." instead of "*.". To redirect all commercial Spanish names (under COM.ES) one would use wildcard entries called "*.COM.ES.".

Note that the redirect zone supports all possible types; it is not limited to A and AAAA records.

Because redirect zones are not referenced directly by name, they are not kept in the zone lookup table with normal master and slave zones. Consequently, it is not currently possible to use **rndc reload *zonename*** to reload a redirect zone. However, when using **rndc reload** without specifying a zone name, redirect zones will be reloaded along with other zones.

`delegation-only`

This is used to enforce the delegation-only status of infrastructure zones (e.g. COM, NET, ORG). Any answer that is received without an explicit or implicit delegation in the authority section will be treated as NXDOMAIN. This does not apply to the zone apex. This should not be applied to leaf zones.

`delegation-only` has no effect on answers received from forwarders.

See caveats on page 98.

Class

The zone's name may optionally be followed by a class. If a class is not specified, class `IN` (for `Internet`), is assumed. This is correct for the vast majority of cases.

The `hesiod` class is named for an information service from MIT's Project Athena. It is used to share information about various systems databases, such as users, groups, printers and so on. The keyword `HS` is a synonym for hesiod.

Another MIT development is Chaosnet, a LAN protocol created in the mid-1970s. Zone data for it can be specified with the `CHAOS` class.

Zone Options

allow-notify
See the description of **allow-notify** in Section 6.7.

allow-query
See the description of **allow-query** in Section 6.7.

allow-query-on
See the description of **allow-query-on** in Section 6.7.

allow-transfer
See the description of **allow-transfer** in Section 6.7.

allow-update
See the description of **allow-update** in Section 6.7.

update-policy
Specifies a "Simple Secure Update" policy. See Section 9.2.

allow-update-forwarding
See the description of **allow-update-forwarding** in Section 6.7.

also-notify

Only meaningful if **notify** is active for this zone. The set of machines that will receive a DNS
NOTIFY message for this zone is made up of all the listed name servers (other than the primary
master) for the zone plus any IP addresses specified with **also-notify**. A port may be specified
with each **also-notify** address to send the notify messages to a port other than the default of
53. A TSIG key may also be specified to cause the NOTIFY to be signed by the given key.
also-notify is not meaningful for stub zones. The default is the empty list.

check-names

This option is used to restrict the character set and syntax of certain domain names in master
files and/or DNS responses received from the network. The default varies according to zone
type. For **master** zones the default is **fail**. For **slave** zones the default is **warn**. It is not
implemented for **hint** zones.

check-mx

See the description of **check-mx** in Section 6.7.

check-spf

See the description of **check-spf** in Section 6.7.

check-wildcard

See the description of **check-wildcard** in Section 6.7.

check-integrity

See the description of **check-integrity** in Section 6.7.

check-sibling

See the description of **check-sibling** in Section 6.7.

zero-no-soa-ttl

See the description of **zero-no-soa-ttl** in Section 6.7.

update-check-ksk

See the description of **update-check-ksk** in Section 6.7.

dnssec-loadkeys-interval

See the description of **dnssec-loadkeys-interval** in Section 6.7.

dnssec-update-mode

See the description of **dnssec-update-mode** in Section 6.7.

dnssec-dnskey-kskonly

See the description of **dnssec-dnskey-kskonly** in Section 6.7.

try-tcp-refresh

See the description of **try-tcp-refresh** in Section 6.7.

database

Specify the type of database to be used for storing the zone data. The string following the
database keyword is interpreted as a list of whitespace-delimited words. The first word identifies the database type, and any subsequent words are passed as arguments to the database to be
interpreted in a way specific to the database type.

The default is `"rbt"`, BIND 9's native in-memory red-black-tree database. This database does not take arguments.

Other values are possible if additional database drivers have been linked into the server. Some sample drivers are included with the distribution but none are linked in by default. For more information, see Section 7.7.

dialup

See the description of **dialup** in Section 6.7.

delegation-only

The flag only applies to forward, hint and stub zones. If set to **yes**, then the zone will also be treated as if it is also a delegation-only type zone.

See caveats on page 98.

forward

Only meaningful if the zone has a forwarders list. The **only** value causes the lookup to fail after trying the forwarders and getting no answer, while **first** would allow a normal lookup to be tried.

forwarders

Used to override the list of global forwarders. If it is not specified in a zone of type **forward**, no forwarding is done for the zone and the global options are not used.

ixfr-base

This was used in BIND 8 to specify the name of the transaction log (journal) file for dynamic update and IXFR. BIND 9 ignores the option and constructs the name of the journal file by appending `".jnl"` to the name of the zone file.

ixfr-tmp-file

This was an undocumented option in BIND 8. Ity is ignored in BIND 9.

journal

Allow the default journal's filename to be overridden. The default is the zone's filename with `".jnl"` appended. This is applicable to **master** and **slave** zones.

max-journal-size

See the description of **max-journal-size** in Section 6.7.

max-transfer-time-in

See the description of **max-transfer-time-in** in Section 6.7.

max-transfer-idle-in

See the description of **max-transfer-idle-in** in Section 6.7.

max-transfer-time-out

See the description of **max-transfer-time-out** in Section 6.7.

max-transfer-idle-out

See the description of **max-transfer-idle-out** in Section 6.7.

notify

See the description of **notify** in Section 6.7.

notify-delay

See the description of **notify-delay** in Section 6.7.

notify-to-soa

See the description of **notify-to-soa** in Section 6.7.

pubkey

In BIND 8, this option was intended for specifying a public zone key for verification of signatures in DNSSEC signed zones when they are loaded from disk. BIND 9 does not verify signatures on load and ignores the option.

zone-statistics

If **yes**, the server will keep statistical information for this zone, which can be dumped to the **statistics-file** defined in the server options. See the description of **zone-statistics** in Section 6.7.

server-addresses

Only meaningful for static-stub zones. This is a list of IP addresses to which queries should be sent in recursive resolution for the zone. A non empty list for this option will internally configure the apex NS RR with associated glue A or AAAA RRs.

For example, if "example.com" is configured as a static-stub zone with 192.0.2.1 and 2001:db8::1234 in a **server-addresses** option, the following RRs will be internally configured.

```
example.com. NS example.com.
example.com. A 192.0.2.1
example.com. AAAA 2001:db8::1234
```

These records are internally used to resolve names under the static-stub zone. For instance, if the server receives a query for "www.example.com" with the RD bit on, the server will initiate recursive resolution and send queries to 192.0.2.1 and/or 2001:db8::1234.

server-names

Only meaningful for static-stub zones. This is a list of domain names of nameservers that act as authoritative servers of the static-stub zone. These names will be resolved to IP addresses when **named** needs to send queries to these servers. To make this supplemental resolution successful, these names must not be a subdomain of the origin name of static-stub zone. That is, when "example.net" is the origin of a static-stub zone, "ns.example" and "master.example.com" can be specified in the **server-names** option, but "ns.example.net" cannot, and will be rejected by the configuration parser.

A non empty list for this option will internally configure the apex NS RR with the specified names. For example, if "example.com" is configured as a static-stub zone with "ns1.example.net" and "ns2.example.net" in a **server-names** option, the following RRs will be internally configured.

```
example.com. NS ns1.example.net.
example.com. NS ns2.example.net.
```

These records are internally used to resolve names under the static-stub zone. For instance, if the server receives a query for "www.example.com" with the RD bit on, the server initiate recursive resolution, resolve "ns1.example.net" and/or "ns2.example.net" to IP addresses, and then send queries to (one or more of) these addresses.

sig-validity-interval

See the description of **sig-validity-interval** in Section 6.7.

sig-signing-nodes

See the description of **sig-signing-nodes** in Section 6.7.

sig-signing-signatures

See the description of **sig-signing-signatures** in Section 6.7.

sig-signing-type

See the description of **sig-signing-type** in Section 6.7.

transfer-source

See the description of **transfer-source** in Section 6.7.

transfer-source-v6

See the description of **transfer-source-v6** in Section 6.7.

alt-transfer-source

See the description of **alt-transfer-source** in Section 6.7.

alt-transfer-source-v6

See the description of **alt-transfer-source-v6** in Section 6.7.

use-alt-transfer-source

See the description of **use-alt-transfer-source** in Section 6.7.

notify-source

See the description of **notify-source** in Section 6.7.

notify-source-v6

See the description of **notify-source-v6** in Section 6.7.

min-refresh-time, max-refresh-time, min-retry-time, max-retry-time

See the description in Section 6.7.

ixfr-from-differences

See the description of **ixfr-from-differences** in Section 6.7. (Note that the **ixfr-from-differences** `master` and `slave` choices are not available at the zone level.)

key-directory

See the description of **key-directory** in Section 6.7.

auto-dnssec

See the description of **auto-dnssec** in Section 6.7.

serial-update-method

See the description of **serial-update-method** in Section 6.7.

inline-signing

If `yes`, this enables "bump in the wire" signing of a zone, where a unsigned zone is transferred in or loaded from disk and a signed version of the zone is served, with possibly, a different serial number. This behavior is disabled by default. (This **inline-signing** feature was introduced in BIND 9.9.)

multi-master

> See the description of **multi-master** in Section 6.7.

masterfile-format

> See the description of **masterfile-format** in Section 6.7.

max-zone-ttl

> See the description of **max-zone-ttl** in Section 6.7.

dnssec-secure-to-insecure

> See the description of **dnssec-secure-to-insecure** in Section 6.7.

7.3   Multiple views

When multiple views are in use, a zone may be referenced by more than one of them. Often, the views will contain different zones with the same name, allowing different clients to receive different answers for the same queries. At times, however, it is desirable for multiple views to contain identical zones. The **in-view** zone option (introduced in BIND 9.10) provides an efficient way to do this: it allows a view to reference a zone that was defined in a previously configured view. Example:

```
view internal {
    match-clients { 10/8; };

    zone example.com {
  type master;
  file "example-external.db";
    };
};

view external {
    match-clients { any; };

    zone example.com {
  in-view internal;
    };
};
```

An **in-view** option cannot refer to a view that is configured later in the configuration file.

A **zone** statement which uses the **in-view** option may not use any other options with the exception of **forward** and **forwarders**. (These options control the behavior of the containing view, rather than changing the zone object itself.)

Zone level acls (e.g. allow-query, allow-transfer) and other configuration details of the zone are all set in the view the referenced zone is defined in. Care need to be taken to ensure that acls are wide enough for all views referencing the zone.

An **in-view** zone cannot be used as a response policy zone.

An **in-view** zone is not intended to reference a **forward** zone.

7.4 Split DNS

This section covers an alternative way without using the **view** statement by using multiple **named** servers to provide different *views* for DNS.

Setting up different visibility of the DNS space to internal and external resolvers is usually referred to as a *Split DNS* setup. There are several reasons an organization would want to set up its DNS this way.

One common reason for setting up a DNS system this way is to hide "internal" DNS information from "external" clients on the Internet. There is some debate as to whether or not this is actually useful. Internal DNS information leaks out in many ways (via email headers, for example) and most savvy "attackers" can find the information they need using other means. However, since listing addresses of internal servers that external clients cannot possibly reach can result in connection delays and other annoyances, an organization may choose to use a Split DNS to present a consistent view of itself to the outside world.

Another common reason for setting up a Split DNS system is to allow internal networks that are behind filters or in RFC 1918 space (reserved IP space, as documented in RFC 1918) to resolve DNS on the Internet. Split DNS can also be used to allow mail from outside back in to the internal network.

Example split DNS setup

Let's say a company named *Example, Inc.* (`example.com`) has several corporate sites that have an internal network with reserved Internet Protocol (IP) space and an external demilitarized zone (DMZ), or "outside" section of a network, that is available to the public.

Example, Inc. wants its internal clients to be able to resolve external hostnames and to exchange mail with people on the outside. The company also wants its internal resolvers to have access to certain internal-only zones that are not available at all outside of the internal network.

In order to accomplish this, the company will set up two sets of name servers. One set will be on the inside network (in the reserved IP space) and the other set will be on bastion hosts, which are "proxy" hosts that can talk to both sides of its network, in the DMZ.

The internal servers will be configured to forward all queries, except queries for `site1.internal`, `site2.internal`, `site1.example.com`, and `site2.example.com`, to the servers in the DMZ. These internal servers will have complete sets of information for `site1.example.com`, `site2.example.com`, `site1.internal`, and `site2.internal`.

To protect the `site1.internal` and `site2.internal` domains, the internal name servers must be configured to disallow all queries to these domains from any external hosts, including the bastion hosts.

The external servers, which are on the bastion hosts, will be configured to serve the "public" version of the `site1` and `site2.example.com` zones. This could include things such as the host records for public servers (`www.example.com` and `ftp.example.com`), and mail exchange (MX) records (`a.mx.example.com` and `b.mx.example.com`).

In addition, the public `site1` and `site2.example.com` zones should have special MX records that contain wildcard (`*`) records pointing to the bastion hosts. This is needed because external mail servers do not have any other way of looking up how to deliver mail to those internal hosts. With the wildcard records, the mail will be delivered to the bastion host, which can then forward it on to internal hosts.

Here's an example of a wildcard MX record:

```
*   IN MX 10 external1.example.com.
```

Now that they accept mail on behalf of anything in the internal network, the bastion hosts will need to know how to deliver mail to internal hosts. In order for this to work properly, the resolvers on the bastion hosts will need to be configured to point to the internal name servers for DNS resolution.

Queries for internal hostnames will be answered by the internal servers, and queries for external hostnames will be forwarded back out to the DNS servers on the bastion hosts.

In order for all this to work properly, internal clients will need to be configured to query *only* the internal name servers for DNS queries. This could also be enforced via selective filtering on the network.

If everything has been set properly, *Example, Inc.*'s internal clients will now be able to:

- Look up any hostnames in the `site1` and `site2.example.com` zones.

- Look up any hostnames in the `site1.internal` and `site2.internal` domains.

- Look up any hostnames on the Internet.

- Exchange mail with both internal and external people.

Hosts on the Internet will be able to:

- Look up any hostnames in the `site1` and `site2.example.com` zones.

- Exchange mail with anyone in the `site1` and `site2.example.com` zones.

Here is an example configuration for the setup just described above. Note that this is only configuration information; for information on how to configure your zone files, see Section 5.5.

Internal DNS server config:

```
acl internals { 172.16.72.0/24; 192.168.1.0/24; };

acl externals { bastion-ips-go-here; };

options {
    ...
    ...
    forward only;
    // forward to external servers
    forwarders {
  bastion-ips-go-here;
    };
```

```
    // sample allow-transfer (no one)
    allow-transfer { none; };
    // restrict query access
    allow-query { internals; externals; };
    // restrict recursion
    allow-recursion { internals; };
    ...
    ...
};

// sample master zone
zone "site1.example.com" {
  type master;
  file "m/site1.example.com";
  // do normal iterative resolution (do not forward)
  forwarders { };
  allow-query { internals; externals; };
  allow-transfer { internals; };
};

// sample slave zone
zone "site2.example.com" {
  type slave;
  file "s/site2.example.com";
  masters { 172.16.72.3; };
  forwarders { };
  allow-query { internals; externals; };
  allow-transfer { internals; };
};

zone "site1.internal" {
  type master;
  file "m/site1.internal";
  forwarders { };
  allow-query { internals; };
  allow-transfer { internals; }
};

zone "site2.internal" {
  type slave;
  file "s/site2.internal";
  masters { 172.16.72.3; };
  forwarders { };
  allow-query { internals };
  allow-transfer { internals; }
};
```

External (bastion host) DNS server config:

```
acl internals { 172.16.72.0/24; 192.168.1.0/24; };

acl externals { bastion-ips-go-here; };
```

```
options {
  ...
  ...
  // sample allow-transfer (no one)
  allow-transfer { none; };
  // default query access
  allow-query { any; };
  // restrict cache access
  allow-query-cache { internals; externals; };
  // restrict recursion
  allow-recursion { internals; externals; };
  ...
  ...
};

// sample slave zone
zone "site1.example.com" {
  type master;
  file "m/site1.foo.com";
  allow-transfer { internals; externals; };
};

zone "site2.example.com" {
  type slave;
  file "s/site2.foo.com";
  masters { another_bastion_host_maybe; };
  allow-transfer { internals; externals; }
};
```

In the `resolv.conf` (or equivalent) on the bastion host(s):

```
search ...
nameserver 172.16.72.2
nameserver 172.16.72.3
nameserver 172.16.72.4
```

7.5 Notify

DNS NOTIFY is a mechanism that allows master servers to notify their slave servers of changes to a zone's data. In response to a **NOTIFY** from a master server, the slave will check to see that its version of the zone is the current version and, if not, initiate a zone transfer.

For more information about DNS **NOTIFY**, see the description of the **notify** option in Section 6.7 and the description of the zone option **also-notify** in Section 6.7. The **NOTIFY** protocol is specified in RFC 1996.

Note
As a slave zone can also be a master to other slaves, **named**, by default, sends **NOTIFY** messages for every zone it loads. Specifying **notify master-only;** will cause **named** to only send **NOTIFY** for master zones that it loads.

7.6 Incremental Zone Transfers (IXFR)

The incremental zone transfer (IXFR) protocol is a way for slave servers to transfer only changed data, instead of having to transfer the entire zone. The IXFR protocol is specified in RFC 1995, "Incremental Zone Transfer in DNS".

When acting as a master, BIND 9 supports IXFR for those zones where the necessary change history information is available. These include master zones maintained by dynamic update and slave zones whose data was obtained by IXFR. For manually maintained master zones, and for slave zones obtained by performing a full zone transfer (AXFR), IXFR is supported only if the option **ixfr-from-differences** is set to **yes**.

When acting as a slave, BIND 9 will attempt to use IXFR unless it is explicitly disabled. For more information about disabling IXFR, see the description of the **request-ixfr** clause of the **server** statement on page 147.

7.7 DLZ (Dynamically Loadable Zones)

DLZ (Dynamically Loadable Zones) is an extension to BIND 9 that allows zone data to be retrieved directly from an external database. There is no required format or schema. DLZ drivers exist for several different database backends including PostgreSQL, MySQL, and LDAP and can be written for any other.

Historically, DLZ drivers had to be statically linked with the **named** binary and were turned on via a configure option at compile time (for example, **"configure --with-dlz-ldap"**). Currently, the drivers provided in the BIND 9 tarball in `contrib/dlz/drivers` are still linked this way.

In BIND 9.8 and higher, it is possible to link some DLZ modules dynamically at runtime, via the DLZ "dlopen" driver, which acts as a generic wrapper around a shared object implementing the DLZ API. The "dlopen" driver is linked into **named** by default, so configure options are no longer necessary when using these dynamically linkable drivers, but are still needed for the older drivers in `contrib/dlz/drivers`.

When the DLZ module provides data to **named**, it does so in text format. The response is converted to DNS wire format by **named**. This conversion, and the lack of any internal caching, places significant limits on the query performance of DLZ modules. Consequently, DLZ is not recommended for use on high-volume servers. However, it can be used in a hidden master configuration, with slaves retrieving zone updates via AXFR.

Note

DLZ has no built-in support for DNS notify; slaves are not automatically informed of changes to the zones in the database.

Configuring DLZ

A DLZ database is configured with a **dlz** statement in `named.conf`:

```
dlz example {
    database "dlopen driver.so args";
    search yes;
};
```

This specifies a DLZ module to search when answering queries; the module is implemented in `driver.so` and is loaded at runtime by the dlopen DLZ driver. Multiple **dlz** statements can be specified; when answering a query, all DLZ modules with `search` set to `yes` will be queried to find out if they contain an answer for the query name; the best available answer will be returned to the client.

Support for multiple Dynamically Loadable Zones and the DLZ `search` option was introduced in BIND 9.10.

The `search` option in the above example can be omitted, because `yes` is the default value.

If `search` is set to `no`, then this DLZ module is *not* searched for the best match when a query is received. Instead, zones in this DLZ must be separately specified in a zone statement. This allows you to configure a zone normally using standard zone option semantics, but specify a different database back-end for storage of the zone's data. For example, to implement NXDOMAIN redirection using a DLZ module for back-end storage of redirection rules:

```
dlz other {
    database "dlopen driver.so args";
    search no;
};

zone "." {
    type redirect;
    dlz other;
};
```

Sample DLZ Driver

For guidance in implementation of DLZ modules, the directory `contrib/dlz/example` contains a basic dynamically-linkable DLZ module--i.e., one which can be loaded at runtime by the "dlopen" DLZ driver. The example sets up a single zone, whose name is passed to the module as an argument in the **dlz** statement:

```
dlz other {
    database "dlopen driver.so example.nil";
};
```

In the above example, the module is configured to create a zone "example.nil", which can answer queries and AXFR requests, and accept DDNS updates. At runtime, prior to any updates, the zone contains an SOA, NS, and a single A record at the apex:

```
example.nil.  3600    IN      SOA     example.nil. hostmaster.example. ↩
    nil. (
                                        123 900 600 86400 3600
                            )
example.nil.  3600    IN      NS      example.nil.
example.nil.  1800    IN      A       10.53.0.1
```

The sample driver is capable of retrieving information about the querying client, and altering its response on the basis of this information. To demonstrate this feature, the example driver responds to queries for "source-addr.`zonename`>/TXT" with the source address of the query. Note, however, that this record will *not* be included in AXFR or ANY responses. Normally, this feature would be used to alter responses in some other fashion, e.g., by providing different address records for a particular name depending on the network from which the query arrived. (The *source-addr* feature was introduced in BIND 9.9.)

Documentation of the DLZ module API can be found in the BIND source at `contrib/dlz/example/README`. This directory also contains the header file `dlz_minimal.h`, which defines the API and should be included by any dynamically-linkable DLZ module.

8 DNS Lookup Tools

The **dig**, **delv**, **host**, and **nslookup** programs are all command line tools for manually querying name servers. They differ in style and output format.

The domain information groper (**dig**) is the most versatile and complete of these lookup tools. It has two modes: simple interactive mode for a single query, and batch mode which executes a query for each in a list of several query lines. All query options are accessible from the command line. The usual simple use of **dig** will take the form

dig @server domain query-type query-class

The **host** utility emphasizes simplicity and ease of use. By default, it converts between host names and Internet addresses, but its functionality can be extended with the use of options. **nslookup** has two modes: interactive and non-interactive. Interactive mode allows the user to query name servers for information about various hosts and domains or to print a list of hosts in a domain. Non-interactive mode is used to print just the name and requested information for a host or domain. Interactive mode is entered when no arguments are given (the default name server will be used) or when the first argument is a hyphen (`-') and the second argument is the host name or Internet address of a name server. Non-interactive mode is used when the name or Internet address of the host to be looked up is given as the first argument. The optional second argument specifies the host name or address of a name server.

Warning
Due to its arcane user interface and frequently inconsistent behavior, it is not recommended to use **nslookup**. Use **dig** instead.

The newer domain entity lookup and validation tool **delv** has **dig**-like semantics for looking up DNS data and performing internal DNSSEC validation. This allows easy validation in environments where the resolver may not be trustworthy, and assists with troubleshooting of DNSSEC problems.

8.1   delv — DNS lookup and validation utility

Synopsis

delv [@server] [-4] [-6] [-a *anchor-file*] [-b *address*] [-c *class*] [-d *level*] [-i] [-m] [-p *port#*] [-q *name*] [-t *type*] [-x *addr*] [name] [type] [class] [queryopt...]

delv [-h]

delv [-v]

delv [queryopt...] [query...]

delv Description

delv (Domain Entity Lookup & Validation) is a tool for sending DNS queries and validating the results, using the same internal resolver and validator logic as **named**. (This tool was introduced in BIND 9.10.)

delv will send to a specified name server all queries needed to fetch and validate the requested data; this includes the original requested query, subsequent queries to follow CNAME or DNAME chains, and queries for DNSKEY, DS and DLV records to establish a chain of trust for DNSSEC validation. It does not perform iterative resolution, but simulates the behavior of a name server configured for DNSSEC validating and forwarding.

By default, responses are validated using built-in DNSSEC trust anchors for the root zone (".") and for the ISC DNSSEC lookaside validation zone ("dlv.isc.org"). Records returned by **delv** are either fully validated or were not signed. If validation fails, an explanation of the failure is included in the output; the validation process can be traced in detail. Because **delv** does not rely on an external server to carry out validation, it can be used to check the validity of DNS responses in environments where local name servers may not be trustworthy.

Unless it is told to query a specific name server, **delv** will try each of the servers listed in /etc/resolv.conf. If no usable server addresses are found, **delv** will send queries to the localhost addresses (127.0.0.1 for IPv4, ::1 for IPv6).

When no command line arguments or options are given, **delv** will perform an NS query for "." (the root zone).

delv Simple Usage

A typical invocation of **delv** looks like:

```
delv @server name type
```

where:

server

> is the name or IP address of the name server to query. This can be an IPv4 address in dotted-decimal notation or an IPv6 address in colon-delimited notation. When the supplied *server* argument is a hostname, **delv** resolves that name before querying that name server (note, however, that this initial lookup is *not* validated by DNSSEC).
>
> If no *server* argument is provided, **delv** consults /etc/resolv.conf; if an address is found there, it queries the name server at that address. If either of the -4 or -6 options are in use, then only addresses for the corresponding transport will be tried. If no usable addresses are found, **delv** will send queries to the localhost addresses (127.0.0.1 for IPv4, ::1 for IPv6).

name

> is the domain name to be looked up.

type

> indicates what type of query is required — ANY, A, MX, etc. *type* can be any valid query type. If no *type* argument is supplied, **delv** will perform a lookup for an A record.

delv Options

-a *anchor-file*

> Specifies a file from which to read DNSSEC trust anchors. The default is /etc/bind.keys, which is included with BIND 9 and contains trust anchors for the root zone (".") and for the ISC DNSSEC lookaside validation zone ("dlv.isc.org").
>
> Keys that do not match the root or DLV trust-anchor names are ignored; these key names can be overridden using the +dlv=NAME or +root=NAME options.

> ---
> **Note**
> When reading the trust anchor file, **delv** treats managed-keys statements and trusted-keys statements identically. That is, for a managed key, it is the *initial* key that is trusted; RFC 5011 key management is not supported. **delv** will not consult the managed-keys database maintained by **named**. This means that if either of the keys in /etc/bind.keys is revoked and rolled over, it will be necessary to update /etc/bind.keys to use DNSSEC validation in **delv**.
> ---

-b *address*

> Sets the source IP address of the query to *address*. This must be a valid address on one of the host's network interfaces or "0.0.0.0" or "::". An optional source port may be specified by appending "#<port>"

-c *class*

> Sets the query class for the requested data. Currently, only class "IN" is supported in **delv** and any other value is ignored.

-d *level*

> Set the systemwide debug level to level. The allowed range is from 0 to 99. The default is 0 (no debugging). Debugging traces from **delv** become more verbose as the debug level increases. See the +mtrace, +rtrace, and +vtrace options below for additional debugging details.

-h

Display the **delv** help usage output and exit.

-i

Insecure mode. This disables internal DNSSEC validation. (Note, however, this does not set the CD bit on upstream queries. If the server being queried is performing DNSSEC validation, then it will not return invalid data; this can cause **delv** to time out. When it is necessary to examine invalid data to debug a DNSSEC problem, use **dig +cd**.)

-m

Enables memory usage debugging.

-p *port#*

Specifies a destination port to use for queries instead of the standard DNS port number 53. This option would be used with a name server that has been configured to listen for queries on a non-standard port number.

-q *name*

Sets the query name to *name*. While the query name can be specified without using the −q, it is sometimes necessary to disambiguate names from types or classes (for example, when looking up the name "ns", which could be misinterpreted as the type NS, or "ch", which could be misinterpreted as class CH).

-t *type*

Sets the query type to *type*, which can be any valid query type supported in BIND 9 except for zone transfer types AXFR and IXFR. As with −q, this is useful to distinguish query name type or class when they are ambiguous. it is sometimes necessary to disambiguate names from types.

The default query type is "A", unless the −x option is supplied to indicate a reverse lookup, in which case it is "PTR".

-v

Print the **delv** version and exit.

-x *addr*

Performs a reverse lookup, mapping an addresses to a name. *addr* is an IPv4 address in dotted-decimal notation, or a colon-delimited IPv6 address. When −x is used, there is no need to provide the *name* or *type* arguments. **delv** automatically performs a lookup for a name like 11.12.13.10.in-addr.arpa and sets the query type to PTR. IPv6 addresses are looked up using nibble format under the IP6.ARPA domain.

-4

Forces **delv** to only use IPv4.

-6

Forces **delv** to only use IPv6.

delv Query Options

delv provides a number of query options which affect the way results are displayed, and in some cases the way lookups are performed.

Each query option is identified by a keyword preceded by a plus sign (+). Some keywords set or reset an option. These may be preceded by the string `no` to negate the meaning of that keyword. Other keywords assign values to options like the timeout interval. They have the form `+keyword=value`. The query options are:

+[no]cdflag

Controls whether to set the CD (checking disabled) bit in queries sent by **delv**. This may be useful when troubleshooting DNSSEC problems from behind a validating resolver. A validating resolver will block invalid responses, making it difficult to retrieve them for analysis. Setting the CD flag on queries will cause the resolver to return invalid responses, which **delv** can then validate internally and report the errors in detail.

+[no]class

Controls whether to display the CLASS when printing a record. The default is to display the CLASS.

+[no]ttl

Controls whether to display the TTL when printing a record. The default is to display the TTL.

+[no]rtrace

Toggle resolver fetch logging. This reports the name and type of each query sent by **delv** in the process of carrying out the resolution and validation process: this includes including the original query and all subsequent queries to follow CNAMEs and to establish a chain of trust for DNSSEC validation.

This is equivalent to setting the debug level to 1 in the "resolver" logging category. Setting the systemwide debug level to 1 using the −d option will product the same output (but will affect other logging categories as well).

+[no]mtrace

Toggle message logging. This produces a detailed dump of the responses received by **delv** in the process of carrying out the resolution and validation process.

This is equivalent to setting the debug level to 10 for the "packets" module of the "resolver" logging category. Setting the systemwide debug level to 10 using the −d option will produce the same output (but will affect other logging categories as well).

+[no]vtrace

Toggle validation logging. This shows the internal process of the validator as it determines whether an answer is validly signed, unsigned, or invalid.

This is equivalent to setting the debug level to 3 for the "validator" module of the "dnssec" logging category. Setting the systemwide debug level to 3 using the −d option will produce the same output (but will affect other logging categories as well).

+[no]short

Provide a terse answer. The default is to print the answer in a verbose form.

+[no]comments
>   Toggle the display of comment lines in the output. The default is to print comments.

+[no]rrcomments
>   Toggle the display of per-record comments in the output (for example, human-readable key information about DNSKEY records). The default is to print per-record comments.

+[no]crypto
>   Toggle the display of cryptographic fields in DNSSEC records. The contents of these field are unnecessary to debug most DNSSEC validation failures and removing them makes it easier to see the common failures. The default is to display the fields. When omitted they are replaced by the string "[omitted]" or in the DNSKEY case the key id is displayed as the replacement, e.g. "[key id = value]".

+[no]trust
>   Controls whether to display the trust level when printing a record. The default is to display the trust level.

+[no]split[=W]
>   Split long hex- or base64-formatted fields in resource records into chunks of *W* characters (where *W* is rounded up to the nearest multiple of 4). *+nosplit* or *+split=0* causes fields not to be split at all. The default is 56 characters, or 44 characters when multiline mode is active.

+[no]all
>   Set or clear the display options +[no]comments, +[no]rrcomments, and +[no]trust as a group.

+[no]multiline
>   Print long records (such as RRSIG, DNSKEY, and SOA records) in a verbose multi-line format with human-readable comments. The default is to print each record on a single line, to facilitate machine parsing of the **delv** output.

+[no]dnssec
>   Indicates whether to display RRSIG records in the **delv** output. The default is to do so. Note that (unlike in **dig**) this does *not* control whether to request DNSSEC records or whether to validate them. DNSSEC records are always requested, and validation will always occur unless suppressed by the use of −i or +noroot and +nodlv.

+[no]root[=ROOT]
>   Indicates whether to perform conventional (non-lookaside) DNSSEC validation, and if so, specifies the name of a trust anchor. The default is to validate using a trust anchor of "." (the root zone), for which there is a built-in key. If specifying a different trust anchor, then −a must be used to specify a file containing the key.

+[no]dlv[=DLV]
>   Indicates whether to perform DNSSEC lookaside validation, and if so, specifies the name of the DLV trust anchor. The default is to perform lookaside validation using a trust anchor of "dlv.isc.org", for which there is a built-in key. If specifying a different name, then −a must be used to specify a file containing the DLV key.

+[no]tcp

> Controls whether to use TCP when sending queries. The default is to use UDP unless a truncated response has been received.

delv Files

`/etc/bind.keys`

`/etc/resolv.conf`

8.2 dig — DNS lookup utility

Synopsis

dig [@server] [-b *address*] [-c *class*] [-f *filename*] [-k *filename*] [-m] [-p *port#*] [-q *name*] [-t *type*] [-v] [-x *addr*] [-y *[hmac:]name:key*] [-4] [-6] [name] [type] [class] [queryopt...]

dig [-h]

dig [global-queryopt...] [query...]

dig Description

dig (domain information groper) is a flexible tool for interrogating DNS name servers. It performs DNS lookups and displays the answers that are returned from the name server(s) that were queried. Most DNS administrators use **dig** to troubleshoot DNS problems because of its flexibility, ease of use and clarity of output. Other lookup tools tend to have less functionality than **dig**.

Although **dig** is normally used with command-line arguments, it also has a batch mode of operation for reading lookup requests from a file. A brief summary of its command-line arguments and options is printed when the -h option is given. Unlike earlier versions, the BIND 9 implementation of **dig** allows multiple lookups to be issued from the command line.

Unless it is told to query a specific name server, **dig** will try each of the servers listed in /etc/ resolv.conf. If no usable server addresses are found, **dig** will send the query to the local host.

When no command line arguments or options are given, **dig** will perform an NS query for "." (the root).

It is possible to set per-user defaults for **dig** via ${HOME}/.digrc. This file is read and any options in it are applied before the command line arguments.

The IN and CH class names overlap with the IN and CH top level domain names. Either use the -t and -c options to specify the type and class, use the -q the specify the domain name, or use "IN." and "CH." when looking up these top level domains.

dig Simple Usage

A typical invocation of **dig** looks like:

```
dig @server name type
```

where:

server

>   is the name or IP address of the name server to query. This can be an IPv4 address in dotted-decimal notation or an IPv6 address in colon-delimited notation. When the supplied `server` argument is a hostname, **dig** resolves that name before querying that name server.

>   If no `server` argument is provided, **dig** consults `/etc/resolv.conf`; if an address is found there, it queries the name server at that address. If either of the `-4` or `-6` options are in use, then only addresses for the corresponding transport will be tried. If no usable addresses are found, **dig** will send the query to the local host. The reply from the name server that responds is displayed.

name

>   is the name of the resource record that is to be looked up.

type

>   indicates what type of query is required — ANY, A, MX, SIG, etc. `type` can be any valid query type. If no `type` argument is supplied, **dig** will perform a lookup for an A record.

dig Options

-4

>   Use IPv4 only.

-6

>   Use IPv6 only.

-b *address[#port]*

>   Set the source IP address of the query. The `address` must be a valid address on one of the host's network interfaces, or "0.0.0.0" or "::". An optional port may be specified by appending "#<port>"

-c *class*

>   Set the query class. The default `class` is IN; other classes are HS for Hesiod records or CH for Chaosnet records.

-f *file*

>   Batch mode: **dig** reads a list of lookup requests to process from the given `file`. Each line in the file should be organized in the same way they would be presented as queries to **dig** using the command-line interface.

-i

Do reverse IPv6 lookups using the obsolete RFC1886 IP6.INT domain, which is no longer in use. Obsolete bit string label queries (RFC2874) are not attempted.

-k *keyfile*

Sign queries using TSIG using a key read from the given file. Key files can be generated using tsig-keygen(8). When using TSIG authentication with **dig**, the name server that is queried needs to know the key and algorithm that is being used. In BIND, this is done by providing appropriate **key** and **server** statements in `named.conf`.

-m

Enable memory usage debugging.

-p *port*

Send the query to a non-standard port on the server, instead of the default port 53. This option would be used to test a name server that has been configured to listen for queries on a non-standard port number.

-q *name*

The domain name to query. This is useful to distinguish the *name* from other arguments.

-t *type*

The resource record type to query. It can be any valid query type which is supported in BIND 9. The default query type is "A", unless the −x option is supplied to indicate a reverse lookup. A zone transfer can be requested by specifying a type of AXFR. When an incremental zone transfer (IXFR) is required, set the *type* to `ixfr=N`. The incremental zone transfer will contain the changes made to the zone since the serial number in the zone's SOA record was *N*.

-v

Print the version number and exit.

-x *addr*

Simplified reverse lookups, for mapping addresses to names. The *addr* is an IPv4 address in dotted-decimal notation, or a colon-delimited IPv6 address. When the −x is used, there is no need to provide the *name*, *class* and *type* arguments. **dig** automatically performs a lookup for a name like `94.2.0.192.in-addr.arpa` and sets the query type and class to PTR and IN respectively. IPv6 addresses are looked up using nibble format under the IP6.ARPA domain (but see also the −i option).

-y *[hmac:]keyname:secret*

Sign queries using TSIG with the given authentication key. *keyname* is the name of the key, and *secret* is the base64 encoded shared secret. *hmac* is the name of the key algorithm; valid choices are `hmac-md5`, `hmac-sha1`, `hmac-sha224`, `hmac-sha256`, `hmac-sha384`, or `hmac-sha512`. If *hmac* is not specified, the default is `hmac-md5`.

Note

You should use the −k option and avoid the −y option, because with −y the shared secret is supplied as a command line argument in clear text. This may be visible in the output from ps(1) or in a history file maintained by the user's shell.

---

dig Query Options

dig provides a number of query options which affect the way in which lookups are made and the results displayed. Some of these set or reset flag bits in the query header, some determine which sections of the answer get printed, and others determine the timeout and retry strategies.

Each query option is identified by a keyword preceded by a plus sign (+). Some keywords set or reset an option. These may be preceded by the string no to negate the meaning of that keyword. Other keywords assign values to options like the timeout interval. They have the form +keyword= value. Keywords may be abbreviated, provided the abbreviation is unambiguous; for example, +cd is equivalent to +cdflag. The query options are:

+[no]aaflag
> A synonym for *+[no]aaonly*.

+[no]aaonly
> Sets the "aa" flag in the query.

+[no]additional
> Display [do not display] the additional section of a reply. The default is to display it.

+[no]adflag
> Set [do not set] the AD (authentic data) bit in the query. This requests the server to return whether all of the answer and authority sections have all been validated as secure according to the security policy of the server. AD=1 indicates that all records have been validated as secure and the answer is not from a OPT-OUT range. AD=0 indicate that some part of the answer was insecure or not validated. As of BIND 9.9, this bit is set by default.

+[no]all
> Set or clear all display flags.

+[no]answer
> Display [do not display] the answer section of a reply. The default is to display it.

+[no]authority
> Display [do not display] the authority section of a reply. The default is to display it.

+[no]badcookie
> Retry lookup with the new server cookie if a BADCOOKIE response is received. (This option was introduced in BIND 9.11.)

+[no]besteffort
> Attempt to display the contents of messages which are malformed. The default is to not display malformed answers.

+bufsize=B
> Set the UDP message buffer size advertised using EDNS0 to B bytes. The maximum and minimum sizes of this buffer are 65535 and 0 respectively. Values outside this range are rounded up or down appropriately. Values other than zero will cause a EDNS query to be sent.

+[no]cdflag
Set [do not set] the CD (checking disabled) bit in the query. This requests the server to not perform DNSSEC validation of responses.

+[no]class
Display [do not display] the CLASS when printing the record.

+[no]cmd
Toggles the printing of the initial comment in the output identifying the version of **dig** and the query options that have been applied. This comment is printed by default.

+[no]comments
Toggle the display of comment lines in the output. The default is to print comments.

+[no]cookie[=####]
Send a COOKIE EDNS option, with optional value. Replaying a COOKIE from a previous response will allow the server to identify a previous client. The default is +cookie.

+cookie is also set when +trace is set to better emulate the default queries from a nameserver. (This option was introduced in BIND 9.11.)

+[no]crypto
Toggle the display of cryptographic fields in DNSSEC records. The contents of these field are unnecessary to debug most DNSSEC validation failures and removing them makes it easier to see the common failures. The default is to display the fields. When omitted they are replaced by the string "[omitted]" or in the DNSKEY case the key id is displayed as the replacement, e.g. "[key id = value]". (This option was introduced in BIND 9.10.)

+[no]defname
Deprecated, treated as a synonym for *+[no]search*

+[no]dnssec
Requests DNSSEC records be sent by setting the DNSSEC OK bit (DO) in the OPT record in the additional section of the query.

+domain=somename
Set the search list to contain the single domain *somename*, as if specified in a **domain** directive in /etc/resolv.conf, and enable search list processing as if the *+search* option were given.

+dscp=value

Set the DSCP code point to be used when sending the query. Valid DSCP code points are in the range [0..63]. By default no code point is explicitly set. (This option was introduced in BIND 9.11.)

+[no]edns[=#]
Specify the EDNS version to query with. Valid values are 0 to 255. Setting the EDNS version will cause a EDNS query to be sent. +noedns clears the remembered EDNS version. EDNS is set to 0 by default.

+[no]ednsflags[=#]

Set the must-be-zero EDNS flags bits (Z bits) to the specified value. Decimal, hex and octal encodings are accepted. Setting a named flag (e.g. DO) will silently be ignored. By default, no Z bits are set. (This option was introduced in BIND 9.10.)

+[no]ednsnegotiation

Enable / disable EDNS version negotiation. By default EDNS version negotiation is enabled. (This option was introduced in BIND 9.10.)

+[no]ednsopt[=code[:value]]

Specify EDNS option with code point `code` and optionally payload of `value` as a hexadecimal string. +noednsopt clears the EDNS options to be sent. (This option was introduced in BIND 9.10.)

+[no]expire

Send an EDNS Expire option. (This option was introduced in BIND 9.10.)

+[no]fail

Do not try the next server if you receive a SERVFAIL. The default is to not try the next server which is the reverse of normal stub resolver behavior.

+[no]header-only

Send a query with a DNS header without a question section. The default is to add a question section. The query type and query name are ignored when this is set. (This option was introduced in BIND 9.11.)

+[no]identify

Show [or do not show] the IP address and port number that supplied the answer when the *+short* option is enabled. If short form answers are requested, the default is not to show the source address and port number of the server that provided the answer.

+[no]ignore

Ignore truncation in UDP responses instead of retrying with TCP. By default, TCP retries are performed.

+[no]keepopen

Keep the TCP socket open between queries and reuse it rather than creating a new TCP socket for each lookup. The default is +nokeepopen.

+[no]multiline

Print records like the SOA records in a verbose multi-line format with human-readable comments. The default is to print each record on a single line, to facilitate machine parsing of the **dig** output.

+ndots=D

Set the number of dots that have to appear in *name* to *D* for it to be considered absolute. The default value is that defined using the ndots statement in /etc/resolv.conf, or 1 if no ndots statement is present. Names with fewer dots are interpreted as relative names and will be searched for in the domains listed in the search or domain directive in /etc/resolv.conf if +search is set.

+[no]nsid

Include an EDNS name server ID (NSID) request when sending a query.

+[no]nssearch

When this option is set, **dig** attempts to find the authoritative name servers for the zone containing the name being looked up and display the SOA record that each name server has for the zone.

+[no]onesoa

Print only one (starting) SOA record when performing an AXFR. The default is to print both the starting and ending SOA records.

+[no]opcode=value

Set [restore] the DNS message opcode to the specified value. The default value is QUERY (0). (This option was introduced in BIND 9.10.)

+[no]qr

Print [do not print] the query as it is sent. By default, the query is not printed.

+[no]question

Print [do not print] the question section of a query when an answer is returned. The default is to print the question section as a comment.

+[no]rdflag

A synonym for *+[no]recurse*.

+[no]recurse

Toggle the setting of the RD (recursion desired) bit in the query. This bit is set by default, which means **dig** normally sends recursive queries. Recursion is automatically disabled when the *+nssearch* or *+trace* query options are used.

+retry=T

Sets the number of times to retry UDP queries to server to *T* instead of the default, 2. Unlike *+tries*, this does not include the initial query.

+[no]rrcomments

Toggle the display of per-record comments in the output (for example, human-readable key information about DNSKEY records). The default is not to print record comments unless multiline mode is active. The rrcomments option was introduced in BIND 9.9.

+[no]search

Use [do not use] the search list defined by the searchlist or domain directive in `resolv.conf` (if any). The search list is not used by default.

'ndots' from `resolv.conf` (default 1) which may be overridden by *+ndots* determines if the name will be treated as relative or not and hence whether a search is eventually performed or not.

+[no]short

Provide a terse answer. The default is to print the answer in a verbose form.

+[no]showsearch

Perform [do not perform] a search showing intermediate results.

+[no]sigchase

Chase DNSSEC signature chains. Requires dig be compiled with -DDIG_SIGCHASE.

+[no]sit[=####]

Send a Source Identity Token EDNS option, with optional value. Replaying a SIT from a previous response will allow the server to identify a previous client. The default is +nosit. Currently using experimental value 65001 for the option code. This experimental option was introduced in BIND 9.10 and obsolete in BIND 9.11; see the dig +cookie instead.

+split=W

Split long hex- or base64-formatted fields in resource records into chunks of *W* characters (where *W* is rounded up to the nearest multiple of 4). *+nosplit* or *+split=0* causes fields not to be split at all. The default is 56 characters, or 44 characters when multiline mode is active. The split option was introduced in BIND 9.9.

+[no]stats

This query option toggles the printing of statistics: when the query was made, the size of the reply and so on. The default behavior is to print the query statistics.

+[no]subnet=addr/prefix

Send an EDNS Client Subnet option with the specified IP address or network prefix. (This option was introduced in BIND 9.10.)

+[no]tcp

Use [do not use] TCP when querying name servers. The default behavior is to use UDP unless an ixfr=N query is requested, in which case the default is TCP. AXFR queries always use TCP.

+timeout=T

Sets the timeout for a query to *T* seconds. The default timeout is 5 seconds. An attempt to set *T* to less than 1 will result in a query timeout of 1 second being applied.

+[no]topdown

When chasing DNSSEC signature chains perform a top-down validation. Requires dig be compiled with -DDIG_SIGCHASE.

+[no]trace

Toggle tracing of the delegation path from the root name servers for the name being looked up. Tracing is disabled by default. When tracing is enabled, **dig** makes iterative queries to resolve the name being looked up. It will follow referrals from the root servers, showing the answer from each server that was used to resolve the lookup.

If @server is also specified, it affects only the initial query for the root zone name servers.

As of BIND 9.9, **+dnssec** is also set when +trace is set to better emulate the default queries from a nameserver.

+tries=T

Sets the number of times to try UDP queries to server to *T* instead of the default, 3. If *T* is less than or equal to zero, the number of tries is silently rounded up to 1.

+trusted-key=####

Specifies a file containing trusted keys to be used with `+sigchase`. Each DNSKEY record must be on its own line.

If not specified, **dig** will look for `/etc/trusted-key.key` then `trusted-key.key` in the current directory.

Requires dig be compiled with -DDIG_SIGCHASE.

+[no]ttlid

Display [do not display] the TTL when printing the record.

+[no]ttlunits

Display [do not display] the TTL in friendly human-readable time units of "s", "m", "h", "d", and "w", representing seconds, minutes, hours, days and weeks. Implies +ttlid. (This option was introduced in BIND 9.11.)

+[no]vc

Use [do not use] TCP when querying name servers. This alternate syntax to `+[no]tcp` is provided for backwards compatibility. The "vc" stands for "virtual circuit".

+[no]zflag

Set [do not set] the last unassigned DNS header flag in a DNS query. This flag is off by default. (This option was introduced in BIND 9.11.)

dig Multiple Queries

The BIND 9 implementation of **dig** supports specifying multiple queries on the command line (in addition to supporting the `-f` batch file option). Each of those queries can be supplied with its own set of flags, options and query options.

In this case, each `query` argument represent an individual query in the command-line syntax described above. Each consists of any of the standard options and flags, the name to be looked up, an optional query type and class and any query options that should be applied to that query.

A global set of query options, which should be applied to all queries, can also be supplied. These global query options must precede the first tuple of name, class, type, options, flags, and query options supplied on the command line. Any global query options (except the `+[no]cmd` option) can be overridden by a query-specific set of query options. For example:

```
dig +qr www.isc.org any -x 127.0.0.1 isc.org ns +noqr
```

shows how **dig** could be used from the command line to make three lookups: an ANY query for `www.isc.org`, a reverse lookup of 127.0.0.1 and a query for the NS records of `isc.org`. A global query option of `+qr` is applied, so that **dig** shows the initial query it made for each lookup. The final query has a local query option of `+noqr` which means that **dig** will not print the initial query when it looks up the NS records for `isc.org`.

dig Idn Support

If **dig** has been built with IDN (internationalized domain name) support, it can accept and display non-ASCII domain names. **dig** appropriately converts character encoding of domain name before sending a request to DNS server or displaying a reply from the server. If you'd like to turn off the IDN support for some reason, defines the `IDN_DISABLE` environment variable. The IDN support is disabled if the variable is set when **dig** runs.

dig Files

`/etc/resolv.conf`

`/etc/trusted-key.key`

`${HOME}/.digrc`

8.3   host — DNS lookup utility

Synopsis

host [-aCdlnrsTwv] [-c *class*] [-N *ndots*] [-R *number*] [-t *type*] [-W *wait*] [-m *flag*]
[-4] [-6] [-v] [-V] name [server]

host Description

host is a simple utility for performing DNS lookups. It is normally used to convert names to IP addresses and vice versa. When no arguments or options are given, **host** prints a short summary of its command line arguments and options.

name is the domain name that is to be looked up. It can also be a dotted-decimal IPv4 address or a colon-delimited IPv6 address, in which case **host** will by default perform a reverse lookup for that address. *server* is an optional argument which is either the name or IP address of the name server that **host** should query instead of the server or servers listed in `/etc/resolv.conf`.

The −a (all) option is equivalent to setting the −v option and asking **host** to make a query of type ANY.

When the −C option is used, **host** will attempt to display the SOA records for zone *name* from all the listed authoritative name servers for that zone. The list of name servers is defined by the NS records that are found for the zone.

The −c option instructs to make a DNS query of class *class*. This can be used to lookup Hesiod or Chaosnet class resource records. The default class is IN (Internet).

Verbose output is generated by **host** when the −d or −v option is used. The two options are equivalent. They have been provided for backwards compatibility. In previous versions, the −d option switched on debugging traces and −v enabled verbose output. As of BIND 9.11, verbose output can also be enabled by setting the *debug* option in `/etc/resolv.conf`.

List mode is selected by the -l option. This makes **host** perform a zone transfer for zone *name*. Transfer the zone printing out the NS, PTR and address records (A/AAAA). If combined with -a all records will be printed.

The -i option specifies that reverse lookups of IPv6 addresses should use the IP6.INT domain as defined in RFC1886. The default is to use IP6.ARPA.

The -N option sets the number of dots that have to be in *name* for it to be considered absolute. The default value is that defined using the ndots statement in /etc/resolv.conf, or 1 if no ndots statement is present. Names with fewer dots are interpreted as relative names and will be searched for in the domains listed in the search or domain directive in /etc/resolv.conf.

The number of UDP retries for a lookup can be changed with the -R option. *number* indicates how many times **host** will repeat a query that does not get answered. If *number* is negative or zero, the number of retries will default to 1. The default value is 1, or as of BIND 9.11, the value of the *attempts* option in /etc/resolv.conf, if set.

Non-recursive queries can be made via the -r option. Setting this option clears the RD — recursion desired — bit in the query which **host** makes. This should mean that the name server receiving the query will not attempt to resolve *name*. The -r option enables **host** to mimic the behavior of a name server by making non-recursive queries and expecting to receive answers to those queries that are usually referrals to other name servers.

By default, **host** uses UDP when making queries. The -T option makes it use a TCP connection when querying the name server. TCP will be automatically selected for queries that require it, such as zone transfer (AXFR) requests.

The -4 option forces **host** to only use IPv4 query transport. The -6 option forces **host** to only use IPv6 query transport.

The -t option is used to select the query type. *type* can be any recognized query type: CNAME, NS, SOA, SIG, KEY, AXFR, etc. When no query type is specified, **host** automatically selects an appropriate query type. By default, it looks for A, AAAA, and MX records, but if the -C option was given, queries will be made for SOA records, and if *name* is a dotted-decimal IPv4 address or colon-delimited IPv6 address, **host** will query for PTR records. If a query type of IXFR is chosen the starting serial number can be specified by appending an equal followed by the starting serial number (e.g. -t IXFR=12345678).

The time to wait for a reply can be controlled through the -W and -w options. The -W option makes **host** wait for *wait* seconds. If *wait* is less than one, the wait interval is set to one second. When the -w option is used, **host** will effectively wait forever for a reply. The time to wait for a response will be set to the number of seconds given by the hardware's maximum value for an integer quantity. By default, **host** will wait for 5 seconds for UDP responses and 10 seconds for TCP connections. Since BIND 9.11, these defaults can be overridden by the *timeout* option in /etc/resolv.conf.

The -s option tells **host** *not* to send the query to the next nameserver if any server responds with a SERVFAIL response, which is the reverse of normal stub resolver behavior.

The -m can be used to set the memory usage debugging flags *record*, *usage* and *trace*.

The -V option causes **host** to print the version number and exit.

host Idn Support

If **host** has been built with IDN (internationalized domain name) support, it can accept and display non-ASCII domain names. **host** appropriately converts character encoding of domain name before sending a request to DNS server or displaying a reply from the server. If you'd like to turn off the IDN support for some reason, defines the `IDN_DISABLE` environment variable. The IDN support is disabled if the variable is set when **host** runs.

host Files

`/etc/resolv.conf`

8.4   nslookup — query Internet name servers interactively

Synopsis

`nslookup` [`-option`] [name | -] [server]

nslookup Description

Nslookup is a program to query Internet domain name servers. **Nslookup** has two modes: interactive and non-interactive. Interactive mode allows the user to query name servers for information about various hosts and domains or to print a list of hosts in a domain. Non-interactive mode is used to print just the name and requested information for a host or domain.

nslookup Arguments

Interactive mode is entered in the following cases:

> a. when no arguments are given (the default name server will be used)
>
> b. when the first argument is a hyphen (-) and the second argument is the host name or Internet address of a name server.

Non-interactive mode is used when the name or Internet address of the host to be looked up is given as the first argument. The optional second argument specifies the host name or address of a name server.

Options can also be specified on the command line if they precede the arguments and are prefixed with a hyphen. For example, to change the default query type to host information, and the initial timeout to 10 seconds, type:

`nslookup -query=hinfo  -timeout=10`

The `-version` option causes **nslookup** to print the version number and immediately exits.

nslookup Interactive Commands

host [server]

> Look up information for host using the current default server or using server, if specified. If host is an Internet address and the query type is A or PTR, the name of the host is returned. If host is a name and does not have a trailing period, the search list is used to qualify the name.
>
> To look up a host not in the current domain, append a period to the name.

server *domain*

lserver *domain*

> Change the default server to *domain*; lserver uses the initial server to look up information about *domain*, while server uses the current default server. If an authoritative answer can't be found, the names of servers that might have the answer are returned.

root

> not implemented

finger

> not implemented

ls

> not implemented

view

> not implemented

help

> not implemented

?

> not implemented

exit

> Exits the program.

set *keyword[=value]*

> This command is used to change state information that affects the lookups. Valid keywords are:

> **all**
>
> > Prints the current values of the frequently used options to **set**. Information about the current default server and host is also printed.

> **class=value**
>
> > Change the query class to one of:

> > **IN**
> >
> > > the Internet class

> > **CH**
> >
> > > the Chaos class

HS
> the Hesiod class

ANY
> wildcard

The class specifies the protocol group of the information.

(Default = IN; abbreviation = cl)

[no]debug
> Turn on or off the display of the full response packet and any intermediate response pack-ets when searching.
>
> (Default = nodebug; abbreviation = [no]deb)

[no]d2
> Turn debugging mode on or off. This displays more about what nslookup is doing.
>
> (Default = nod2)

domain=name
> Sets the search list to *name*.

[no]search
> If the lookup request contains at least one period but doesn't end with a trailing period, append the domain names in the domain search list to the request until an answer is received.
>
> (Default = search)

port=value
> Change the default TCP/UDP name server port to *value*.
>
> (Default = 53; abbreviation = po)

querytype=value

type=value
> Change the type of the information query.
>
> (Default = A; abbreviations = q, ty)

[no]recurse
> Tell the name server to query other servers if it does not have the information.
>
> (Default = recurse; abbreviation = [no]rec)

ndots=number
> Set the number of dots (label separators) in a domain that will disable searching. Absolute names always stop searching.

retry=number
> Set the number of retries to number.

timeout=number
> Change the initial timeout interval for waiting for a reply to number seconds.

[no]vc
> Always use a virtual circuit when sending requests to the server.
>
> (Default = novc)

[no]`fail`
> Try the next nameserver if a nameserver responds with SERVFAIL or a referral (nofail) or terminate query (fail) on such a response.
>
> (Default = nofail)

nslookup Files

`/etc/resolv.conf`

9 Dynamic Updates

This chapter covers transaction level authentication using shared secrets and DNS UPDATE which may be used to add or delete resource records from a zone over DNS (instead of editing a zone file). Commonly the authentication is used for the dynamic updates, but it also may be used for other server-to-server or client-to-server communications.

9.1 Dynamic Update

Dynamic Update is a method for adding, replacing or deleting records in a master server by sending it a special form of DNS messages. The format and meaning of these messages is specified in RFC 2136.

Dynamic update is enabled by including an **allow-update** or an **update-policy** clause in the **zone** statement.

If the zone's **update-policy** is set to `local`, updates to the zone will be permitted for the key `local-ddns`, which will be generated by **named** at startup. See Section 9.2 for more details.

Dynamic updates using Kerberos signed requests can be made using the TKEY/GSS protocol by setting either the **tkey-gssapi-keytab** option, or alternatively by setting both the **tkey-gssapi-credential** and **tkey-domain** options. Once enabled, Kerberos signed requests will be matched against the update policies for the zone, using the Kerberos principal as the signer for the request.

Updating of secure zones (zones using DNSSEC) follows RFC 3007: RRSIG, NSEC and NSEC3 records affected by updates are automatically regenerated by the server using an online zone key. Update authorization is based on transaction signatures and an explicit server policy.

The journal file

All changes made to a zone using dynamic update are stored in the zone's journal file. This file is automatically created by the server when the first dynamic update takes place. The name of the journal file is formed by appending the extension `.jnl` to the name of the corresponding zone file unless specifically overridden. The journal file is in a binary format and should not be edited manually.

The server will also occasionally write ("dump") the complete contents of the updated zone to its zone file. This is not done immediately after each dynamic update, because that would be too slow when a large zone is updated frequently. Instead, the dump is delayed by up to 15 minutes, allowing additional updates to take place. During the dump process, transient files will be created with the extensions .jnw and .jbk; under ordinary circumstances, these will be removed when the dump is complete, and can be safely ignored.

When a server is restarted after a shutdown or crash, it will replay the journal file to incorporate into the zone any updates that took place after the last zone dump.

Changes that result from incoming incremental zone transfers are also journalled in a similar way.

The zone files of dynamic zones cannot normally be edited by hand because they are not guaranteed to contain the most recent dynamic changes — those are only in the journal file. The only way to ensure that the zone file of a dynamic zone is up to date is to run:

```
rndc stop
```

If you have to make changes to a dynamic zone manually, the following procedure will work. Disable dynamic updates to the zone using:

```
rndc freeze zone
```

This will update the zone's master file with the changes stored in its .jnl file. Edit the zone file. To reload the changed zone and re-enable dynamic updates, run:

```
rndc thaw zone
```

rndc sync *zone* (introduced in BIND 9.9) will update the zone file with changes from the journal file without stopping dynamic updates; this may be useful for viewing the current zone state. To remove the .jnl file after updating the zone file, use **rndc sync -clean**.

9.2 Dynamic Update Policies

BIND 9 supports two alternative methods of granting clients the right to perform dynamic updates to a zone, configured by the **allow-update** and **update-policy** option, respectively.

The **allow-update** clause works the same way as in previous versions of BIND. It grants given clients the permission to update any record of any name in the zone.

The **update-policy** clause allows more fine-grained control over what updates are allowed. A set of rules is specified, where each rule either grants or denies permissions for one or more names to be updated by one or more identities. If the dynamic update request message is signed (that is, it includes either a TSIG or SIG(0) record), the identity of the signer can be determined.

Rules are specified in the **update-policy** zone option, and are only meaningful for master zones. When the **update-policy** statement is present, it is a configuration error for the **allow-update** statement to be present. The **update-policy** only examines the signer of a message; the source address is not relevant.

There is a pre-defined **update-policy** rule which can be switched on with the command **update-policy local;**. Switching on this rule in a zone causes **named** to generate a TSIG session key and place it in a

file, and to allow that key to update the zone. (By default, the file is `/var/run/named/session.`
`key`, the key name is "local-ddns" and the key algorithm is HMAC-SHA256, but these values are
configurable with the **session-keyfile**, **session-keyname** and **session-keyalg** options, respectively).

A client running on the local system, and with appropriate permissions, may read that file and use
the key to sign update requests. The zone's update policy will be set to allow that key to change any
record within the zone. Assuming the key name is "local-ddns", this policy is equivalent to:

```
update-policy { grant local-ddns zonesub any; };
```

The command **nsupdate -l** sends update requests to localhost, and signs them using the session key.

Other rule definitions look like this:

```
( grant | deny ) identity nametype   name    types
```

Each rule grants or denies privileges. Once a message has successfully matched a rule, the operation
is immediately granted or denied and no further rules are examined. A rule is matched when the
signer matches the identity field, the name matches the name field in accordance with the nametype
field, and the type matches the types specified in the type field.

No signer is required for `tcp-self` or `6to4-self` however the standard reverse mapping / prefix
conversion must match the identity field.

The identity field specifies a name or a wildcard name. Normally, this is the name of the TSIG or
SIG(0) key used to sign the update request. When a TKEY exchange has been used to create a shared
secret, the identity of the shared secret is the same as the identity of the key used to authenticate the
TKEY exchange. TKEY is also the negotiation method used by GSS-TSIG, which establishes an
identity that is the Kerberos principal of the client, such as **"user@host.domain"**. When the
`identity` field specifies a wildcard name, it is subject to DNS wildcard expansion, so the rule will
apply to multiple identities. The `identity` field must contain a fully-qualified domain name.

For nametypes `krb5-self`, `ms-self`, `krb5-subdomain`, and `ms-subdomain` the `identity`
field specifies the Windows or Kerberos realm of the machine belongs to.

The `nametype` field has 13 values: `name`, `subdomain`, `wildcard`, `self`, `selfsub`, `selfw`
`ild`, `krb5-self`, `ms-self`, `krb5-subdomain`, `ms-subdomain`, `tcp-self`, `6to4-self`,
`zonesub`, and `external`.

name

> Exact-match semantics. This rule matches when the name being updated is identical to the
> contents of the `name` field.

subdomain

> This rule matches when the name being updated is a subdomain of, or identical to, the contents
> of the `name` field.

zonesub

> This rule is similar to subdomain, except that it matches when the name being updated is a
> subdomain of the zone in which the **update-policy** statement appears. This obviates the need
> to type the zone name twice, and enables the use of a standard **update-policy** statement in
> multiple zones without modification. When this rule is used, the `name` field is omitted.

wildcard

The *name* field is subject to DNS wildcard expansion, and this rule matches when the name being updated is a valid expansion of the wildcard.

self

This rule matches when the name being updated matches the contents of the *identity* field. The *name* field is ignored, but should be the same as the *identity* field. The self nametype is most useful when allowing using one key per name to update, where the key has the same name as the name to be updated. The *identity* would be specified as * (an asterisk) in this case.

selfsub

This rule is similar to self except that subdomains of self can also be updated.

selfwild

This rule is similar to self except that only subdomains of self can be updated.

ms-self

This rule takes a Windows machine principal (machine$@REALM) for machine in REALM and and converts it machine.realm allowing the machine to update machine.realm. The REALM to be matched is specified in the *identity* field.

ms-subdomain

This rule takes a Windows machine principal (machine$@REALM) for machine in REALM and converts it to machine.realm allowing the machine to update subdomains of machine.realm. The REALM to be matched is specified in the *identity* field.

krb5-self

This rule takes a Kerberos machine principal (host/machine@REALM) for machine in REALM and and converts it machine.realm allowing the machine to update machine.realm. The REALM to be matched is specified in the *identity* field.

krb5-subdomain

This rule takes a Kerberos machine principal (host/machine@REALM) for machine in REALM and converts it to machine.realm allowing the machine to update subdomains of machine.realm. The REALM to be matched is specified in the *identity* field.

tcp-self

Allow updates that have been sent via TCP and for which the standard mapping from the initiating IP address into the IN-ADDR.ARPA and IP6.ARPA namespaces match the name to be updated.

Note

It is theoretically possible to spoof these TCP sessions.

6to4-self

Allow the 6to4 prefix to be update by any TCP connection from the 6to4 network or from the corresponding IPv4 address. This is intended to allow NS or DNAME RRsets to be added to the reverse tree.

Note
It is theoretically possible to spoof these TCP sessions.

---

external

This rule allows **named** to defer the decision of whether to allow a given update to an external daemon. The method of communicating with the daemon is specified in the `identity` field, the format of which is "`local:path`", where `path` is the location of a UNIX-domain socket. (Currently, "local" is the only supported mechanism.)

Requests to the external daemon are sent over the UNIX-domain socket as datagrams with the following format:

```
Protocol version number (4 bytes, network byte order, currently  ↩
    1)
Request length (4 bytes, network byte order)
Signer (null-terminated string)
Name (null-terminated string)
TCP source address (null-terminated string)
Rdata type (null-terminated string)
Key (null-terminated string)
TKEY token length (4 bytes, network byte order)
TKEY token (remainder of packet)
```

The daemon replies with a four-byte value in network byte order, containing either 0 or 1; 0 indicates that the specified update is not permitted, and 1 indicates that it is.

In all cases, the `name` field must specify a fully-qualified domain name.

If no types are explicitly specified, this rule matches all types except RRSIG, NS, SOA, NSEC and NSEC3. Types may be specified by name, including "ANY" (ANY matches all types except NSEC and NSEC3, which can never be updated). Note that when an attempt is made to delete all records associated with a name, the rules are checked for each existing record type.

Dynamic Update Security

Access to the dynamic update facility should be strictly limited. In earlier versions of BIND, the only way to do this was based on the IP address of the host requesting the update, by listing an IP address or network prefix in the **allow-update** zone option. This method is insecure since the source address of the update UDP packet is easily forged. Also note that if the IP addresses allowed by the **allow-update** option include the address of a slave server which performs forwarding of dynamic updates, the master can be trivially attacked by sending the update to the slave, which will forward it to the master with its own source IP address causing the master to approve it without question.

For these reasons, it is strongly recommended that updates be cryptographically authenticated by means of transaction signatures (TSIG). That is, the **allow-update** option should list only TSIG key names, not IP addresses or network prefixes. Alternatively, the **update-policy** option can be used.

Some sites choose to keep all dynamically-updated DNS data in a subdomain and delegate that subdomain to a separate zone. This way, the top-level zone containing critical data such as the IP addresses of public web and mail servers need not allow dynamic update at all.

9.3 TSIG

TSIG (Transaction SIGnatures) is a mechanism for authenticating DNS messages, originally specified in RFC 2845. It allows DNS messages to be cryptographically signed using a shared secret. TSIG can be used in any DNS transaction, as a way to restrict access to certain server functions (e.g., recursive queries) to authorized clients when IP-based access control is insufficient or needs to be overridden, or as a way to ensure message authenticity when it is critical to the integrity of the server, such as with dynamic UPDATE messages or zone transfers from a master to a slave server.

This is a guide to setting up TSIG in BIND. It describes the configuration syntax and the process of creating TSIG keys.

named supports TSIG for server-to-server communication, and some of the tools included with BIND support it for sending messages to **named**:

- nsupdate(1) supports TSIG via the −k, −l and −y command line options, or via the **key** command when running interactively.

- dig(1) supports TSIG via the −k and −y command line options.

Generating a Shared Key

TSIG keys can be generated using the **tsig-keygen** (for BIND 9.10 or newer) or **ddns-confgen** (for BIND 9.9) command; the output of the command is a **key** directive suitable for inclusion in `named.conf`. For BIND 9.10 and newer, the key name, algorithm and size can be specified by command line parameters; the defaults are "tsig-key", HMAC-SHA256, and 256 bits, respectively. For BIND 9.9, key name and algorithm can be specified by command line parameters; the defaults are "ddns-key" and HMAC-SHA256, respectively. By default, the output of **ddns-confgen** also includes additional configuration text for setting up dynamic DNS in **named**; the −q suppresses this. See Chapter 9 for further details.

Any string which is a valid DNS name can be used as a key name. For example, a key to be shared between servers called *host1* and *host2* could be called "host1-host2.".[1] This key could be generated with BIND 9.10 (or newer) using:

```
$ tsig-keygen host1-host2. > host1-host2.key
```

Or generated using BIND 9.9 with:

```
$ ddns-confgen -q -k host1-host2. > host1-host2.key
```

This key may then be copied to both hosts. The key name and secret must be identical on both hosts.

 Warning
Copying a shared secret from one server to another is beyond the scope of the DNS. A secure transport mechanism should be used: secure FTP, SSL, ssh, telephone, encrypted email, etc.

---

[1]There is no particular reason for the trailing period in this key name example. It is not required. But be sure to be consistent if using it.

tsig-keygen can also be run as **ddns-confgen**, in which case its output includes additional configuration text for setting up dynamic DNS in **named**.

Loading A New Key

For a key shared between servers called *host1* and *host2*, the following could be added to each server's `named.conf` file:

```
key "host1-host2." {
  algorithm hmac-sha256;
  secret "DAopyf1mhCbFVZw7pgmNPBoLUq8wEUT7UuPoLENP2HY=";
};
```

(This is the same key generated above using **tsig-keygen** or **ddns-confgen**.)

Since this text contains a secret, it is recommended that either `named.conf` not be world-readable, or that the **key** directive be stored in a file which is not world-readable, and which is included in `named.conf` via the **include** directive.

Once a key has been added to `named.conf` and the server has been restarted or reconfigured, the server can recognize the key. If the server receives a message signed by the key, it will be able to verify the signature. If the signature is valid, the response will be signed using the same key.

TSIG keys that are known to a server can be listed using the command **rndc tsig-list**.

Instructing the Server to Use a Key

A server sending a request to another server must be told whether to use a key, and if so, which key to use.

For example, a key may be specified for each server in the **masters** statement in the definition of a slave zone; in this case, all SOA QUERY messages, NOTIFY messages, and zone transfer requests (AXFR or IXFR) will be signed using the specified key. Keys may also be specified in the **also-notify** statement of a master or slave zone, causing NOTIFY messages to be signed using the specified key.

Keys can also be specified in a **server** directive. Adding the following on *host1*, if the IP address of *host2* is 10.1.2.3, would cause *all* requests from *host1* to *host2*, including normal DNS queries, to be signed using the **host1-host2.** key:

```
server 10.1.2.3 {
  keys { host1-host2. ;};
};
```

Multiple keys may be present in the **keys** statement, but only the first one is used. As this directive does not contain secrets, it can be used in a world-readable file.

Requests sent by *host2* to *host1* would *not* be signed, unless a similar **server** directive were in *host2*'s configuration file.

Whenever any server sends a TSIG-signed DNS request, it will expect the response to be signed with the same key. If a response is not signed, or if the signature is not valid, the response will be rejected.

TSIG-Based Access Control

TSIG keys may be specified in ACL definitions and ACL directives such as **allow-query**, **allow-transfer** and **allow-update**. The above key would be denoted in an ACL element as **key host1-host2.**

An example of an **allow-update** directive using a TSIG key:

```
allow-update { !{ !localnets; any; }; key host1-host2. ;};
```

This allows dynamic updates to succeed only if the UPDATE request comes from an address in **localnets**, *and* if it is signed using the **host1-host2.** key.

See Section 9.2 for a discussion of the more flexible **update-policy** statement.

Errors

Processing of TSIG-signed messages can result in several errors:

- If a TSIG-aware server receives a message signed by an unknown key, the response will be unsigned, with the TSIG extended error code set to BADKEY.

- If a TSIG-aware server receives a message from a known key but with an invalid signature, the response will be unsigned, with the TSIG extended error code set to BADSIG.

- If a TSIG-aware server receives a message with a time outside of the allowed range, the response will be signed, with the TSIG extended error code set to BADTIME, and the time values will be adjusted so that the response can be successfully verified.

In all of the above cases, the server will return a response code of NOTAUTH (not authenticated[2]).

Q: *I'm trying to use TSIG to authenticate dynamic updates or zone transfers. I'm sure I have the keys set up correctly, but the server is rejecting the TSIG. Why?*

A: This may be a clock skew problem. Check that the the clocks on the client and server are properly synchronized (e.g., using NTP).

9.4 TKEY

TKEY (Transaction KEY) is a mechanism for automatically negotiating a shared secret between two hosts, originally specified in RFC 2930.

There are several TKEY "modes" that specify how a key is to be generated or assigned. BIND 9 implements only one of these modes: Diffie-Hellman key exchange. Both hosts are required to have a KEY record with algorithm DH (though this record is not required to be present in a zone).

The TKEY process is initiated by a client or server by sending a query of type TKEY to a TKEY-aware server. The query must include an appropriate KEY record in the additional section, and must

---

[2]NOTAUTH is an overloaded rcode.

be signed using either TSIG or SIG(0) with a previously established key. The server's response, if successful, will contain a TKEY record in its answer section. After this transaction, both participants will have enough information to calculate a shared secret using Diffie-Hellman key exchange. The shared secret can then be used by to sign subsequent transactions between the two servers.

TSIG keys known by the server, including TKEY-negotiated keys, can be listed using **rndc tsig-list**.

TKEY-negotiated keys can be deleted from a server using **rndc tsig-delete**. This can also be done via the TKEY protocol itself, by sending an authenticated TKEY query specifying the "key deletion" mode.

9.5 SIG(0)

BIND partially supports DNSSEC SIG(0) transaction signatures as specified in RFC 2535 and RFC 2931. SIG(0) uses public/private keys to authenticate messages. Access control is performed in the same manner as TSIG keys; privileges can be granted or denied in ACL directives based on the key name.

When a SIG(0) signed message is received, it will only be verified if the key is known and trusted by the server. The server will not attempt to recursively fetch or validate the key.

SIG(0) signing of multiple-message TCP streams is not supported.

The only tool shipped with BIND 9 that generates SIG(0) signed messages is **nsupdate**.

9.6 nsupdate — Dynamic DNS update utility

Synopsis

```
nsupdate [-d] [-D] [-L level] [-g | -o | -l | -y [hmac:]keyname:secret | -k keyf
ile] [-t timeout] [-u udptimeout] [-r udpretries] [-R randomdev] [-v] [-T] [-P] [-
V] [filename]
```

nsupdate Description

nsupdate is used to submit Dynamic DNS Update requests as defined in RFC 2136 to a name server. This allows resource records to be added or removed from a zone without manually editing the zone file. A single update request can contain requests to add or remove more than one resource record.

Zones that are under dynamic control via **nsupdate** or a DHCP server should not be edited by hand. Manual edits could conflict with dynamic updates and cause data to be lost.

The resource records that are dynamically added or removed with **nsupdate** have to be in the same zone. Requests are sent to the zone's master server. This is identified by the MNAME field of the zone's SOA record.

Transaction signatures can be used to authenticate the Dynamic DNS updates. These use the TSIG resource record type described in RFC 2845 or the SIG(0) record described in RFC 2535 and RFC 2931 or GSS-TSIG as described in RFC 3645.

TSIG relies on a shared secret that should only be known to **nsupdate** and the name server. For instance, suitable key and server statements would be added to /etc/named.conf so that the name server can associate the appropriate secret key and algorithm with the IP address of the client application that will be using TSIG authentication. You can use **ddns-confgen** to generate suitable configuration fragments. **nsupdate** uses the -y or -k options to provide the TSIG shared secret. These options are mutually exclusive.

SIG(0) uses public key cryptography. To use a SIG(0) key, the public key must be stored in a KEY record in a zone served by the name server.

GSS-TSIG uses Kerberos credentials. Standard GSS-TSIG mode is switched on with the -g flag. A non-standards-compliant variant of GSS-TSIG used by Windows 2000 can be switched on with the -o flag.

nsupdate Options

-d

> Debug mode. This provides tracing information about the update requests that are made and the replies received from the name server.

-D

> Extra debug mode.

-k *keyfile*

> The file containing the TSIG authentication key. Keyfiles may be in two formats: a single file containing a named.conf-format **key** statement, which may be generated automatically by **ddns-confgen**, or a pair of files whose names are of the format K{name}.+157.+{random}.key and K{name}.+157.+{random}.private, which can be generated by **dnssec-keygen**. The -k may also be used to specify a SIG(0) key used to authenticate Dynamic DNS update requests. In this case, the key specified is not an HMAC-MD5 key.

-l

> Local-host only mode. This sets the server address to localhost (disabling the **server** so that the server address cannot be overridden). Connections to the local server will use a TSIG key found in /var/run/named/session.key, which is automatically generated by **named** if any local master zone has set **update-policy** to **local**. The location of this key file can be overridden with the -k option.

-L *level*

> Set the logging debug level. If zero, logging is disabled.

-p *port*

> Set the port to use for connections to a name server. The default is 53.

-P

> Print the list of private BIND-specific resource record types whose format is understood by **nsupdate**. See also the -T option. (The -P option was introduced in BIND 9.10.)

-r *udpretries*

The number of UDP retries. The default is 3. If zero, only one update request will be made.

-R *randomdev*

Where to obtain randomness. If the operating system does not provide a /dev/random or equivalent device, the default source of randomness is keyboard input. randomdev specifies the name of a character device or file containing random data to be used instead of the default. The special value keyboard indicates that keyboard input should be used. This option may be specified multiple times.

-t *timeout*

The maximum time an update request can take before it is aborted. The default is 300 seconds. Zero can be used to disable the timeout.

-T

Print the list of IANA standard resource record types whose format is understood by **nsupdate**. **nsupdate** will exit after the lists are printed. The -T option can be combined with the -P option. (The -T option was introduced in BIND 9.10.)

Other types can be entered using "TYPEXXXXX" where "XXXXX" is the decimal value of the type with no leading zeros. The rdata, if present, will be parsed using the UNKNOWN rdata format, (<backslash> <hash> <space> <length> <space> <hexstring>).

-u *udptimeout*

The UDP retry interval. The default is 3 seconds. If zero, the interval will be computed from the timeout interval and number of UDP retries.

-v

Use TCP even for small update requests. By default, **nsupdate** uses UDP to send update requests to the name server unless they are too large to fit in a UDP request in which case TCP will be used. TCP may be preferable when a batch of update requests is made.

-V

Print the version number and exit.

-y *[hmac:]keyname:secret*

Literal TSIG authentication key. *keyname* is the name of the key, and *secret* is the base64 encoded shared secret. *hmac* is the name of the key algorithm; valid choices are hmac-md5, hmac-sha1, hmac-sha224, hmac-sha256, hmac-sha384, or hmac-sha512. If *hmac* is not specified, the default is hmac-md5.

Warning
Use of the -y option is discouraged because the shared secret is supplied as a command line argument in clear text. This may be visible in the output from ps(1) or in a history file maintained by the user's shell.

---

nsupdate Input Format

nsupdate reads input from *filename* or standard input. Each command is supplied on exactly one line of input. Some commands are for administrative purposes. The others are either update instructions or prerequisite checks on the contents of the zone. These checks set conditions that some name or set of resource records (RRset) either exists or is absent from the zone. These conditions must be met if the entire update request is to succeed. Updates will be rejected if the tests for the prerequisite conditions fail.

Every update request consists of zero or more prerequisites and zero or more updates. This allows a suitably authenticated update request to proceed if some specified resource records are present or missing from the zone. A blank input line (or the **send** command) causes the accumulated commands to be sent as one Dynamic DNS update request to the name server.

The command formats and their meaning are as follows:

server servername [port]
> Sends all dynamic update requests to the name server *servername*. When no server statement is provided, **nsupdate** will send updates to the master server of the correct zone. The MNAME field of that zone's SOA record will identify the master server for that zone. *port* is the port number on *servername* where the dynamic update requests get sent. If no port number is specified, the default DNS port number of 53 is used.

local address [port]
> Sends all dynamic update requests using the local *address*. When no local statement is provided, **nsupdate** will send updates using an address and port chosen by the system. *port* can additionally be used to make requests come from a specific port. If no port number is specified, the system will assign one.

zone zonename
> Specifies that all updates are to be made to the zone *zonename*. If no *zone* statement is provided, **nsupdate** will attempt determine the correct zone to update based on the rest of the input.

class classname
> Specify the default class. If no *class* is specified, the default class is *IN*.

ttl seconds
> Specify the default time to live for records to be added. The value *none* will clear the default ttl.

key [hmac:] keyname secret
> Specifies that all updates are to be TSIG-signed using the *keyname secret* pair. If *hmac* is specified, then it sets the signing algorithm in use; the default is hmac-md5. The **key** command overrides any key specified on the command line via -y or -k.

gsstsig
> Use GSS-TSIG to sign the updated. This is equivalent to specifying -g on the command line.

oldgsstsig
> Use the Windows 2000 version of GSS-TSIG to sign the updated. This is equivalent to specifying -o on the command line.

realm [realm_name]
> When using GSS-TSIG use *realm_name* rather than the default realm in `krb5.conf`. If no realm is specified the saved realm is cleared.

check-names [yes_or_no]

> Turn on or off check-names processing on records to be added. Check-names has no effect on prerequisites or records to be deleted. By default check-names processing is on. If check-names processing fails the record will not be added to the UPDATE message.

[prereq] nxdomain domain-name
> Requires that no resource record of any type exists with name *domain-name*.

[prereq] yxdomain domain-name
> Requires that *domain-name* exists (has as at least one resource record, of any type).

[prereq] nxrrset domain-name [class] type
> Requires that no resource record exists of the specified *type*, *class* and *domain-name*. If *class* is omitted, IN (internet) is assumed.

[prereq] yxrrset domain-name [class] type
> This requires that a resource record of the specified *type*, *class* and *domain-name* must exist. If *class* is omitted, IN (internet) is assumed.

[prereq] yxrrset domain-name [class] type data...
> The *data* from each set of prerequisites of this form sharing a common *type*, *class*, and *domain-name* are combined to form a set of RRs. This set of RRs must exactly match the set of RRs existing in the zone at the given *type*, *class*, and *domain-name*. The *data* are written in the standard text representation of the resource record's RDATA.

[update] del[ete] domain-name [ttl] [class] [type [data...]]
> Deletes any resource records named *domain-name*. If *type* and *data* is provided, only matching resource records will be removed. The internet class is assumed if *class* is not supplied. The *ttl* is ignored, and is only allowed for compatibility.

[update] add domain-name ttl [class] type data...
> Adds a new resource record with the specified *ttl*, *class* and *data*.

show
> Displays the current message, containing all of the prerequisites and updates specified since the last send.

send
> Sends the current message. This is equivalent to entering a blank line.

answer
> Displays the answer.

debug
> Turn on debugging.

version
> Print version number.

help
> Print a list of commands.

Lines beginning with a semicolon are comments and are ignored.

nsupdate Examples

The examples below show how **nsupdate** could be used to insert and delete resource records from the example.com zone. Notice that the input in each example contains a trailing blank line so that a group of commands are sent as one dynamic update request to the master name server for example.com.

```
# nsupdate
> update delete oldhost.example.com A
> update add newhost.example.com 86400 A 172.16.1.1
> send
```

Any A records for oldhost.example.com are deleted. And an A record for newhost.example.com with IP address 172.16.1.1 is added. The newly-added record has a 1 day TTL (86400 seconds).

```
# nsupdate
> prereq nxdomain nickname.example.com
> update add nickname.example.com 86400 CNAME somehost.example.com
> send
```

The prerequisite condition gets the name server to check that there are no resource records of any type for nickname.example.com. If there are, the update request fails. If this name does not exist, a CNAME for it is added. This ensures that when the CNAME is added, it cannot conflict with the long-standing rule in RFC 1034 that a name must not exist as any other record type if it exists as a CNAME. (The rule has been updated for DNSSEC in RFC 2535 to allow CNAMEs to have RRSIG, DNSKEY and NSEC records.)

nsupdate Files

`/etc/resolv.conf`
> used to identify default name server

`/var/run/named/session.key`
> sets the default TSIG key for use in local-only mode

`K{name}.+157.+{random}.key`
> base-64 encoding of HMAC-MD5 key created by dnssec-keygen(8).

`K{name}.+157.+{random}.private`
> base-64 encoding of HMAC-MD5 key created by dnssec-keygen(8).

nsupdate Bugs

The TSIG key is redundantly stored in two separate files. This is a consequence of nsupdate using the DST library for its cryptographic operations, and may change in future releases.

9.7 ddns-confgen — ddns key generation tool

Synopsis

tsig-keygen [-a *algorithm*] [-h] [-r *randomfile*] [name]

ddns-confgen [-a *algorithm*] [-h] [-k *keyname*] [-q] [-r *randomfile*] [-s *name* | -z *zone*]

ddns-confgen Description

tsig-keygen and **ddns-confgen** are invocation methods for a utility that generates keys for use in TSIG signing. The resulting keys can be used, for example, to secure dynamic DNS updates to a zone or for the **rndc** command channel.

The **tsig-keygen** tool was introduced in BIND 9.10.

When run as **tsig-keygen**, a domain name can be specified on the command line which will be used as the name of the generated key. If no name is specified, the default is tsig-key.

When run as **ddns-confgen**, the generated key is accompanied by configuration text and instructions that can be used with **nsupdate** and **named** when setting up dynamic DNS, including an example **update-policy** statement. (This usage similar to the **rndc-confgen** command for setting up command channel security.)

Note that **named** itself can configure a local DDNS key for use with **nsupdate -l**: it does this when a zone is configured with **update-policy local;**. **ddns-confgen** is only needed when a more elaborate configuration is required: for instance, if **nsupdate** is to be used from a remote system.

ddns-confgen Options

-a *algorithm*
> Specifies the algorithm to use for the TSIG key. Available choices are: hmac-md5, hmac-sha1, hmac-sha224, hmac-sha256, hmac-sha384 and hmac-sha512. The default is hmac-sha256. Options are case-insensitive, and the "hmac-" prefix may be omitted.

-h
> Prints a short summary of options and arguments.

-k *keyname*

Specifies the key name of the DDNS authentication key. The default is `ddns-key` when neither the `-s` nor `-z` option is specified; otherwise, the default is `ddns-key` as a separate label followed by the argument of the option, e.g., `ddns-key.example.com`. The key name must have the format of a valid domain name, consisting of letters, digits, hyphens and periods.

-q

(**ddns-confgen** only.) Quiet mode: Print only the key, with no explanatory text or usage examples; This is essentially identical to **tsig-keygen**.

-r *randomfile*

Specifies a source of random data for generating the authorization. If the operating system does not provide a `/dev/random` or equivalent device, the default source of randomness is keyboard input. `randomdev` specifies the name of a character device or file containing random data to be used instead of the default. The special value `keyboard` indicates that keyboard input should be used.

-s *name*

(**ddns-confgen** only.) Generate configuration example to allow dynamic updates of a single hostname. The example **named.conf** text shows how to set an update policy for the specified *name* using the "name" nametype. The default key name is ddns-key.*name*. Note that the "self" nametype cannot be used, since the name to be updated may differ from the key name. This option cannot be used with the `-z` option.

-z *zone*

(**ddns-confgen** only.) Generate configuration example to allow dynamic updates of a zone: The example **named.conf** text shows how to set an update policy for the specified *zone* using the "zonesub" nametype, allowing updates to all subdomain names within that *zone*. This option cannot be used with the `-s` option.

10   DNSSEC

Cryptographic authentication of DNS information is possible through the DNS Security (*DNSSEC-bis*) extensions, defined in RFC 4033, RFC 4034, and RFC 4035. This section describes the creation and use of DNSSEC signed zones.

In order to set up a DNSSEC secure zone, there are a series of steps which must be followed. BIND 9 ships with several tools that are used in this process, which are explained in more detail below. In all cases, the −h option prints a full list of parameters. Note that the DNSSEC tools require the keyset files to be in the working directory or the directory specified by the −d option, and that the tools shipped with BIND 9.2.x and earlier are not compatible with the current ones.

There must also be communication with the administrators of the parent and/or child zone to transmit keys. A zone's security status must be indicated by the parent zone for a DNSSEC capable resolver to trust its data. This is done through the presence or absence of a DS record at the delegation point.

For other servers to trust data in this zone, they must either be statically configured with this zone's zone key or the zone key of another zone above this one in the DNS tree.

10.1   Generating Keys

The **dnssec-keygen** program (covered later in this chapter) is used to generate keys.

A secure zone must contain one or more zone keys. The zone keys will sign all other records in the zone, as well as the zone keys of any secure delegated zones. Zone keys must have the same name as the zone, a name type of **ZONE**, and must be usable for authentication. It is recommended that zone keys use a cryptographic algorithm designated as "mandatory to implement" by the IETF; currently the only one is RSASHA1.

The following command will generate a 768-bit RSASHA1 key for the child.example zone:

dnssec-keygen −a RSASHA1 −b 768 −n ZONE child.example.

Two output files will be produced: Kchild.example.+005+12345.key and Kchild.example.+005+12345.private (where 12345 is an example of a key tag). The key filenames contain the key name (child.example.), algorithm (3 is DSA, 1 is RSAMD5, 5 is RSASHA1, etc.), and the key tag (12345 in this case). The private key (in the .private file) is used to generate signatures, and the public key (in the .key file) is used for signature verification.

To generate another key with the same properties (but with a different key tag), repeat the above command.

The **dnssec-keyfromlabel** program is used to get a key pair from a crypto hardware and build the key files. Its usage is similar to **dnssec-keygen**.

The public keys should be inserted into the zone file by including the `.key` files using **$INCLUDE** statements.

10.2   Signing the Zone

The **dnssec-signzone** program (covered later in this chapter) is used to sign a zone.

Any `keyset` files corresponding to secure subzones should be present. The zone signer will generate `NSEC`, `NSEC3` and `RRSIG` records for the zone, as well as `DS` for the child zones if `'-g'` is specified. If `'-g'` is not specified, then DS RRsets for the secure child zones need to be added manually.

The following command signs the zone, assuming it is in a file called `zone.child.example`. By default, all zone keys which have an available private key are used to generate signatures.

dnssec-signzone -o child.example zone.child.example

One output file is produced: `zone.child.example.signed`. This file should be referenced by `named.conf` as the input file for the zone.

dnssec-signzone will also produce a keyset and dsset files and optionally a dlvset file. These are used to provide the parent zone administrators with the `DNSKEY`s (or their corresponding `DS` records) that are the secure entry point to the zone.

10.3   Configuring Servers

To enable **named** to respond appropriately to DNS requests from DNSSEC aware clients, **dnssec-enable** must be set to yes. (This is the default setting.)

To enable **named** to validate answers from other servers, the **dnssec-enable** option must be set to **yes**, and the **dnssec-validation** options must be set to **yes** or **auto**.

If **dnssec-validation** is set to **auto**, then a default trust anchor for the DNS root zone will be used. If it is set to **yes**, however, then at least one trust anchor must be configured with a **trusted-keys** or **managed-keys** statement in `named.conf`, or DNSSEC validation will not occur. The default setting is **yes**.

trusted-keys are copies of DNSKEY RRs for zones that are used to form the first link in the cryptographic chain of trust. All keys listed in **trusted-keys** (and corresponding zones) are deemed to exist and only the listed keys will be used to validated the DNSKEY RRset that they are from.

managed-keys are trusted keys which are automatically kept up to date via RFC 5011 trust anchor maintenance.

trusted-keys and **managed-keys** are described in more detail in Section 6.10 and Section 6.11.

Unlike BIND 8, BIND 9 does not verify signatures on load, so zone keys for authoritative zones do not need to be specified in the configuration file.

After DNSSEC gets established, a typical DNSSEC configuration will look something like the following. It has one or more public keys for the root. This allows answers from outside the organization to be validated. It will also have several keys for parts of the namespace the organization controls. These are here to ensure that **named** is immune to compromises in the DNSSEC components of the security of parent zones.

```
managed-keys {
  /* Root Key */
  "." initial-key 257 3 3 "BNY4wrWM1nCfJ+CXd0rVXyYmobt7sEEfK3clRbGaTwS
        JxrGkxJWoZu6I7PzJu/E9gx4UC1zGAH1XKdE4zYIpRh
        aBKnvcC2U9mZhkdUpd1Vso/HAdjNe8LmMlnzY3zy2Xy
        4klWOADTPzSv9eamj8V18PHGjBLaVtYvk/ln5ZApjYg
        hf+6FElrmLkdaz MQ2OCnACR817DF4BBa7UR/beDHyp
        5iWTXWSi6XmoJLbG9Scqc7l7OKDqlvXR3M/lUUVRbke
        glIPJSidmK3ZyCllh4XSKbje/45SKucHgnwU5jefMtq
        66gKodQj+MiA21AfUVe7u99WzTLzY3qlxDhxYQQ20FQ
        97S+LKUTpQcq27R7AT3/V5hRQxScINqwcz4jYqZD2fQ
        dgxbcDTClU0CRBdiieyLMNzXG3";
};

trusted-keys {
  /* Key for our organization's forward zone */
  example.com. 257 3 5 "AwEAAaxPMcR2x0HbQV4WeZB6oEDX+r0QM6
        5KbhTjrW1ZaARmPhEZZe3Y9ifgEuq7vZ/z
        GZUdEGNWy+JZzus0lUptwgjGwhUS1558Hb
        4JKUbbOTcM8pwX1j0EiX3oDFVmjHO444gL
        kBOUKUf/mC7HvfwYH/Be22GnClrinKJp1O
        g4ywzO9WglMk7jbfW33gUKvirTHr25GL7S
        TQUzBb5Usxt8lgnyTUHslt3JwCY5hKZ6Cq
        FxmAVZP20igTixin/1LcrgX/KMEGd/biuv
        F4qJCyduieHukuY3H4XMAcR+xia2nIUPvm
        /oyWR8BW/hWdzOvnSCThlHf3xiYleDbt/o
        1OTQ09A0=";

  /* Key for our reverse zone. */
  2.0.192.IN-ADDRPA.NET. 257 3 5 "AQOnS4xn/IgOUpBPJ3bogzwc
        xOdNax071L18QqZnQQQAVVr+i
        LhGTnNGp3HoWQLUIzKrJVZ3zg
        gy3WwNT6kZo6c0tszYqbtvchm
        gQC8CzKojM/W16i6MG/eafGU3
        siaOdS0yOI6BgPsw+YZdzlYMa
        IJGf4M4dyoKIhzdZyQ2bYQrjy
        Q4LB01C7aOnsMyYKHHYeRvPxj
        IQXmdqgOJGq+vsevG06zW+1xg
        YJh9rCIfnmlGX/KMgxLPG2vXT
        D/RnLX+D3T3UL7HJYHJhAZD5L
        59VvjSPsZJHeDCUyWYrvPZesZ
        DIRvhDD52SKvbheeTJUm6Ehkz
        ytNN2SN96QRk8j/iI8ib";
```

```
};

options {
  ...
  dnssec-enable yes;
  dnssec-validation yes;
};
```

Note

None of the keys listed in this example are valid. In particular, the root key is not valid.

When DNSSEC validation is enabled and properly configured, the resolver will reject any answers from signed, secure zones which fail to validate, and will return SERVFAIL to the client.

Responses may fail to validate for any of several reasons, including missing, expired, or invalid signatures, a key which does not match the DS RRset in the parent zone, or an insecure response from a zone which, according to its parent, should have been secure.

Note

When the validator receives a response from an unsigned zone that has a signed parent, it must confirm with the parent that the zone was intentionally left unsigned. It does this by verifying, via signed and validated NSEC/NSEC3 records, that the parent zone contains no DS records for the child.

If the validator *can* prove that the zone is insecure, then the response is accepted. However, if it cannot, then it must assume an insecure response to be a forgery; it rejects the response and logs an error.

The logged error reads "insecurity proof failed" and "got insecure response; parent indicates it should be secure". (Prior to BIND 9.7, the logged error was "not insecure". This referred to the zone, not the response.)

10.4 dnssec-checkds — DNSSEC delegation consistency checking tool

Synopsis

```
dnssec-checkds [-l domain] [-f file] [-d dig path] [-D dsfromkey path] zone
dnssec-dsfromkey [-l domain] [-f file] [-d dig path] [-D dsfromkey path] zone
```

dnssec-checkds Description

dnssec-checkds verifies the correctness of Delegation Signer (DS) or DNSSEC Lookaside Validation (DLV) resource records for keys in a specified zone. This utility was introduced in BIND 9.9.

Note

This tool depends on Python; it will not be built or installed on systems that do not have a python interpreter.

---

dnssec-checkds Options

-f *file*

If a *file* is specified, then the zone is read from that file to find the DNSKEY records. If not, then the DNSKEY records for the zone are looked up in the DNS.

-l *domain*

Check for a DLV record in the specified lookaside domain, instead of checking for a DS record in the zone's parent. For example, to check for DLV records for "example.com" in ISC's DLV zone, use: **dnssec-checkds -l dlv.isc.org example.com**

-d *dig path*

Specifies a path to a **dig** binary. Used for testing.

-D *dsfromkey path*

Specifies a path to a **dnssec-dsfromkey** binary. Used for testing.

10.5 dnssec-coverage — checks future DNSKEY coverage for a zone

Synopsis

```
dnssec-coverage [-K directory] [-l length] [-f file] [-d DNSKEY TTL] [-m max
TTL] [-r interval] [-c compilezone path] [-k] [-z] [zone]
```

dnssec-coverage Description

dnssec-coverage verifies that the DNSSEC keys for a given zone or a set of zones have timing metadata set properly to ensure no future lapses in DNSSEC coverage. This utility was introduced in BIND 9.9.

Note

This tool depends on Python; it will not be built or installed on systems that do not have a python interpreter.

If zone is specified, then keys found in the key repository matching that zone are scanned, and an ordered list is generated of the events scheduled for that key (i.e., publication, activation, inactivation, deletion). The list of events is walked in order of occurrence. Warnings are generated if any event is scheduled which could cause the zone to enter a state in which validation failures might occur: for example, if the number of published or active keys for a given algorithm drops to zero, or if a key is deleted from the zone too soon after a new key is rolled, and cached data signed by the prior key has not had time to expire from resolver caches.

If zone is not specified, then all keys in the key repository will be scanned, and all zones for which there are keys will be analyzed. (Note: This method of reporting is only accurate if all the zones that have keys in a given repository share the same TTL parameters.)

dnssec-coverage Options

-K `directory`

> Sets the directory in which keys can be found. Defaults to the current working directory.

-f `file`

> If a file is specified, then the zone is read from that file; the largest TTL and the DNSKEY TTL are determined directly from the zone data, and the −m and −d options do not need to be specified on the command line.

-l `duration`

> The length of time to check for DNSSEC coverage. Key events scheduled further into the future than duration will be ignored, and assumed to be correct. (The −l was introduced in BIND 9.10.)

> The value of duration can be set in seconds, or in larger units of time by adding a suffix: 'mi' for minutes, 'h' for hours, 'd' for days, 'w' for weeks, 'mo' for months, 'y' for years.

-m `maximum TTL`

> Sets the value to be used as the maximum TTL for the zone or zones being analyzed when determining whether there is a possibility of validation failure. When a zone-signing key is deactivated, there must be enough time for the record in the zone with the longest TTL to have expired from resolver caches before that key can be purged from the DNSKEY RRset. If that condition does not apply, a warning will be generated.

> The length of the TTL can be set in seconds, or in larger units of time by adding a suffix: 'mi' for minutes, 'h' for hours, 'd' for days, 'w' for weeks, 'mo' for months, 'y' for years.

> This option is mandatory unless the −f has been used to specify a zone file. (If −f has been specified, this option may still be used; it will override the value found in the file.)

-d `DNSKEY TTL`

> Sets the value to be used as the DNSKEY TTL for the zone or zones being analyzed when determining whether there is a possibility of validation failure. When a key is rolled (that is, replaced with a new key), there must be enough time for the old DNSKEY RRset to have expired from resolver caches before the new key is activated and begins generating signatures. If that condition does not apply, a warning will be generated.

The length of the TTL can be set in seconds, or in larger units of time by adding a suffix: 'mi' for minutes, 'h' for hours, 'd' for days, 'w' for weeks, 'mo' for months, 'y' for years.

This option is mandatory unless the −f has been used to specify a zone file, or a default key TTL was set with the −L to **dnssec-keygen**. (If either of those is true, this option may still be used; it will override the value found in the zone or key file.)

-r *resign interval*

Sets the value to be used as the resign interval for the zone or zones being analyzed when determining whether there is a possibility of validation failure. This value defaults to 22.5 days, which is also the default in **named**. However, if it has been changed by the `sig-validity-interval` option in `named.conf`, then it should also be changed here.

The length of the interval can be set in seconds, or in larger units of time by adding a suffix: 'mi' for minutes, 'h' for hours, 'd' for days, 'w' for weeks, 'mo' for months, 'y' for years.

-k

Only check KSK coverage; ignore ZSK events. Cannot be used with −z. (The −k was introduced in BIND 9.10.)

-z

Only check ZSK coverage; ignore KSK events. Cannot be used with −k. (The −z was introduced in BIND 9.10.)

-c *compilezone path*

Specifies a path to a **named-compilezone** binary. Used for testing.

10.6 dnssec-dsfromkey — DNSSEC DS RR generation tool

Synopsis

`dnssec-dsfromkey [-v level] [-1] [-2] [-a alg] [-C] [-1 domain] [-T TTL]` keyfile

`dnssec-dsfromkey -s [-1] [-2] [-a alg] [-K directory] [-1 domain] [-s] [-c class] [-T TTL] [-f file] [-A] [-v level]` dnsname

`dnssec-dsfromkey [-h] [-V]`

dnssec-dsfromkey Description

dnssec-dsfromkey outputs the Delegation Signer (DS) resource record (RR), as defined in RFC 3658 and RFC 4509, for the given key(s).

dnssec-dsfromkey Options

-1

Use SHA-1 as the digest algorithm (the default is to use both SHA-1 and SHA-256).

-2

Use SHA-256 as the digest algorithm.

-a *algorithm*

Select the digest algorithm. The value of `algorithm` must be one of SHA-1 (SHA1), SHA-256 (SHA256), GOST or SHA-384 (SHA384). These values are case insensitive.

-C

Generate CDS records rather than DS records. This is mutually exclusive with generating lookaside records.

-T *TTL*

Specifies the TTL of the DS records. (The `-T` option was introduced in BIND 9.9.)

-K *directory*

Look for key files (or, in keyset mode, `keyset-` files) in `directory`.

-f *file*

Zone file mode: in place of the keyfile name, the argument is the DNS domain name of a zone master file, which can be read from `file`. If the zone name is the same as `file`, then it may be omitted.

If `file` is set to `"-"`, then the zone data is read from the standard input. This makes it possible to use the output of the **dig** command as input, as in:

dig dnskey example.com | dnssec-dsfromkey -f - example.com

(This standard input feature was introduced in BIND 9.9.)

-A

Include ZSKs when generating DS records. Without this option, only keys which have the KSK flag set will be converted to DS records and printed. Useful only in zone file mode.

-l *domain*

Generate a DLV set instead of a DS set. The specified `domain` is appended to the name for each record in the set. The DNSSEC Lookaside Validation (DLV) RR is described in RFC 4431. This is mutually exclusive with generating CDS records.

-s

Keyset mode: in place of the keyfile name, the argument is the DNS domain name of a keyset file.

-c *class*

Specifies the DNS class (default is IN). Useful only in keyset or zone file mode.

-v *level*

Sets the debugging level.

-h

Prints usage information.

-V

Prints version information.

dnssec-dsfromkey Example

To build the SHA-256 DS RR from the **Kexample.com.+003+26160** keyfile name, the following command would be issued:

dnssec-dsfromkey -2 Kexample.com.+003+26160

The command would print something like:

```
example.com. IN DS 26160 5 2 3A1EADA7A74B8D0BA86726B0C227AA85A  ←
    B8BBD2B2004F41A868A54F0 C5EA0B94
```

dnssec-dsfromkey Files

The keyfile can be designed by the key identification Knnnn.+aaa+iiiii or the full file name Knnnn.+aaa+iiiii.key as generated by dnssec-keygen(8).

The keyset file name is built from the directory, the string keyset- and the dnsname.

dnssec-dsfromkey Caveat

A keyfile error can give a "file not found" even if the file exists.

10.7   dnssec-importkey — import external DNSKEY records

Synopsis

```
dnssec-importkey [-K directory] [-L ttl] [-P date/offset] [-D date/offset] [-
h] [-v level] [-V] keyfile
```

```
dnssec-importkey -f filename [-K directory] [-L ttl] [-P date/offset] [-D date/
offset] [-h] [-v level] [-V] [dnsname]
```

dnssec-importkey Description

dnssec-importkey reads a public DNSKEY record and generates a pair of .key/.private files. The DNSKEY record may be read from an existing .key file, in which case a corresponding .private file will be generated, or it may be read from any other file or from the standard input, in which case both .key and .private files will be generated.

The newly-created .private file does *not* contain private key data, and cannot be used for signing. However, having a .private file makes it possible to set publication (-P) and deletion (-D) times for the key, which means the public key can be added to and removed from the DNSKEY RRset on schedule even if the true private key is stored offline.

This tool was introduced in BIND 9.10.

dnssec-importkey Options

-f `filename`

Zone file mode: instead of a public keyfile name, the argument is the DNS domain name of a zone master file, which can be read from `file`. If the domain name is the same as `file`, then it may be omitted.

If `file` is set to `"-"`, then the zone data is read from the standard input.

-K `directory`

Sets the directory in which the key files are to reside.

-L `ttl`

Sets the default TTL to use for this key when it is converted into a DNSKEY RR. If the key is imported into a zone, this is the TTL that will be used for it, unless there was already a DNSKEY RRset in place, in which case the existing TTL would take precedence. Setting the default TTL to `0` or `none` removes it.

-h

Emit usage message and exit.

-v `level`

Sets the debugging level.

-V

Prints version information.

dnssec-importkey Timing Options

Dates can be expressed in the format YYYYMMDD or YYYYMMDDHHMMSS. If the argument begins with a '+' or '-', it is interpreted as an offset from the present time. For convenience, if such an offset is followed by one of the suffixes 'y', 'mo', 'w', 'd', 'h', or 'mi', then the offset is computed in years (defined as 365 24-hour days, ignoring leap years), months (defined as 30 24-hour days), weeks, days, hours, or minutes, respectively. Without a suffix, the offset is computed in seconds. To explicitly prevent a date from being set, use 'none' or 'never'.

-P `date/offset`

Sets the date on which a key is to be published to the zone. After that date, the key will be included in the zone but will not be used to sign it.

-D `date/offset`

Sets the date on which the key is to be deleted. After that date, the key will no longer be included in the zone. (It may remain in the key repository, however.)

dnssec-importkey Files

A keyfile can be designed by the key identification `Knnnn.+aaa+iiiii` or the full file name `Knnnn.+aaa+iiiii.key` as generated by dnssec-keygen(8).

10.8 dnssec-keyfromlabel — DNSSEC key generation tool

Synopsis

dnssec-keyfromlabel -l *label* [-3] [-a *algorithm*] [-A *date/offset*] [-c *class*] [-D *date/offset*] [-E *engine*] [-f *flag*] [-G] [-I *date/offset*] [-i *interval*] [-k] [-K *directory*] [-L *ttl*] [-n *nametype*] [-P *date/offset*] [-p *protocol*] [-R *date/offset*] [-S *key*] [-t *type*] [-v *level*] [-V] [-y] name

dnssec-keyfromlabel Description

dnssec-keyfromlabel generates a key pair of files that referencing a key object stored in a cryptographic hardware service module (HSM). The private key file can be used for DNSSEC signing of zone data as if it were a conventional signing key created by **dnssec-keygen**, but the key material is stored within the HSM, and the actual signing takes place there.

The name of the key is specified on the command line. This must match the name of the zone for which the key is being generated.

dnssec-keyfromlabel Options

-a *algorithm*

Selects the cryptographic algorithm. The value of algorithm must be one of RSAMD5, RSASHA1, DSA, NSEC3RSASHA1, NSEC3DSA, RSASHA256, RSASHA512, ECCGOST, ECDSAP256SHA256 or ECDSAP384SHA384. These values are case insensitive.

If no algorithm is specified, then RSASHA1 will be used by default, unless the −3 option is specified, in which case NSEC3RSASHA1 will be used instead. (If −3 is used and an algorithm is specified, that algorithm will be checked for compatibility with NSEC3.)

Note 1: that for DNSSEC, RSASHA1 is a mandatory to implement algorithm, and DSA is recommended.

Note 2: DH automatically sets the -k flag.

-3

Use an NSEC3-capable algorithm to generate a DNSSEC key. If this option is used and no algorithm is explicitly set on the command line, NSEC3RSASHA1 will be used by default.

-E *engine*

Specifies the cryptographic hardware to use.

When BIND is built with OpenSSL PKCS#11 support, this defaults to the string "pkcs11", which identifies an OpenSSL engine that can drive a cryptographic accelerator or hardware service module. When BIND 9.10 or later is built with native PKCS#11 cryptography (--enable-native-pkcs11), it defaults to the path of the PKCS#11 provider library specified via "--with-pkcs11". (The native PKCS#11 support was introduced in BIND 9.10. See Section 10.17 for further details.)

-l *label*

Specifies the label for a key pair in the crypto hardware.

When BIND 9 is built with OpenSSL-based PKCS#11 support, the label is an arbitrary string that identifies a particular key. It may be preceded by an optional OpenSSL engine name, followed by a colon, as in "pkcs11:*keylabel*".

When BIND 9 is built with native PKCS#11 support, the label is a PKCS#11 URI string in the format "pkcs11:keyword=*value*[;keyword=*value*;...]" Keywords include "token", which identifies the HSM; "object", which identifies the key; and "pin-source", which identifies a file from which the HSM's PIN code can be obtained. The label will be stored in the on-disk "private" file.

If the label contains a `pin-source` field, tools using the generated key files will be able to use the HSM for signing and other operations without any need for an operator to manually enter a PIN.

Warning

Making the HSM's PIN accessible in this manner may reduce the security advantage of using an HSM; be sure this is what you want to do before making use of this feature.

-n *nametype*

Specifies the owner type of the key. The value of `nametype` must either be ZONE (for a DNSSEC zone key (KEY/DNSKEY)), HOST or ENTITY (for a key associated with a host (KEY)), USER (for a key associated with a user(KEY)) or OTHER (DNSKEY). These values are case insensitive.

-C

Compatibility mode: generates an old-style key, without any metadata. By default, **dnssec-keyfromlabel** will include the key's creation date in the metadata stored with the private key, and other dates may be set there as well (publication date, activation date, etc). Keys that include this data may be incompatible with older versions of BIND; the −C option suppresses them.

-c *class*

Indicates that the DNS record containing the key should have the specified class. If not specified, class IN is used.

-f *flag*

Set the specified flag in the flag field of the KEY/DNSKEY record. The only recognized flags are KSK (Key Signing Key) and REVOKE.

-G

Generate a key, but do not publish it or sign with it. This option is incompatible with -P and -A.

-h

Prints a short summary of the options and arguments to **dnssec-keyfromlabel**.

-K `directory`

Sets the directory in which the key files are to be written.

-k

Generate KEY records rather than DNSKEY records.

-L `ttl`

Sets the default TTL to use for this key when it is converted into a DNSKEY RR. If the key is imported into a zone, this is the TTL that will be used for it, unless there was already a DNSKEY RRset in place, in which case the existing TTL would take precedence. Setting the default TTL to 0 or none removes it. (The -L option was introduced in BIND 9.9.)

-p `protocol`

Sets the protocol value for the key. The protocol is a number between 0 and 255. The default is 3 (DNSSEC). Other possible values for this argument are listed in RFC 2535 and its successors.

-S `key`

Generate a key as an explicit successor to an existing key. The name, algorithm, size, and type of the key will be set to match the predecessor. The activation date of the new key will be set to the inactivation date of the existing one. The publication date will be set to the activation date minus the prepublication interval, which defaults to 30 days.

-t `type`

Indicates the use of the key. type must be one of AUTHCONF, NOAUTHCONF, NOAUTH, or NOCONF. The default is AUTHCONF. AUTH refers to the ability to authenticate data, and CONF the ability to encrypt data.

-v `level`

Sets the debugging level.

-V

Prints version information.

-y

Allows DNSSEC key files to be generated even if the key ID would collide with that of an existing key, in the event of either key being revoked. (This is only safe to use if you are sure you won't be using RFC 5011 trust anchor maintenance with either of the keys involved.)

dnssec-keyfromlabel Timing Options

Dates can be expressed in the format YYYYMMDD or YYYYMMDDHHMMSS. If the argument begins with a '+' or '-', it is interpreted as an offset from the present time. For convenience, if such an offset is followed by one of the suffixes 'y', 'mo', 'w', 'd', 'h', or 'mi', then the offset is computed in years (defined as 365 24-hour days, ignoring leap years), months (defined as 30 24-hour days), weeks, days, hours, or minutes, respectively. Without a suffix, the offset is computed in seconds. To explicitly prevent a date from being set, use 'none' or 'never'.

-P `date/offset`

Sets the date on which a key is to be published to the zone. After that date, the key will be included in the zone but will not be used to sign it. If not set, and if the -G option has not been used, the default is "now".

-A *date/offset*

>   Sets the date on which the key is to be activated. After that date, the key will be included in the zone and used to sign it. If not set, and if the -G option has not been used, the default is "now".

-R *date/offset*

>   Sets the date on which the key is to be revoked. After that date, the key will be flagged as revoked. It will be included in the zone and will be used to sign it.

-I *date/offset*

>   Sets the date on which the key is to be retired. After that date, the key will still be included in the zone, but it will not be used to sign it.

-D *date/offset*

>   Sets the date on which the key is to be deleted. After that date, the key will no longer be included in the zone. (It may remain in the key repository, however.)

-i *interval*

>   Sets the prepublication interval for a key. If set, then the publication and activation dates must be separated by at least this much time. If the activation date is specified but the publication date isn't, then the publication date will default to this much time before the activation date; conversely, if the publication date is specified but activation date isn't, then activation will be set to this much time after publication.

>   If the key is being created as an explicit successor to another key, then the default prepublication interval is 30 days; otherwise it is zero.

>   As with date offsets, if the argument is followed by one of the suffixes 'y', 'mo', 'w', 'd', 'h', or 'mi', then the interval is measured in years, months, weeks, days, hours, or minutes, respectively. Without a suffix, the interval is measured in seconds.

dnssec-keyfromlabel Generated Key Files

When **dnssec-keyfromlabel** completes successfully, it prints a string of the form `Knnnn.+aaa+iiiii` to the standard output. This is an identification string for the key files it has generated.

- `nnnn` is the key name.

- `aaa` is the numeric representation of the algorithm.

- `iiiii` is the key identifier (or footprint).

dnssec-keyfromlabel creates two files, with names based on the printed string. `Knnnn.+aaa+iiiii.key` contains the public key, and `Knnnn.+aaa+iiiii.private` contains the private key.

The `.key` file contains a DNS KEY record that can be inserted into a zone file (directly or with a $INCLUDE statement).

The `.private` file contains algorithm-specific fields. For obvious security reasons, this file does not have general read permission.

10.9 dnssec-keygen — DNSSEC key generation tool

Synopsis

dnssec-keygen [-a *algorithm*] [-b *keysize*] [-n *nametype*] [-3] [-A *date/offset*]
[-C] [-c *class*] [-D *date/offset*] [-E *engine*] [-f *flag*] [-G] [-g *generator*] [-h] [-I
date/offset] [-i *interval*] [-K *directory*] [-L *ttl*] [-k] [-P *date/offset*] [-p *pro
tocol*] [-q] [-R *date/offset*] [-r *randomdev*] [-S *key*] [-s *strength*] [-t *type*] [-v
level] [-V] [-z] name

dnssec-keygen Description

dnssec-keygen generates keys for DNSSEC (Secure DNS), as defined in RFC 2535 and RFC 4034. It
can also generate keys for use with TSIG (Transaction Signatures) as defined in RFC 2845, or TKEY
(Transaction Key) as defined in RFC 2930.

The name of the key is specified on the command line. For DNSSEC keys, this must match the name
of the zone for which the key is being generated.

dnssec-keygen Options

-a *algorithm*

Selects the cryptographic algorithm. For DNSSEC keys, the value of algorithm must be one
of RSAMD5, RSASHA1, DSA, NSEC3RSASHA1, NSEC3DSA, RSASHA256, RSASHA512,
ECCGOST, ECDSAP256SHA256 or ECDSAP384SHA384. For TSIG/TKEY, the value must
be DH (Diffie Hellman), HMAC-MD5, HMAC-SHA1, HMAC-SHA224, HMAC-SHA256,
HMAC-SHA384, or HMAC-SHA512. These values are case insensitive.

If no algorithm is specified, then RSASHA1 will be used by default, unless the −3 option is
specified, in which case NSEC3RSASHA1 will be used instead. (If −3 is used and an algorithm
is specified, that algorithm will be checked for compatibility with NSEC3.)

Note 1: for DNSSEC, RSASHA1 is a mandatory to implement algorithm, and DSA is recommended. For TSIG, HMAC-MD5 is mandatory.

Note 2: DH, HMAC-MD5, and HMAC-SHA1 through HMAC-SHA512 automatically set the
-T KEY option.

-b *keysize*

Specifies the number of bits in the key. The choice of key size depends on the algorithm used.
RSA keys must be between 512 and 2048 bits. Diffie Hellman keys must be between 128 and
4096 bits. DSA keys must be between 512 and 1024 bits and an exact multiple of 64. HMAC
keys must be between 1 and 512 bits. Elliptic curve algorithms don't need this parameter.

The key size does not need to be specified if using a default algorithm. The default key size is
1024 bits for zone signing keys (ZSKs) and 2048 bits for key signing keys (KSKs, generated
with −f KSK). However, if an algorithm is explicitly specified with the −a, then there is no
default key size, and the −b must be used.

-n *nametype*

> Specifies the owner type of the key. The value of `nametype` must either be ZONE (for a DNSSEC zone key (KEY/DNSKEY)), HOST or ENTITY (for a key associated with a host (KEY)), USER (for a key associated with a user(KEY)) or OTHER (DNSKEY). These values are case insensitive. Defaults to ZONE for DNSKEY generation.

-3

> Use an NSEC3-capable algorithm to generate a DNSSEC key. If this option is used and no algorithm is explicitly set on the command line, NSEC3RSASHA1 will be used by default. Note that RSASHA256, RSASHA512, ECCGOST, ECDSAP256SHA256 and ECD-SAP384SHA384 algorithms are NSEC3-capable.

-C

> Compatibility mode: generates an old-style key, without any metadata. By default, **dnssec-keygen** will include the key's creation date in the metadata stored with the private key, and other dates may be set there as well (publication date, activation date, etc). Keys that include this data may be incompatible with older versions of BIND; the $-C$ option suppresses them.

-c *class*

> Indicates that the DNS record containing the key should have the specified class. If not specified, class IN is used.

-E *engine*

> Specifies the cryptographic hardware to use, when applicable.

> When BIND is built with OpenSSL PKCS#11 support, this defaults to the string "pkcs11", which identifies an OpenSSL engine that can drive a cryptographic accelerator or hardware service module. When BIND 9.10 or later is built with native PKCS#11 cryptography (--enable-native-pkcs11), it defaults to the path of the PKCS#11 provider library specified via "--with-pkcs11". (The native PKCS#11 support was introduced in BIND 9.10. See Section 10.17 for further details.)

-e

> If generating an RSAMD5/RSASHA1 key, use a large exponent. The $-e$ was removed in BIND 9.9 and is not in later versions.

-f *flag*

> Set the specified flag in the flag field of the KEY/DNSKEY record. The only recognized flags are KSK (Key Signing Key) and REVOKE.

-G

> Generate a key, but do not publish it or sign with it. This option is incompatible with -P and -A.

-g *generator*

> If generating a Diffie Hellman key, use this generator. Allowed values are 2 and 5. If no generator is specified, a known prime from RFC 2539 will be used if possible; otherwise the default is 2.

-h

> Prints a short summary of the options and arguments to **dnssec-keygen**.

-K *directory*

Sets the directory in which the key files are to be written.

-k

Deprecated in favor of -T KEY.

-L *ttl*

Sets the default TTL to use for this key when it is converted into a DNSKEY RR. If the key is imported into a zone, this is the TTL that will be used for it, unless there was already a DNSKEY RRset in place, in which case the existing TTL would take precedence. If this value is not set and there is no existing DNSKEY RRset, the TTL will default to the SOA TTL. Setting the default TTL to 0 or none is the same as leaving it unset. (The -L option was introduced in BIND 9.9.)

-p *protocol*

Sets the protocol value for the generated key. The protocol is a number between 0 and 255. The default is 3 (DNSSEC). Other possible values for this argument are listed in RFC 2535 and its successors.

-q

Quiet mode: Suppresses unnecessary output, including progress indication. Without this option, when **dnssec-keygen** is run interactively to generate an RSA or DSA key pair, it will print a string of symbols to stderr indicating the progress of the key generation. A '.' indicates that a random number has been found which passed an initial sieve test; '+' means a number has passed a single round of the Miller-Rabin primality test; a space means that the number has passed all the tests and is a satisfactory key.

-r *randomdev*

Specifies the source of randomness. If the operating system does not provide a /dev/random or equivalent device, the default source of randomness is keyboard input. randomdev specifies the name of a character device or file containing random data to be used instead of the default. The special value keyboard indicates that keyboard input should be used.

-S *key*

Create a new key which is an explicit successor to an existing key. The name, algorithm, size, and type of the key will be set to match the existing key. The activation date of the new key will be set to the inactivation date of the existing one. The publication date will be set to the activation date minus the prepublication interval, which defaults to 30 days.

-s *strength*

Specifies the strength value of the key. The strength is a number between 0 and 15, and currently has no defined purpose in DNSSEC.

-T *rrtype*

Specifies the resource record type to use for the key. rrtype must be either DNSKEY or KEY. The default is DNSKEY when using a DNSSEC algorithm, but it can be overridden to KEY for use with SIG(0).

Using any TSIG algorithm (HMAC-* or DH) forces this option to KEY.

-t *type*

Indicates the use of the key. `type` must be one of AUTHCONF, NOAUTHCONF, NOAUTH, or NOCONF. The default is AUTHCONF. AUTH refers to the ability to authenticate data, and CONF the ability to encrypt data.

-v *level*

Sets the debugging level.

-V

Prints version information.

dnssec-keygen Timing Options

Dates can be expressed in the format YYYYMMDD or YYYYMMDDHHMMSS. If the argument begins with a '+' or '-', it is interpreted as an offset from the present time. For convenience, if such an offset is followed by one of the suffixes 'y', 'mo', 'w', 'd', 'h', or 'mi', then the offset is computed in years (defined as 365 24-hour days, ignoring leap years), months (defined as 30 24-hour days), weeks, days, hours, or minutes, respectively. Without a suffix, the offset is computed in seconds. To explicitly prevent a date from being set, use 'none' or 'never'.

-P *date/offset*

Sets the date on which a key is to be published to the zone. After that date, the key will be included in the zone but will not be used to sign it. If not set, and if the -G option has not been used, the default is "now".

-A *date/offset*

Sets the date on which the key is to be activated. After that date, the key will be included in the zone and used to sign it. If not set, and if the -G option has not been used, the default is "now". If set, if and -P is not set, then the publication date will be set to the activation date minus the prepublication interval.

-R *date/offset*

Sets the date on which the key is to be revoked. After that date, the key will be flagged as revoked. It will be included in the zone and will be used to sign it.

-I *date/offset*

Sets the date on which the key is to be retired. After that date, the key will still be included in the zone, but it will not be used to sign it.

-D *date/offset*

Sets the date on which the key is to be deleted. After that date, the key will no longer be included in the zone. (It may remain in the key repository, however.)

-i *interval*

Sets the prepublication interval for a key. If set, then the publication and activation dates must be separated by at least this much time. If the activation date is specified but the publication date isn't, then the publication date will default to this much time before the activation date; conversely, if the publication date is specified but activation date isn't, then activation will be set to this much time after publication.

If the key is being created as an explicit successor to another key, then the default prepublication interval is 30 days; otherwise it is zero.

As with date offsets, if the argument is followed by one of the suffixes 'y', 'mo', 'w', 'd', 'h', or 'mi', then the interval is measured in years, months, weeks, days, hours, or minutes, respectively. Without a suffix, the interval is measured in seconds.

dnssec-keygen Generated Keys

When **dnssec-keygen** completes successfully, it prints a string of the form `Knnnn.+aaa+iiiii` to the standard output. This is an identification string for the key it has generated.

- `nnnn` is the key name.

- `aaa` is the numeric representation of the algorithm.

- `iiiii` is the key identifier (or footprint).

dnssec-keygen creates two files, with names based on the printed string. `Knnnn.+aaa+iiiii.key` contains the public key, and `Knnnn.+aaa+iiiii.private` contains the private key.

The `.key` file contains a DNS KEY record that can be inserted into a zone file (directly or with a $INCLUDE statement).

The `.private` file contains algorithm-specific fields. For obvious security reasons, this file does not have general read permission.

Both `.key` and `.private` files are generated for symmetric encryption algorithms such as HMAC-MD5, even though the public and private key are equivalent.

dnssec-keygen Example

To generate a 768-bit DSA key for the domain **example.com**, the following command would be issued:

```
dnssec-keygen -a DSA -b 768 -n ZONE example.com
```

The command would print a string of the form:

```
Kexample.com.+003+26160
```

In this example, **dnssec-keygen** creates the files `Kexample.com.+003+26160.key` and `Kexample.com.+003+26160.private`.

10.10 dnssec-revoke — set the REVOKED bit on a DNSSEC key

Synopsis

```
dnssec-revoke [-hr] [-v level] [-V] [-K directory] [-E engine] [-f] [-R] keyfile
```

dnssec-revoke Description

dnssec-revoke reads a DNSSEC key file, sets the REVOKED bit on the key as defined in RFC 5011, and creates a new pair of key files containing the now-revoked key.

dnssec-revoke Options

-h

Emit usage message and exit.

-K `directory`

Sets the directory in which the key files are to reside.

-r

After writing the new keyset files remove the original keyset files.

-v `level`

Sets the debugging level.

-V

Prints version information.

-E `engine`

Specifies the cryptographic hardware to use, when applicable.

When BIND is built with OpenSSL PKCS#11 support, this defaults to the string "pkcs11", which identifies an OpenSSL engine that can drive a cryptographic accelerator or hardware service module. When BIND 9.10 or later is built with native PKCS#11 cryptography (--enable-native-pkcs11), it defaults to the path of the PKCS#11 provider library specified via "--with-pkcs11". (The native PKCS#11 support was introduced in BIND 9.10. See Section 10.17 for further details.)

-f

Force overwrite: Causes **dnssec-revoke** to write the new key pair even if a file already exists matching the algorithm and key ID of the revoked key.

-R

Print the key tag of the key with the REVOKE bit set but do not revoke the key.

10.11   dnssec-settime — set DNSSEC key timing metadata

Synopsis

```
dnssec-settime [-f] [-K directory] [-L ttl] [-P date/offset] [-A date/offset]
[-R date/offset] [-I date/offset] [-D date/offset] [-h] [-V] [-v level] [-E eng
ine] keyfile
```

dnssec-settime Description

dnssec-settime reads a DNSSEC private key file and sets the key timing metadata as specified by the −P, −A, −R, −I, and −D options. The metadata can then be used by **dnssec-signzone** or other signing software to determine when a key is to be published, whether it should be used for signing a zone, etc.

If none of these options is set on the command line, then **dnssec-settime** simply prints the key timing metadata already stored in the key.

When key metadata fields are changed, both files of a key pair (Knnnn.+aaa+iiiii.key and Knnnn.+aaa+iiiii.private) are regenerated. Metadata fields are stored in the private file. A human-readable description of the metadata is also placed in comments in the key file. The private file's permissions are always set to be inaccessible to anyone other than the owner (mode 0600).

dnssec-settime Options

-f

> Force an update of an old-format key with no metadata fields. Without this option, **dnssec-settime** will fail when attempting to update a legacy key. With this option, the key will be recreated in the new format, but with the original key data retained. The key's creation date will be set to the present time. If no other values are specified, then the key's publication and activation dates will also be set to the present time.

-K *directory*
> Sets the directory in which the key files are to reside.

-L *ttl*
> Sets the default TTL to use for this key when it is converted into a DNSKEY RR. If the key is imported into a zone, this is the TTL that will be used for it, unless there was already a DNSKEY RRset in place, in which case the existing TTL would take precedence. If this value is not set and there is no existing DNSKEY RRset, the TTL will default to the SOA TTL. Setting the default TTL to 0 or none removes it from the key. (The −L option was introduced in BIND 9.9.)

-h

> Emit usage message and exit.

-V

> Prints version information.

-v *level*
> Sets the debugging level.

-E *engine*
> Specifies the cryptographic hardware to use, when applicable.

> When BIND is built with OpenSSL PKCS#11 support, this defaults to the string "pkcs11", which identifies an OpenSSL engine that can drive a cryptographic accelerator or hardware

service module. When BIND 9.10 or later is built with native PKCS#11 cryptography (--enable-native-pkcs11), it defaults to the path of the PKCS#11 provider library specified via "--with-pkcs11". (The native PKCS#11 support was introduced in BIND 9.10. See Section 10.17 for further details.)

dnssec-settime Timing Options

Dates can be expressed in the format YYYYMMDD or YYYYMMDDHHMMSS. If the argument begins with a '+' or '-', it is interpreted as an offset from the present time. For convenience, if such an offset is followed by one of the suffixes 'y', 'mo', 'w', 'd', 'h', or 'mi', then the offset is computed in years (defined as 365 24-hour days, ignoring leap years), months (defined as 30 24-hour days), weeks, days, hours, or minutes, respectively. Without a suffix, the offset is computed in seconds. To unset a date, use 'none' or 'never'.

-P *date/offset*

> Sets the date on which a key is to be published to the zone. After that date, the key will be included in the zone but will not be used to sign it.

-A *date/offset*

> Sets the date on which the key is to be activated. After that date, the key will be included in the zone and used to sign it.

-R *date/offset*

> Sets the date on which the key is to be revoked. After that date, the key will be flagged as revoked. It will be included in the zone and will be used to sign it.

-I *date/offset*

> Sets the date on which the key is to be retired. After that date, the key will still be included in the zone, but it will not be used to sign it.

-D *date/offset*

> Sets the date on which the key is to be deleted. After that date, the key will no longer be included in the zone. (It may remain in the key repository, however.)

-S *predecessor key*

> Select a key for which the key being modified will be an explicit successor. The name, algorithm, size, and type of the predecessor key must exactly match those of the key being modified. The activation date of the successor key will be set to the inactivation date of the predecessor. The publication date will be set to the activation date minus the prepublication interval, which defaults to 30 days.

-i *interval*

> Sets the prepublication interval for a key. If set, then the publication and activation dates must be separated by at least this much time. If the activation date is specified but the publication date isn't, then the publication date will default to this much time before the activation date; conversely, if the publication date is specified but activation date isn't, then activation will be set to this much time after publication.

> If the key is being set to be an explicit successor to another key, then the default prepublication interval is 30 days; otherwise it is zero.

As with date offsets, if the argument is followed by one of the suffixes 'y', 'mo', 'w', 'd', 'h', or 'mi', then the interval is measured in years, months, weeks, days, hours, or minutes, respectively. Without a suffix, the interval is measured in seconds.

dnssec-settime Printing Options

dnssec-settime can also be used to print the timing metadata associated with a key.

-u
> Print times in UNIX epoch format.

-p `C/P/A/R/I/D/all`
> Print a specific metadata value or set of metadata values. The -p option may be followed by one or more of the following letters to indicate which value or values to print: C for the creation date, P for the publication date, A for the activation date, R for the revocation date, I for the inactivation date, or D for the deletion date. To print all of the metadata, use -p all.

10.12 dnssec-signzone — DNSSEC zone signing tool

Synopsis

```
dnssec-signzone [-a] [-c class] [-d directory] [-D] [-E engine] [-e end-time] [-
f output-file] [-g] [-h] [-K directory] [-k key] [-L serial] [-l domain] [-M dom
ain] [-i interval] [-I input-format] [-j jitter] [-N soa-serial-format] [-o ori
gin] [-O output-format] [-P] [-p] [-Q] [-R] [-r randomdev] [-S] [-s start-time] [-T
ttl] [-t] [-u] [-v level] [-V] [-X extended end-time] [-x] [-z] [-3 salt] [-H iterat
ions] [-A] zonefile [key...]
```

dnssec-signzone Description

dnssec-signzone signs a zone. It generates NSEC and RRSIG records and produces a signed version of the zone. The security status of delegations from the signed zone (that is, whether the child zones are secure or not) is determined by the presence or absence of a `keyset` file for each child zone.

dnssec-signzone Options

-a
> Verify all generated signatures.

-c `class`
> Specifies the DNS class of the zone.

-C

    Compatibility mode: Generate a `keyset-`*`zonename`* file in addition to `dsset-`*`zonename`* when signing a zone, for use by older versions of **dnssec-signzone**.

-d *directory*

    Look for `dsset-` or `keyset-` files in `directory`.

-D

    Output only those record types automatically managed by **dnssec-signzone**, i.e. RRSIG, NSEC, NSEC3 and NSEC3PARAM records. If smart signing (`-S`) is used, DNSKEY records are also included. The resulting file can be included in the original zone file with **$INCLUDE**. This option cannot be combined with `-O raw`, `-O map`, or serial number updating. (The `-D` option was introduced in BIND 9.9.)

-E *engine*

    When applicable, specifies the hardware to use for cryptographic operations, such as a secure key store used for signing.

    When BIND is built with OpenSSL PKCS#11 support, this defaults to the string "pkcs11", which identifies an OpenSSL engine that can drive a cryptographic accelerator or hardware service module. When BIND 9.10 or later is built with native PKCS#11 cryptography (--enable-native-pkcs11), it defaults to the path of the PKCS#11 provider library specified via "--with-pkcs11". (The native PKCS#11 support was introduced in BIND 9.10. See Section 10.17 for further details.)

-g

    Generate DS records for child zones from `dsset-` or `keyset-` file. Existing DS records will be removed.

-K *directory*

    Key repository: Specify a directory to search for DNSSEC keys. If not specified, defaults to the current directory.

-k *key*

    Treat specified key as a key signing key ignoring any key flags. This option may be specified multiple times.

-l *domain*

    Generate a DLV set in addition to the key (DNSKEY) and DS sets. The domain is appended to the name of the records.

-M *maxttl*

    Sets the maximum TTL for the signed zone. Any TTL higher than *maxttl* in the input zone will be reduced to *maxttl* in the output. This provides certainty as to the largest possible TTL in the signed zone, which is useful to know when rolling keys because it is the longest possible time before signatures that have been retrieved by resolvers will expire from resolver caches. Zones that are signed with this option should be configured to use a matching `max-zone-ttl` in `named.conf`. (Note: This option is incompatible with `-D`, because it modifies non-DNSSEC data in the output zone.) (The `-M` option was introduced in BIND 9.10.)

-s *start-time*

Specify the date and time when the generated RRSIG records become valid. This can be either an absolute or relative time. An absolute start time is indicated by a number in YYYYMMD-DHHMMSS notation; 20000530144500 denotes 14:45:00 UTC on May 30th, 2000. A relative start time is indicated by +N, which is N seconds from the current time. If no start-time is specified, the current time minus 1 hour (to allow for clock skew) is used.

-e *end-time*

Specify the date and time when the generated RRSIG records expire. As with start-time, an absolute time is indicated in YYYYMMDDHHMMSS notation. A time relative to the start time is indicated with +N, which is N seconds from the start time. A time relative to the current time is indicated with now+N. If no end-time is specified, 30 days from the start time is used as a default. end-time must be later than start-time.

-X *extended end-time*

Specify the date and time when the generated RRSIG records for the DNSKEY RRset will expire. This is to be used in cases when the DNSKEY signatures need to persist longer than signatures on other records; e.g., when the private component of the KSK is kept offline and the KSK signature is to be refreshed manually. (The −X option was introduced in BIND 9.9.)

As with start-time, an absolute time is indicated in YYYYMMDDHHMMSS notation. A time relative to the start time is indicated with +N, which is N seconds from the start time. A time relative to the current time is indicated with now+N. If no extended end-time is specified, the value of end-time is used as the default. (end-time, in turn, defaults to 30 days from the start time.) extended end-time must be later than start-time.

-f *output-file*

The name of the output file containing the signed zone. The default is to append .signed to the input filename. If output-file is set to "-", then the signed zone is written to the standard output, with a default output format of "full".

-h

Prints a short summary of the options and arguments to **dnssec-signzone**.

-V

Prints version information.

-i *interval*

When a previously-signed zone is passed as input, records may be resigned. The interval option specifies the cycle interval as an offset from the current time (in seconds). If a RRSIG record expires after the cycle interval, it is retained. Otherwise, it is considered to be expiring soon, and it will be replaced.

The default cycle interval is one quarter of the difference between the signature end and start times. So if neither end-time or start-time are specified, **dnssec-signzone** generates signatures that are valid for 30 days, with a cycle interval of 7.5 days. Therefore, if any existing RRSIG records are due to expire in less than 7.5 days, they would be replaced.

-I *input-format*

The format of the input zone file. Possible formats are **"text"** (default), **"raw"**, and **"map"**. This option is primarily intended to be used for dynamic signed zones so that the dumped zone file in a non-text format containing updates can be signed directly. The use of this option does not make much sense for non-dynamic zones. (The **"map"** format was introduced in BIND 9.10.)

-j *jitter*

When signing a zone with a fixed signature lifetime, all RRSIG records issued at the time of signing expires simultaneously. If the zone is incrementally signed, i.e. a previously-signed zone is passed as input to the signer, all expired signatures have to be regenerated at about the same time. The `jitter` option specifies a jitter window that will be used to randomize the signature expire time, thus spreading incremental signature regeneration over time.

Signature lifetime jitter also to some extent benefits validators and servers by spreading out cache expiration, i.e. if large numbers of RRSIGs don't expire at the same time from all caches there will be less congestion than if all validators need to refetch at mostly the same time.

-L *serial*

When writing a signed zone to "raw" or "map" format, set the "source serial" value in the header to the specified serial number. (This is expected to be used primarily for testing purposes.) (The −L option was introduced in BIND 9.9.)

-n *ncpus*

Specifies the number of threads to use. By default, one thread is started for each detected CPU.

-N *soa-serial-format*

The SOA serial number format of the signed zone. Possible formats are **"keep"** (default), **"increment"**, **"unixtime"**, and **"date"**.

"keep"

Do not modify the SOA serial number.

"increment"

Increment the SOA serial number using RFC 1982 arithmetics.

"unixtime"

Set the SOA serial number to the number of seconds since epoch.

"date"

Set the SOA serial number to today's date in YYYYMMDDNN format. The **"date"** format was introduced in BIND 9.11.

-o *origin*

The zone origin. If not specified, the name of the zone file is assumed to be the origin.

-O *output-format*

The format of the output file containing the signed zone. Possible formats are **"text"** (default), which is the standard textual representation of the zone; **"full"**, which is text output in a format suitable for processing by external scripts; and **"map"**, **"raw"**, and **"raw=N"**, which store the zone in binary formats for rapid loading by **named**. **"raw=N"** (introduced in BIND 9.9) specifies the format version of the raw zone file: if N is 0, the raw file can be read by any version of **named**; if N is 1, the file can be read by release 9.9.0 or higher; the default is 1. (The **"map"** format was introduced in BIND 9.10.)

-p

Use pseudo-random data when signing the zone. This is faster, but less secure, than using real random data. This option may be useful when signing large zones or when the entropy source is limited.

-P

Disable post sign verification tests.

The post sign verification test ensures that for each algorithm in use there is at least one non revoked self signed KSK key, that all revoked KSK keys are self signed, and that all records in the zone are signed by the algorithm. This option skips these tests.

-Q

Remove signatures from keys that are no longer active.

Normally, when a previously-signed zone is passed as input to the signer, and a DNSKEY record has been removed and replaced with a new one, signatures from the old key that are still within their validity period are retained. This allows the zone to continue to validate with cached copies of the old DNSKEY RRset. The -Q forces **dnssec-signzone** to remove signatures from keys that are no longer active. This enables ZSK rollover using the procedure described in RFC 4641, section 4.2.1.1 ("Pre-Publish Key Rollover").

-R

Remove signatures from keys that are no longer published.

This option is similar to -Q, except it forces **dnssec-signzone** to signatures from keys that are no longer published. This enables ZSK rollover using the procedure described in RFC 4641, section 4.2.1.2 ("Double Signature Zone Signing Key Rollover").

-r `randomdev`

Specifies the source of randomness. If the operating system does not provide a `/dev/random` or equivalent device, the default source of randomness is keyboard input. `randomdev` specifies the name of a character device or file containing random data to be used instead of the default. The special value `keyboard` indicates that keyboard input should be used.

-S

Smart signing: Instructs **dnssec-signzone** to search the key repository for keys that match the zone being signed, and to include them in the zone if appropriate.

When a key is found, its timing metadata is examined to determine how it should be used, according to the following rules. Each successive rule takes priority over the prior ones:

If no timing metadata has been set for the key, the key is published in the zone and used to sign the zone.

If the key's publication date is set and is in the past, the key is published in the zone.

If the key's activation date is set and in the past, the key is published (regardless of publication date) and used to sign the zone.

If the key's revocation date is set and in the past, and the key is published, then the key is revoked, and the revoked key is used to sign the zone.

If either of the key's unpublication or deletion dates are set and in the past, the key is NOT published or used to sign the zone, regardless of any other metadata.

-T *ttl*

Specifies a TTL to be used for new DNSKEY records imported into the zone from the key repository. If not specified, the default is the TTL value from the zone's SOA record. This option is ignored when signing without −S, since DNSKEY records are not imported from the key repository in that case. It is also ignored if there are any pre-existing DNSKEY records at the zone apex, in which case new records' TTL values will be set to match them, or if any of the imported DNSKEY records had a default TTL value. In the event of a a conflict between TTL values in imported keys, the shortest one is used.

-t

Print statistics at completion.

-u

Update NSEC/NSEC3 chain when re-signing a previously signed zone. With this option, a zone signed with NSEC can be switched to NSEC3, or a zone signed with NSEC3 can be switch to NSEC or to NSEC3 with different parameters. Without this option, **dnssec-signzone** will retain the existing chain when re-signing.

-v *level*

Sets the debugging level.

-x

Only sign the DNSKEY RRset with key-signing keys, and omit signatures from zone-signing keys. (This is similar to the **dnssec-dnskey-kskonly yes;** zone option in **named**.)

-z

Ignore KSK flag on key when determining what to sign. This causes KSK-flagged keys to sign all records, not just the DNSKEY RRset. (This is similar to the **update-check-ksk no;** zone option in **named**.)

-3 *salt*

Generate an NSEC3 chain with the given hex encoded salt. A dash (*salt*) can be used to indicate that no salt is to be used when generating the NSEC3 chain.

-H *iterations*

When generating an NSEC3 chain, use this many iterations. The default is 10.

-A

When generating an NSEC3 chain set the OPTOUT flag on all NSEC3 records and do not generate NSEC3 records for insecure delegations.

Using this option twice (i.e., −AA) turns the OPTOUT flag off for all records. This is useful when using the −u option to modify an NSEC3 chain which previously had OPTOUT set.

zonefile

> The file containing the zone to be signed.

key

> Specify which keys should be used to sign the zone. If no keys are specified, then the zone will be examined for DNSKEY records at the zone apex. If these are found and there are matching private keys, in the current directory, then these will be used for signing.

dnssec-signzone Example

The following command signs the **example.com** zone with the DSA key generated by **dnssec-keygen** (Kexample.com.+003+17247). Because the **-S** option is not being used, the zone's keys must be in the master file (db.example.com). This invocation looks for dsset files, in the current directory, so that DS records can be imported from them (**-g**).

```
% dnssec-signzone -g -o example.com db.example.com \
Kexample.com.+003+17247
db.example.com.signed
%
```

In the above example, **dnssec-signzone** creates the file db.example.com.signed. This file should be referenced in a zone statement in a named.conf file.

This example re-signs a previously signed zone with default parameters. The private keys are assumed to be in the current directory.

```
% cp db.example.com.signed db.example.com
% dnssec-signzone -o example.com db.example.com
db.example.com.signed
%
```

10.13   dnssec-verify — DNSSEC zone verification tool

Synopsis

dnssec-verify [-c *class*] [-E *engine*] [-I *input-format*] [-o *origin*] [-v *level*] [-V] [-x] [-z] zonefile

dnssec-verify Description

dnssec-verify verifies that a zone is fully signed for each algorithm found in the DNSKEY RRset for the zone, and that the NSEC / NSEC3 chains are complete. This utility was introduced in BIND 9.9.

dnssec-verify Options

-c *class*
: Specifies the DNS class of the zone.

-E *engine*
: Specifies the cryptographic hardware to use, when applicable.

   When BIND is built with OpenSSL PKCS#11 support, this defaults to the string "pkcs11", which identifies an OpenSSL engine that can drive a cryptographic accelerator or hardware service module. When BIND 9.10 or later is built with native PKCS#11 cryptography (--enable-native-pkcs11), it defaults to the path of the PKCS#11 provider library specified via "--with-pkcs11". (The native PKCS#11 support was introduced in BIND 9.10. See Section 10.17 for further details.)

-I *input-format*
: The format of the input zone file. Possible formats are **"text"** (default) and **"raw"**. This option is primarily intended to be used for dynamic signed zones so that the dumped zone file in a non-text format containing updates can be verified independently. The use of this option does not make much sense for non-dynamic zones.

-o *origin*
: The zone origin. If not specified, the name of the zone file is assumed to be the origin.

-v *level*
: Sets the debugging level.

-V
: Prints version information.

-x
: Only verify that the DNSKEY RRset is signed with key-signing keys. Without this flag, it is assumed that the DNSKEY RRset will be signed by all active keys. When this flag is set, it will not be an error if the DNSKEY RRset is not signed by zone-signing keys. This corresponds to the −x option in **dnssec-signzone**.

-z
: Ignore the KSK flag on the keys when determining whether the zone if correctly signed. Without this flag it is assumed that there will be a non-revoked, self-signed DNSKEY with the KSK flag set for each algorithm and that RRsets other than DNSKEY RRset will be signed with a different DNSKEY without the KSK flag set.

   With this flag set, we only require that for each algorithm, there will be at least one non-revoked, self-signed DNSKEY, regardless of the KSK flag state, and that other RRsets will be signed by a non-revoked key for the same algorithm that includes the self-signed key; the same key may be used for both purposes. This corresponds to the −z option in **dnssec-signzone**.

zonefile
: The file containing the zone to be signed.

10.14   nsec3hash — generate NSEC3 hash

Synopsis

```
nsec3hash salt algorithm iterations domain
```

nsec3hash Description

nsec3hash generates an NSEC3 hash based on a set of NSEC3 parameters. This can be used to check the validity of NSEC3 records in a signed zone.

nsec3hash Arguments

salt
> The salt provided to the hash algorithm.

algorithm
> A number indicating the hash algorithm. Currently the only supported hash algorithm for NSEC3 is SHA-1, which is indicated by the number 1; consequently "1" is the only useful value for this argument.

iterations
> The number of additional times the hash should be performed.

domain
> The domain name to be hashed.

10.15   DNSSEC, Dynamic Zones, and Automatic Signing

As of BIND 9.7.0 it is possible to change a dynamic zone from insecure to signed and back again. A secure zone can use either NSEC or NSEC3 chains.

Converting from insecure to secure

Changing a zone from insecure to secure can be done in two ways: using a dynamic DNS update, or the **auto-dnssec** zone option.

For either method, you need to configure **named** so that it can see the K* files which contain the public and private parts of the keys that will be used to sign the zone. These files will have been generated by **dnssec-keygen**. You can do this by placing them in the key directory, as specified in `named.conf`:

```
zone example.net {
        type master;
        update-policy local;
        file "dynamic/example.net/example.net";
        key-directory "dynamic/example.net";
};
```

If one KSK and one ZSK DNSKEY key have been generated, this configuration will cause all records in the zone to be signed with the ZSK, and the DNSKEY RRset to be signed with the KSK as well. An NSEC chain will be generated as part of the initial signing process.

Dynamic DNS update method

To insert the keys via dynamic update:

```
% nsupdate
> ttl 3600
> update add example.net DNSKEY 256 3 7  ↵
    AwEAAZn17pUF0KpbPA2c7Gz76Vb18v0teKT3EyAGfBfL8eQ8al35zz3Y  ↵
    I1m/SAQBxIqMfLtIwqWPdgthsu36azGQAX8=
> update add example.net DNSKEY 257 3 7 AwEAAd/7odU/64  ↵
    o2LGsifbLtQmtO8dFDtTAZXSX2+X3e/UNlq9IHq3Y0 XtC0Iuawl/  ↵
    qkaKVxXe2lo8Ct+dM6UehyCqk=
> send
```

While the update request will complete almost immediately, the zone will not be completely signed until **named** has had time to walk the zone and generate the NSEC and RRSIG records. The NSEC record at the apex will be added last, to signal that there is a complete NSEC chain.

If you wish to sign using NSEC3 instead of NSEC, you should add an NSEC3PARAM record to the initial update request. If you wish the NSEC3 chain to have the OPTOUT bit set, set it in the flags field of the NSEC3PARAM record.

```
% nsupdate
> ttl 3600
> update add example.net DNSKEY 256 3 7  ↵
    AwEAAZn17pUF0KpbPA2c7Gz76Vb18v0teKT3EyAGfBfL8eQ8al35zz3Y  ↵
    I1m/SAQBxIqMfLtIwqWPdgthsu36azGQAX8=
> update add example.net DNSKEY 257 3 7 AwEAAd/7odU/64  ↵
    o2LGsifbLtQmtO8dFDtTAZXSX2+X3e/UNlq9IHq3Y0 XtC0Iuawl/  ↵
    qkaKVxXe2lo8Ct+dM6UehyCqk=
> update add example.net NSEC3PARAM 1 1 100 1234567890
> send
```

Again, this update request will complete almost immediately; however, the record won't show up until **named** has had a chance to build/remove the relevant chain. A private type record will be created to record the state of the operation (see below for more details), and will be removed once the operation completes.

While the initial signing and NSEC/NSEC3 chain generation is happening, other updates are possible as well.

Fully automatic zone signing

To enable automatic signing, add the **auto-dnssec** option to the zone statement in `named.conf`. **auto-dnssec** has two possible arguments: `allow` or `maintain`.

With **auto-dnssec allow**, **named** can search the key directory for keys matching the zone, insert them into the zone, and use them to sign the zone. It will do so only when it receives an **rndc sign <zonename>**.

auto-dnssec maintain includes the above functionality, but will also automatically adjust the zone's DNSKEY records on schedule according to the keys' timing metadata. (See dnssec-keygen(8) and dnssec-settime(8) for more information.)

As of BIND 9.9, **named** will periodically search the key directory for keys matching the zone, and if the keys' metadata indicates that any change should be made the zone, such as adding, removing, or revoking a key, then that action will be carried out. By default, the key directory is checked for changes every 60 minutes; this period can be adjusted with the `dnssec-loadkeys-interval`, up to a maximum of 24 hours. The **rndc loadkeys** forces **named** to check for key updates immediately.

If keys are present in the key directory the first time the zone is loaded, the zone will be signed immediately, without waiting for an **rndc sign** or **rndc loadkeys** command. (Those commands can still be used when there are unscheduled key changes, however.)

When new keys are added to a zone, the TTL is set to match that of any existing DNSKEY RRset. If there is no existing DNSKEY RRset, then the TTL will be set to the TTL specified when the key was created (using the **dnssec-keygen -L** option), if any, or to the SOA TTL.

If you wish the zone to be signed using NSEC3 instead of NSEC, submit an NSEC3PARAM record via dynamic update prior to the scheduled publication and activation of the keys. If you wish the NSEC3 chain to have the OPTOUT bit set, set it in the flags field of the NSEC3PARAM record. The NSEC3PARAM record will not appear in the zone immediately, but it will be stored for later reference. When the zone is signed and the NSEC3 chain is completed, the NSEC3PARAM record will appear in the zone. (This support was introduced in BIND 9.9.)

Using the **auto-dnssec** option requires the zone to be configured to allow dynamic updates, by adding an **allow-update** or **update-policy** statement to the zone configuration. If this has not been done, the configuration will fail.

Private-type records

The state of the signing process is signaled by private-type records (with a default type value of 65534). When signing is complete, these records will have a nonzero value for the final octet (for those records which have a nonzero initial octet).

The private type record format: If the first octet is non-zero then the record indicates that the zone needs to be signed with the key matching the record, or that all signatures that match the record should be removed.

```
algorithm (octet 1)
```

```
key id in network order (octet 2 and 3)
removal flag (octet 4)
complete flag (octet 5)
```

Only records flagged as "complete" can be removed via dynamic update. Attempts to remove other private type records will be silently ignored.

If the first octet is zero (this is a reserved algorithm number that should never appear in a DNSKEY record) then the record indicates changes to the NSEC3 chains are in progress. The rest of the record contains an NSEC3PARAM record. The flag field tells what operation to perform based on the flag bits.

```
0x01 OPTOUT
0x80 CREATE
0x40 REMOVE
0x20 NONSEC
```

DNSKEY rollovers

As with insecure-to-secure conversions, rolling DNSSEC keys can be done in two ways: using a dynamic DNS update, or the **auto-dnssec** zone option.

Dynamic DNS update method

To perform key rollovers via dynamic update, you need to add the K* files for the new keys so that **named** can find them. You can then add the new DNSKEY RRs via dynamic update. **named** will then cause the zone to be signed with the new keys. When the signing is complete the private type records will be updated so that the last octet is non zero.

If this is for a KSK you need to inform the parent and any trust anchor repositories of the new KSK.

You should then wait for the maximum TTL in the zone before removing the old DNSKEY. If it is a KSK that is being updated, you also need to wait for the DS RRset in the parent to be updated and its TTL to expire. This ensures that all clients will be able to verify at least one signature when you remove the old DNSKEY.

The old DNSKEY can be removed via UPDATE. Take care to specify the correct key. **named** will clean out any signatures generated by the old key after the update completes.

Automatic key rollovers

When a new key reaches its activation date (as set by **dnssec-keygen** or **dnssec-settime**), if the **auto-dnssec** zone option is set to maintain, **named** will automatically carry out the key rollover. If the key's algorithm has not previously been used to sign the zone, then the zone will be fully signed as quickly as possible. However, if the new key is replacing an existing key of the same algorithm, then the zone will be re-signed incrementally, with signatures from the old key being replaced with signatures from the new key as their signature validity periods expire. By default, this rollover completes in 30 days, after which it will be safe to remove the old key from the DNSKEY RRset.

NSEC3PARAM rollovers via UPDATE

Add the new NSEC3PARAM record via dynamic update. When the new NSEC3 chain has been generated, the NSEC3PARAM flag field will be zero. At this point you can remove the old NSEC3PARAM record. The old chain will be removed after the update request completes.

Converting from NSEC to NSEC3

To do this, you just need to add an NSEC3PARAM record. When the conversion is complete, the NSEC chain will have been removed and the NSEC3PARAM record will have a zero flag field. The NSEC3 chain will be generated before the NSEC chain is destroyed.

Converting from NSEC3 to NSEC

To do this, use **nsupdate** to remove all NSEC3PARAM records with a zero flag field. The NSEC chain will be generated before the NSEC3 chain is removed.

Converting from secure to insecure

To convert a signed zone to unsigned using dynamic DNS, delete all the DNSKEY records from the zone apex using **nsupdate**. All signatures, NSEC or NSEC3 chains, and associated NSEC3PARAM records will be removed automatically. This will take place after the update request completes.

This requires the **dnssec-secure-to-insecure** option to be set to **yes** in named.conf.

In addition, if the **auto-dnssec maintain** zone statement is used, it should be removed or changed to **allow** instead (or it will re-sign).

Periodic re-signing

In any secure zone which supports dynamic updates, **named** will periodically re-sign RRsets which have not been re-signed as a result of some update action. The signature lifetimes will be adjusted so as to spread the re-sign load over time rather than all at once.

NSEC3 and OPTOUT

named only supports creating new NSEC3 chains where all the NSEC3 records in the zone have the same OPTOUT state. **named** supports UPDATES to zones where the NSEC3 records in the chain have mixed OPTOUT state. **named** does not support changing the OPTOUT state of an individual NSEC3 record, the entire chain needs to be changed if the OPTOUT state of an individual NSEC3 needs to be changed.

10.16   Dynamic Trust Anchor Management

BIND 9.7.0 introduces support for dynamic trust anchor management as defined in RFC 5011. Using this feature allows **named** to keep track of changes to critical DNSSEC keys without any need for the operator to make changes to configuration files.

Validating Resolver

To configure a validating resolver to use RFC 5011 to maintain a trust anchor, configure the trust anchor using a **managed-keys** statement. Information about this can be found in Section 6.11.

Authoritative Server

To set up an authoritative zone for RFC 5011 trust anchor maintenance, generate two (or more) key signing keys (KSKs) for the zone. Sign the zone with one of them; this is the "active" KSK. All KSKs which do not sign the zone are "stand-by" keys.

Any validating resolver which is configured to use the active KSK as an RFC 5011-managed trust anchor will take note of the stand-by KSKs in the zone's DNSKEY RRset, and store them for future reference. The resolver will recheck the zone periodically, and after 30 days, if the new key is still there, then the key will be accepted by the resolver as a valid trust anchor for the zone. Any time after this 30-day acceptance timer has completed, the active KSK can be revoked, and the zone can be "rolled over" to the newly accepted key.

The easiest way to place a stand-by key in a zone is to use the "smart signing" features of **dnssec-keygen** and **dnssec-signzone**. If a key with a publication date in the past, but an activation date which is unset or in the future, "**dnssec-signzone -S**" will include the DNSKEY record in the zone, but will not sign with it:

```
$ dnssec-keygen -K keys -f KSK -P now -A now+2y example.net
$ dnssec-signzone -S -K keys example.net
```

To revoke a key, use the **dnssec-revoke** command. This adds the REVOKED bit to the key flags and re-generates the K*.key and K*.private files.

After revoking the active key, the zone must be signed with both the revoked KSK and the new active KSK. (Smart signing takes care of this automatically.)

Once a key has been revoked and used to sign the DNSKEY RRset in which it appears, that key will never again be accepted as a valid trust anchor by the resolver. However, validation can proceed using the new active key (which had been accepted by the resolver when it was a stand-by key).

When a key has been revoked, its key ID changes, increasing by 128, and wrapping around at 65535. So, for example, the key "Kexample.com.+005+10000" becomes "Kexample.com.+005+10128".

If two keys have IDs exactly 128 apart, and one is revoked, then the two key IDs will collide, causing several problems. To prevent this, **dnssec-keygen** will not generate a new key if another key is present which may collide. This checking will only occur if the new keys are written to the same directory which holds all other keys in use for that zone.

Older versions of BIND 9 did not have this precaution. Exercise caution if using key revocation on keys that were generated by previous releases, or if using keys stored in multiple directories or on multiple machines.

It is expected that a future release of BIND 9 will address this problem in a different way, by storing revoked keys with their original unrevoked key IDs.

10.17 PKCS#11 (Cryptoki) support

PKCS#11 (Public Key Cryptography Standard #11) defines a platform-independent API for the control of hardware security modules (HSMs) and other cryptographic support devices.

BIND 9 is known to work with three HSMs: The AEP Keyper, which has been tested with Debian Linux, Solaris x86 and Windows Server 2003; the Thales nShield, tested with Debian Linux; and the Sun SCA 6000 cryptographic acceleration board, tested with Solaris x86. In addition, BIND can be used with all current versions of SoftHSM, a software-based HSM simulator library produced by the OpenDNSSEC project.

PKCS#11 makes use of a "provider library": a dynamically loadable library which provides a low-level PKCS#11 interface to drive the HSM hardware. The PKCS#11 provider library comes from the HSM vendor, and it is specific to the HSM to be controlled.

There are two available mechanisms for PKCS#11 support in BIND 9: OpenSSL-based PKCS#11 and native PKCS#11. When using the first mechanism, BIND uses a modified version of OpenSSL, which loads the provider library and operates the HSM indirectly; any cryptographic operations not supported by the HSM can be carried out by OpenSSL instead. The second mechanism enables BIND to bypass OpenSSL completely; BIND loads the provider library itself, and uses the PKCS#11 API to drive the HSM directly.

Prerequisites

See the documentation provided by your HSM vendor for information about installing, initializing, testing and troubleshooting the HSM.

Native PKCS#11

Native PKCS#11 mode will only work with an HSM capable of carrying out *every* cryptographic operation BIND 9 may need. The HSM's provider library must have a complete implementation of the PKCS#11 API, so that all these functions are accessible. As of this writing, only the Thales nShield HSM and SoftHSMv2 can be used in this fashion. For other HSMs, including the AEP Keyper, Sun SCA 6000 and older versions of SoftHSM, use OpenSSL-based PKCS#11. (Note: Eventually, when more HSMs become capable of supporting native PKCS#11, it is expected that OpenSSL-based PKCS#11 will be deprecated.)

Support for using native PKCS#11 was introduced in BIND 9.10. To build BIND with native PKCS#11, configure as follows:

```
$ cd bind9
$ ./configure --enable-native-pkcs11 \
  --with-pkcs11=provider-library-path
```

This will cause all BIND tools, including **named** and the **dnssec-*** and **pkcs11-*** tools, to use the PKCS#11 provider library specified in *provider-library-path* for cryptography. (The provider library path can be overridden using the −E in **named** and the **dnssec-*** tools, or the −m in the **pkcs11-*** tools.)

Building SoftHSMv2

SoftHSMv2, the latest development version of SoftHSM, is available from https://github.com/opendnssec/-SoftHSMv2 . It is a software library developed by the OpenDNSSEC project (http://www.opendnssec.org) which provides a PKCS#11 interface to a virtual HSM, implemented in the form of a SQLite3 database on the local filesystem. It provides less security than a true HSM, but it allows you to experiment with native PKCS#11 when an HSM is not available. SoftHSMv2 can be configured to use either OpenSSL or the Botan library to perform cryptographic functions, but when using it for native PKCS#11 in BIND, OpenSSL is required.

By default, the SoftHSMv2 configuration file is *prefix*/etc/softhsm2.conf (where *prefix* is configured at compile time). This location can be overridden by the SOFTHSM2_CONF environment variable. The SoftHSMv2 cryptographic store must be installed and initialized before using it with BIND.

```
$   cd SoftHSMv2
$   configure --with-crypto-backend=openssl --prefix=/opt/pkcs11/usr -- ↵
    enable-gost
$   make
$   make install
$   /opt/pkcs11/usr/bin/softhsm-util --init-token 0 --slot 0 --label ↵
    softhsmv2
```

OpenSSL-based PKCS#11

OpenSSL-based PKCS#11 mode uses a modified version of the OpenSSL library; stock OpenSSL does not fully support PKCS#11. ISC provides a patch to OpenSSL to correct this. This patch is based on work originally done by the OpenSolaris project; it has been modified by ISC to provide new features such as PIN management and key-by-reference.

There are two "flavors" of PKCS#11 support provided by the patched OpenSSL, one of which must be chosen at configuration time. The correct choice depends on the HSM hardware:

- Use 'crypto-accelerator' with HSMs that have hardware cryptographic acceleration features, such as the SCA 6000 board. This causes OpenSSL to run all supported cryptographic operations in the HSM.

- Use 'sign-only' with HSMs that are designed to function primarily as secure key storage devices, but lack hardware acceleration. These devices are highly secure, but are not necessarily any faster at cryptography than the system CPU — often, they are slower. It is therefore most efficient to use them only for those cryptographic functions that require access to the secured private key, such as zone signing, and to use the system CPU for all other computationally-intensive operations. The AEP Keyper is an example of such a device.

The modified OpenSSL code is included in the BIND 9 release, in the form of a context diff against the latest versions of OpenSSL. OpenSSL 0.9.8, 1.0.0, and 1.0.1 are supported; there are separate diffs for each version. In the examples to follow, we use OpenSSL 0.9.8, but the same methods work with OpenSSL 1.0.0 and 1.0.1.

Note
The latest OpenSSL versions as of this writing (January 2015) are 0.9.8zc, 1.0.0o, and 1.0.1j. ISC will provide updated patches as new versions of OpenSSL are released. The version number in the following examples is expected to change.

Before building BIND 9 with PKCS#11 support, it will be necessary to build OpenSSL with the patch in place, and configure it with the path to your HSM's PKCS#11 provider library.

Patching OpenSSL

```
$ wget http://www.openssl.org/source/openssl-0.9.8zc.tar.gz
```

Extract the tarball:

```
$ tar zxf openssl-0.9.8zc.tar.gz
```

Apply the patch from the BIND 9 release:

```
$ patch -p1 -d openssl-0.9.8zc \
        < bind9/bin/pkcs11/openssl-0.9.8zc-patch
```

Note
The patch file may not be compatible with the "patch" utility on all operating systems. You may need to install GNU patch.

When building OpenSSL, place it in a non-standard location so that it does not interfere with OpenSSL libraries elsewhere on the system. In the following examples, we choose to install into "/opt/pkcs11/usr". We will use this location when we configure BIND 9.

Later, when building BIND 9, the location of the custom-built OpenSSL library will need to be specified via configure.

Building OpenSSL for the AEP Keyper on Linux

The AEP Keyper is a highly secure key storage device, but does not provide hardware cryptographic acceleration. It can carry out cryptographic operations, but it is probably slower than your system's CPU. Therefore, we choose the 'sign-only' flavor when building OpenSSL.

The Keyper-specific PKCS#11 provider library is delivered with the Keyper software. In this example, we place it /opt/pkcs11/usr/lib:

```
$ cp pkcs11.GCC4.0.2.so.4.05 /opt/pkcs11/usr/lib/libpkcs11.so
```

This library is only available for Linux as a 32-bit binary. If we are compiling on a 64-bit Linux system, it is necessary to force a 32-bit build, by specifying -m32 in the build options.

Finally, the Keyper library requires threads, so we must specify -pthread.

```
$ cd openssl-0.9.8zc
$ ./Configure linux-generic32 -m32 -pthread \
    --pk11-libname=/opt/pkcs11/usr/lib/libpkcs11.so \
    --pk11-flavor=sign-only \
    --prefix=/opt/pkcs11/usr
```

After configuring, run "**make**" and "**make test**". If "**make test**" fails with "pthread_atfork() not found", you forgot to add the -pthread above.

Building OpenSSL for the SCA 6000 on Solaris

The SCA-6000 PKCS#11 provider is installed as a system library, libpkcs11. It is a true crypto accelerator, up to 4 times faster than any CPU, so the flavor shall be 'crypto-accelerator'.

In this example, we are building on Solaris x86 on an AMD64 system.

```
$ cd openssl-0.9.8zc
$ ./Configure solaris64-x86_64-cc \
    --pk11-libname=/usr/lib/64/libpkcs11.so \
    --pk11-flavor=crypto-accelerator \
    --prefix=/opt/pkcs11/usr
```

(For a 32-bit build, use "solaris-x86-cc" and /usr/lib/libpkcs11.so.)

After configuring, run **make** and **make test**.

Building OpenSSL for SoftHSM

SoftHSM (version 1) is a software library developed by the OpenDNSSEC project (http://www.opendnssec.org) which provides a PKCS#11 interface to a virtual HSM, implemented in the form of a SQLite3 database on the local filesystem. SoftHSM uses the Botan library to perform cryptographic functions. Though less secure than a true HSM, it can allow you to experiment with PKCS#11 when an HSM is not available.

The SoftHSM cryptographic store must be installed and initialized before using it with OpenSSL, and the SOFTHSM_CONF environment variable must always point to the SoftHSM configuration file:

```
$  cd softhsm-1.3.7
$  configure --prefix=/opt/pkcs11/usr
$  make
$  make install
$  export SOFTHSM_CONF=/opt/pkcs11/softhsm.conf
$  echo "0:/opt/pkcs11/softhsm.db" > $SOFTHSM_CONF
$  /opt/pkcs11/usr/bin/softhsm --init-token 0 --slot 0 --label softhsm
```

SoftHSM can perform all cryptographic operations, but since it only uses your system CPU, there is no advantage to using it for anything but signing. Therefore, we choose the 'sign-only' flavor when building OpenSSL.

```
$ cd openssl-0.9.8zc
$ ./Configure linux-x86_64 -pthread \
      --pk11-libname=/opt/pkcs11/usr/lib/libsofthsm.so \
      --pk11-flavor=sign-only \
      --prefix=/opt/pkcs11/usr
```

After configuring, run "**make**" and "**make test**".

Once you have built OpenSSL, run "**apps/openssl engine pkcs11**" to confirm that PKCS#11 support was compiled in correctly. The output should be one of the following lines, depending on the flavor selected:

```
(pkcs11) PKCS #11 engine support (sign only)
```

Or:

```
(pkcs11) PKCS #11 engine support (crypto accelerator)
```

Next, run "**apps/openssl engine pkcs11 -t**". This will attempt to initialize the PKCS#11 engine. If it is able to do so successfully, it will report "`[ available ]`".

If the output is correct, run "**make install**" which will install the modified OpenSSL suite to `/opt/pkcs11/usr`.

Configuring BIND 9 for Linux with the AEP Keyper

To link with the PKCS#11 provider, threads must be enabled in the BIND 9 build.

The PKCS#11 library for the AEP Keyper is currently only available as a 32-bit binary. If we are building on a 64-bit host, we must force a 32-bit build by adding "-m32" to the CC options on the "configure" command line.

```
$ cd ../bind9
$ ./configure CC="gcc -m32" --enable-threads \
     --with-openssl=/opt/pkcs11/usr \
     --with-pkcs11=/opt/pkcs11/usr/lib/libpkcs11.so
```

Configuring BIND 9 for Solaris with the SCA 6000

To link with the PKCS#11 provider, threads must be enabled in the BIND 9 build.

```
$ cd ../bind9
$ ./configure CC="cc -xarch=amd64" --enable-threads \
      --with-openssl=/opt/pkcs11/usr \
      --with-pkcs11=/usr/lib/64/libpkcs11.so
```

(For a 32-bit build, omit CC="cc -xarch=amd64".)

If configure complains about OpenSSL not working, you may have a 32/64-bit architecture mismatch. Or, you may have incorrectly specified the path to OpenSSL (it should be the same as the --prefix argument to the OpenSSL Configure).

Configuring BIND 9 for SoftHSM

```
$ cd ../bind9
$ ./configure --enable-threads \
      --with-openssl=/opt/pkcs11/usr \
      --with-pkcs11=/opt/pkcs11/usr/lib/libsofthsm.so
```

After configuring, run "**make**", "**make test**" and "**make install**".

(Note: If "make test" fails in the "pkcs11" system test, you may have forgotten to set the SOFTHSM_CONF environment variable.)

PKCS#11 Tools

BIND 9 includes a minimal set of tools to operate the HSM, including **pkcs11-keygen** to generate a new key pair within the HSM, **pkcs11-list** to list objects currently available, **pkcs11-destroy** to remove objects, and **pkcs11-tokens** to list available tokens.

In UNIX/Linux builds, these tools are built only if BIND 9 is configured with the --with-pkcs11 option. (Note: If --with-pkcs11 is set to "yes", rather than to the path of the PKCS#11 provider, then the tools will be built but the provider will be left undefined. Use the -m option or the PKCS11_PROVIDER environment variable to specify the path to the provider.)

Using the HSM

For OpenSSL-based PKCS#11, we must first set up the runtime environment so the OpenSSL and PKCS#11 libraries can be loaded:

```
$ export LD_LIBRARY_PATH=/opt/pkcs11/usr/lib:${LD_LIBRARY_PATH}
```

This causes **named** and other binaries to load the OpenSSL library from /opt/pkcs11/usr/lib rather than from the default location. This step is not necessary when using native PKCS#11.

Some HSMs require other environment variables to be set. For example, when operating an AEP Keyper, it is necessary to specify the location of the "machine" file, which stores information about the Keyper for use by the provider library. If the machine file is in /opt/Keyper/PKCS11Provider/ machine, use:

```
$ export KEYPER_LIBRARY_PATH=/opt/Keyper/PKCS11Provider
```

Such environment variables must be set whenever running any tool that uses the HSM, including **pkcs11-keygen**, **pkcs11-list**, **pkcs11-destroy**, **dnssec-keyfromlabel**, **dnssec-signzone**, **dnssec-keygen**, and **named**.

We can now create and use keys in the HSM. In this case, we will create a 2048 bit key and give it the label "sample-ksk":

```
$ pkcs11-keygen -b 2048 -l sample-ksk
```

To confirm that the key exists:

```
$ pkcs11-list
Enter PIN:
object[0]: handle 2147483658 class 3 label[8] 'sample-ksk' id[0]
object[1]: handle 2147483657 class 2 label[8] 'sample-ksk' id[0]
```

Before using this key to sign a zone, we must create a pair of BIND 9 key files. The "dnssec-keyfromlabel" utility does this. In this case, we will be using the HSM key "sample-ksk" as the key-signing key for "example.net":

```
$ dnssec-keyfromlabel -l sample-ksk -f KSK example.net
```

The resulting K*.key and K*.private files can now be used to sign the zone. Unlike normal K* files, which contain both public and private key data, these files will contain only the public key data, plus an identifier for the private key which remains stored within the HSM. Signing with the private key takes place inside the HSM.

If you wish to generate a second key in the HSM for use as a zone-signing key, follow the same procedure above, using a different keylabel, a smaller key size, and omitting "-f KSK" from the **dnssec-keyfromlabel** arguments:

(Note: When using OpenSSL-based PKCS#11, the label is an arbitrary string which identifies the key. With native PKCS#11, the label is a PKCS#11 URI string which may include other details about the key and the HSM, including its PIN. See dnssec-keyfromlabel(8) for details.)

```
$ pkcs11-keygen -b 1024 -l sample-zsk
$ dnssec-keyfromlabel -l sample-zsk example.net
```

Alternatively, you may prefer to generate a conventional on-disk key, using **dnssec-keygen**:

```
$ dnssec-keygen example.net
```

This provides less security than an HSM key, but since HSMs can be slow or cumbersome to use for security reasons, it may be more efficient to reserve HSM keys for use in the less frequent key-signing operation. The zone-signing key can be rolled more frequently, if you wish, to compensate for a reduction in key security. (Note: When using native PKCS#11, there is no speed advantage to using on-disk keys, as cryptographic operations will be done by the HSM regardless.)

Now you can sign the zone. (Note: If not using the -S option to **dnssec-signzone**, it will be necessary to add the contents of both K*.key files to the zone master file before signing it.)

```
$ dnssec-signzone -S example.net
Enter PIN:
Verifying the zone using the following algorithms:
NSEC3RSASHA1.
Zone signing complete:
Algorithm: NSEC3RSASHA1: ZSKs: 1, KSKs: 1 active, 0 revoked, 0 stand-by
example.net.signed
```

Specifying the engine on the command line

When using OpenSSL-based PKCS#11, the "engine" to be used by OpenSSL can be specified in **named** and all of the BIND **dnssec-*** tools by using the "-E <engine>" command line option. If BIND 9 is built with the --with-pkcs11 option, this option defaults to "pkcs11". Specifying the engine will generally not be necessary unless for some reason you wish to use a different OpenSSL engine.

If you wish to disable use of the "pkcs11" engine — for troubleshooting purposes, or because the HSM is unavailable — set the engine to the empty string. For example:

```
$ dnssec-signzone -E '' -S example.net
```

This causes **dnssec-signzone** to run as if it were compiled without the --with-pkcs11 option.

When built with native PKCS#11 mode, the "engine" option has a different meaning: it specifies the path to the PKCS#11 provider library. This may be useful when testing a new provider library.

Running named with automatic zone re-signing

If you want **named** to dynamically re-sign zones using HSM keys, and/or to to sign new records inserted via nsupdate, then **named** must have access to the HSM PIN. In OpenSSL-based PKCS#11, this is accomplished by placing the PIN into the openssl.cnf file (in the above examples, /opt/pkcs11/usr/ssl/openssl.cnf).

The location of the openssl.cnf file can be overridden by setting the OPENSSL_CONF environment variable before running **named**.

Sample openssl.cnf:

```
openssl_conf = openssl_def
[ openssl_def ]
engines = engine_section
[ engine_section ]
pkcs11 = pkcs11_section
[ pkcs11_section ]
PIN = <PLACE PIN HERE>
```

This will also allow the dnssec-* tools to access the HSM without PIN entry. (The pkcs11-* tools access the HSM directly, not via OpenSSL, so a PIN will still be required to use them.)

In native PKCS#11 mode, the PIN can be provided in a file specified as an attribute of the key's label. For example, if a key had the label **pkcs11:object=local-zsk;pin-source=/etc/hsmpin**, then the PIN would be read from the file /etc/hsmpin.

 Warning
Placing the HSM's PIN in a text file in this manner may reduce the security advantage of using an HSM. Be sure this is what you want to do before configuring the system in this way.

---

11   The BIND Lightweight Resolver

11.1   The Lightweight Resolver Library

Traditionally applications have been linked with a stub resolver library that sends recursive DNS queries to a local caching name server.

IPv6 once introduced new complexity into the resolution process, such as following A6 chains and DNAME records, and simultaneous lookup of IPv4 and IPv6 addresses. Though most of the complexity was then removed, these are hard or impossible to implement in a traditional stub resolver.

BIND 9 therefore can also provide resolution services to local clients using a combination of a lightweight resolver library and a resolver daemon process running on the local host. These communicate using a simple UDP-based protocol, the "lightweight resolver protocol" that is distinct from and simpler than the full DNS protocol.

11.2   Running a Resolver Daemon

To use the lightweight resolver interface, the system must run the resolver daemon **lwresd** or a local name server configured with a **lwres** statement.

By default, applications using the lightweight resolver library will make UDP requests to the IPv4 loopback address (127.0.0.1) on port 921. The address can be overridden by **lwserver** lines in `/etc/resolv.conf`.

The daemon currently only looks in the DNS, but in the future it may use other sources such as `/etc/hosts`, NIS, etc.

The **lwresd** daemon is essentially a caching-only name server that responds to requests using the lightweight resolver protocol rather than the DNS protocol. Because it needs to run on each host, it is designed to require no or minimal configuration. Unless configured otherwise, it uses the name servers listed on **nameserver** lines in `/etc/resolv.conf` as forwarders, but is also capable of doing the resolution autonomously if none are specified.

The **lwresd** daemon may also be configured with a `named.conf` style configuration file, in `/etc/lwresd.conf` by default. A name server may also be configured to act as a lightweight resolver daemon using the **lwres** statement in `named.conf` (as covered in Section 11.3).

In BIND 9.11, the number of client queries that the **lwresd** daemon is able to serve can be set using the `lwres-tasks` and `lwres-clients` statements in the configuration.

11.3   lwres Statement

lwres Statement Grammar

This is the grammar of the **lwres** statement in the `named.conf` file:

```
lwres {
    listen-on { ip_addr port ip_port dscp ip_dscp ;
    ip_addr port ip_port dscp ip_dscp ;  ...   };
    view view_name;
    search { domain_name ;   domain_name ;  ...   };
    ndots number;
    lwres-tasks number;
    lwres-clients number;
};
```

lwres Statement Definition and Usage

The **lwres** configures the name server to also act as a lightweight resolver server. There may be multiple **lwres** statements configuring lightweight resolver servers with different properties.

The **listen-on** specifies a list of IPv4 addresses (and ports) that this instance of a lightweight resolver daemon should accept requests on. If no port is specified, port 921 is used. If this statement is omitted, requests will be accepted on 127.0.0.1, port 921.

The **view** binds this instance of a lightweight resolver daemon to a view in the DNS namespace, so that the response will be constructed in the same manner as a normal DNS query matching this view. If this statement is omitted, the default view is used, and if there is no default view, an error is triggered.

The **search** is equivalent to the **search** statement in `/etc/resolv.conf`. It provides a list of domains which are appended to relative names in queries.

The **ndots** is equivalent to the **ndots** statement in `/etc/resolv.conf`. It indicates the minimum number of dots in a relative domain name that should result in an exact match lookup before search path elements are appended.

The `lwres-tasks` statement specifies the number of worker threads the lightweight resolver will dedicate to serving clients. By default the number is the same as the number of CPUs on the system; this can be overridden using the `-n` command line option when starting the server.

The `lwres-clients` specifies the number of client objects per thread the lightweight resolver should create to serve client queries. By default, if the lightweight resolver runs as a part of **named**, 256 client objects are created for each task; if it runs as **lwresd**, 1024 client objects are created for each thread. The maximum value is 32768; higher values will be silently ignored and the maximum will be used instead.

Warning

Setting too high a value may overconsume system resources.

The maximum number of client queries that the lightweight resolver can handle at any one time equals `lwres-tasks` times `lwres-clients`.

The `lwres-tasks` and `lwres-clients` options were introduced in BIND 9.11.

11.4   lwresd — lightweight resolver daemon

Synopsis

`lwresd [-c config-file] [-C config-file] [-d debug-level] [-f] [-g] [-i pid-file]`
`[-m flag] [-n #cpus] [-P port] [-p port] [-s] [-t directory] [-u user] [-v] [-4] [-`
`6]`

lwresd Description

lwresd is the daemon providing name lookup services to clients that use the BIND 9 lightweight resolver library. It is essentially a stripped-down, caching-only name server that answers queries using the BIND 9 lightweight resolver protocol rather than the DNS protocol.

lwresd listens for resolver queries on a UDP port on the IPv4 loopback interface, 127.0.0.1. This means that **lwresd** can only be used by processes running on the local machine. By default, UDP port number 921 is used for lightweight resolver requests and responses.

Incoming lightweight resolver requests are decoded by the server which then resolves them using the DNS protocol. When the DNS lookup completes, **lwresd** encodes the answers in the lightweight resolver format and returns them to the client that made the request.

If `/etc/resolv.conf` contains any `nameserver` entries, **lwresd** sends recursive DNS queries to those servers. This is similar to the use of forwarders in a caching name server. If no `nameserver` entries are present, or if forwarding fails, **lwresd** resolves the queries autonomously starting at the root name servers, using a built-in list of root server hints.

lwresd Options

-4

Use IPv4 only even if the host machine is capable of IPv6. `-4` and `-6` are mutually exclusive.

-6

Use IPv6 only even if the host machine is capable of IPv4. `-4` and `-6` are mutually exclusive.

-c *config-file*
> Use *config-file* as the configuration file instead of the default, /etc/lwresd.conf. -c can not be used with -C.

-C *config-file*
> Use *config-file* as the configuration file instead of the default, /etc/resolv.conf. -C can not be used with -c.

-d *debug-level*
> Set the daemon's debug level to *debug-level*. Debugging traces from **lwresd** become more verbose as the debug level increases.

-f

> Run the server in the foreground (i.e. do not daemonize).

-g

> Run the server in the foreground and force all logging to stderr.

-i *pid-file*
> Use *pid-file* as the PID file instead of the default, /var/run/lwresd/lwresd.pid.

-m *flag*
> Turn on memory usage debugging flags. Possible flags are *usage*, *trace*, *record*, *size*, and *mctx*. These correspond to the ISC_MEM_DEBUGXXXX flags described in <isc/mem.h>.

-n *#cpus*
> Create *#cpus* worker threads to take advantage of multiple CPUs. If not specified, **lwresd** will try to determine the number of CPUs present and create one thread per CPU. If it is unable to determine the number of CPUs, a single worker thread will be created.

-P *port*
> Listen for lightweight resolver queries on port *port*. If not specified, the default is port 921.

-p *port*
> Send DNS lookups to port *port*. If not specified, the default is port 53. This provides a way of testing the lightweight resolver daemon with a name server that listens for queries on a non-standard port number.

-s

> Write memory usage statistics to stdout on exit.

> **Note**
> This option is mainly of interest to BIND 9 developers and may be removed or changed in a future release.

-t *directory*
> Chroot to *directory* after processing the command line arguments, but before reading the configuration file.

Warning

This option should be used in conjunction with the −u option, as chrooting a process running as root doesn't enhance security on most systems; the way chroot(2) is defined allows a process with root privileges to escape a chroot jail.

-u *user*

Setuid to *user* after completing privileged operations, such as creating sockets that listen on privileged ports.

-v

Report the version number and exit.

lwresd Files

/etc/resolv.conf

The default configuration file.

/var/run/lwresd.pid

The default process-id file.

Index

CPSIA information can be obtained at www.ICGtesting.com
Printed in the USA
BVOW04s0244030216

435191BV00043B/139/P

9 781937 516031